LINCOLN BIBLE INSTITUTE

F.W. Hyne Davy

P9-DBI-649

THE
FRANCISCANS
IN ENGLAND

THE
FRANCISCANS
IN ENGLAND
1224–1538

BY EDWARD HUTTON

LONDON
CONSTABLE & COMPANY LTD

First published 1926

Printed in Great Britain at
The Mayflower Press, Plymouth. William Brendon & Son, Ltd.

282.42
H98

THIS
LABOUR OF LOVE
IS OFFERED
IN DEEP HUMILITY
UPON THE DCC ANNIVERSARY
OF THE DEATH OF
THE BLESSED
SAINT FRANCIS
OF ASSISI
FOR THE REPOSE OF THE SOUL
OF
HENRY VIII,
KING OF ENGLAND

He gathered the worms out of the way, lest they be trodden under foot.

GOLDEN LEGEND: ST. FRANCIS.

14968

My debts to previous writers are fully acknowledged in the notes to this volume. I wish particularly to thank the Very Reverend Father Cuthbert, O.S.F.C., for his kind permission, of which I have often availed myself, to use his translation of Friar Thomas of Eccleston's *Chronicle*.

*

CONTENTS

The Franciscans in England

I

THE COMING OF THE FRIARS

" IN the year of Our Lord 1224," says Friar Thomas
of Eccleston, " in the time of the Lord Pope
Honorius, that is in the very year in which the Rule
of the Blessed Francis was confirmed by him, in the
eighth year of the Lord King Henry, son of John, on
the Tuesday after the Feast of the Nativity of the
Blessed Virgin (Sept. 8), which that year was upon a
Sunday, the Friars Minor first came into England, at
Dover."

Thomas of Eccleston, the first historian of the Franciscan Order in England, was himself a Friar, probably
one of the earliest to enter the Order in England. Unfortunately we know very little of him. He himself
tells us that he was an inmate of the London convent
when William of Nottingham was Minister (1240–50),
and that he was a student at Oxford during the life-time
of Grosseteste. The date of his chronicle *De Adventu
Fratrum Minorum in Angliam*,[1] which he dedicated to
his learned friend Friar Simon of Esseby, is, if not later,
not much earlier than 1260, and he tells us in his
preface that he had been collecting material for it for

[1] *Monumenta Franciscana*, Vol. I, ed. J. S. Brewer (Longman, 1855):
De Adventu Fratrum Minorum in Angliam.

twenty-five years. In his book, then, we have the work of a contemporary, and often of an eye-witness, of the beginnings of the Order in England, whose sincerity speaks for itself.

Now Friar Thomas tells us that the Franciscans first landed in England in the year 1224, upon the Tuesday after the feast of the Nativity of the Blessed Virgin on September 8th, upon September 10th, that is, for the feast that year fell upon a Sunday. The date of the year and the day of the month are, as we shall see, important and significant beyond what appears at first sight.

Wadding, the Irish Franciscan[1] of the seventeenth century, asserts in his *Annales Minorum* that the Friars first came to England in 1219. To support him there is no real evidence, certainly nothing that for a moment can be set against the words of a contemporary such as Friar Thomas. The assertion that St. Francis appointed Agnellus of Pisa Minister of England in 1219 is unsupported, though not impossible,[2] the letter of St. Francis[3] to Agnellus being undated, while the statements of Mathew Paris ad annum 1243 that "the Friars built their first houses in England scarcely twenty-four years ago" evidently refers to the Dominicans who landed in England in 1220. In support of Friar

---

[1] WADDING : *Annales Minorum* (fol. Romæ, 1731–45).

[2] It is possible, as I suggest later, that Agnellus was appointed first in 1219 and confirmed in 1224. See *infra* p. 13, n. 2. It should be noted that the *Chronicle of the Grey Friars of London* gives us two entries under different dates : XVI An. Johan. Reg. (1215) : "Thys yere beganne the Freere Minors in Ynglond," and VII An. Hen. III (1223) : "Thys yere came the Freeres Minors into Ynglond." The fifteenth-century MS., *Prima Fundatio Fratrum Minorum Londoniæ*, printed in *Monumenta Franciscana* (Rolls Series), I., 493 *et seq.*, also states that St. Francis died "Anno Domini MCCXXVI et secundo anno post introitam fratrum minorum in Angliam."

[3] WADDING, *op. cit.*, I, 303, see *infra*.

Thomas, on the contrary we have the statement of the Franciscan author of the *Lanercost Chronicle*, who was certainly living within a hundred years of the landing of the Friars. He asserts that the Friars Minor first landed in 1224 *post festum natalis Virginis*, and, though later he substitutes the feast of St. Bartholomew (Aug. 24) for that of the Nativity of the Blessed Virgin, he repeats his assertion that the year was 1224.

Altogether then, as we might expect, what evidence we have goes to support the statement of Friar Thomas of Eccleston, who records that the Franciscans first landed in England at Dover upon September 10, 1224.

That date is, as I have said, full of significance.

In the early days of August in that year St. Francis, with his friars Masseo, Angelo and Leo, had set out for La Verna, the mountain which Orlando da Chiusi had given him on the confines of Tuscany, to keep there the Lent of St. Michael which begins upon the morrow of the feast of the Assumption (Aug. 15). Some of the most beautiful pages of the *Fioretti* record that journey and the long vigil of the saint in the little cell only to be reached by a plank bridge over the chasm, on the south side of the mountain. When this cell was made St. Francis said to his three friars, " Go ye to your own place and leave me here alone. . . . But Brother Leo, thou shalt come to me once a day with a little bread and water, and at night once again at the hour of Matins ; and then thou shalt come to me in silence and when thou art at the bridgehead thou shalt say : *Domine labia mea aperies*, and if I answer thee, cross over and come to the cell, and we will say Matins together ; and if I answer thee not, then depart straightway " : and so it was. But there came a morning " as the time of the feast of the Most Holy Cross

[11]

drew near in the month of September,"[1] when he got no answer, and when, contrary to St. Francis' bidding but out of the deep love he bore him, he crossed the bridge over the chasm nevertheless, and entered into the cell. "And not finding St. Francis he thought that he might be praying somewhere in the wood; wherefore he came out again and by the light of the moon went softly searching through the wood; and at last he heard the voice of St. Francis, and drawing near saw him on his knees in prayer with face and hands raised up to Heaven; and in fervour of spirit he was saying: 'Who art thou, O most sweet my God? What am I most vile worm and Thine unprofitable servant?' and these selfsame words he said again and again and he spake no word beside." It was the vision of the two lights of the knowledge and understanding of himself and of the knowledge and understanding of the Creator and of the three gifts of "holy obedience, most high poverty and glorious chastity."

This vision which Brother Leo saw, and which St. Francis explained to him when he was discovered by the rustling of the leaves beneath his feet, was the forerunner in those September days of the greatest of all, in which St. Francis received the Stigmata, which befell in the dawn of September 14th, the feast of the Most Holy Cross.

The story of how St. Francis received the Stigmata is too well known to need repetition here; and indeed I have only alluded at such length to the famous sojourn of St. Francis upon La Verna and to the wonders he experienced there, because it was actually in the midst of these, while he was thus rapt in God

[1] The feast of the Exaltation of the Holy Cross falls upon September 14.

upon that far mountain, that his friars first set foot in England, landing as they did at Dover, " as the time of the feast of the most Holy Cross drew near," upon September 10th. It is good to remind oneself that it was in those very days, the holiest the Order was ever to know, the Franciscans came to these shores.

The little band which landed at Dover upon that September day consisted of four clerics and five lay brethren. They were led by Friar Agnellus of Pisa, who was about thirty years of age and in deacon's orders. He had been chosen by St. Francis himself to go to England as Minister Provincial; according to Friar Thomas, in the general chapter immediately preceding, that is, in 1223; others[1] assert, however, that he had been appointed in 1219 and assign the following letter[2] to that date : " Ego frater Franciscus

[1] See WADDING, *op. cit.*, I, 303, and *Analecta Franciscana* II, 14–15.

[2] Christopher Davenport, known in religion as Fra Francesco a S. Clara, gives the letter as quoted, in his *Historia Minor. Prov. Ang. FF. Min.* (Duaci, 1658). He adds that the original was preserved in the Episcopio at St. Omer. Wadding tells us that in the convent of La Verna there was preserved a picture of Blessed Agnellus holding the letter appointing him Minister Provincial of England which he received from St. Francis, written in large characters, in his hands. This picture still exists at La Verna, in the corridor leading from the choir of S. Francesco towards the Foresterie. It is in the twelfth medallion on the left, 78 cm.×91 cm.; beneath one sees the "obbedienza," or letter measuring 15 cm.×21 cm. This medallion is probably the work of Gerino da Pistoja who was at La Verna between 1501 and 1509. The text of the letter is hard to read, but has been deciphered by more than one student. P. Giovanni Giaccherini, O·F·M·, gives it as follows : " Fratri Agnello de Pisis provincie Tuscie ordinis minorum frater Francyscus de Assisio M[inister] G[eneralis] licet indignus salutem, etc., Ad meritum obedientie salutaris t(ibi) precipio ut Angliam eas idem (sic) officium M(inistri) exercendo. ValeTdicoT." In the lower margin is the imprint of an oval seal. The two signs dividing the word Valedico are two tau crosses.

The existence of this painting seems to prove the existence of a letter from St. Francis appointing Agnellus Minister Provincial in England. But it does not throw any light on the question of date. It is also to be

de Assisio Minister Generalis præcipio tibi fratri Agnello de Pisa per obedientiam ut vadas ad Angliam et ibi facias officium Ministeratus. Vale. Frater Franciscus de Assisio."

That letter, if not itself genuine, represents one that is of similar tenour, but its date is uncertain. Agnellus may have been appointed Minister of England at the famous General Council of Mats in 1219, but if so, he did not actually enter his province till five years later. We know from Friar Thomas and others that he accompanied Friar Pacifico to France when at the head of a little company of friars he arrived in that country in 1219; and he was actually custos of Paris when the order (perhaps the very letter quoted by Wadding) which contains a definite command—*ut vadas ad Angliam*—came in 1224 for him to set out for England. Tronci, the historian of Pisa, preserves some part of this when he says, ad ann. 1211 : " In this year the patriarch S. Francis came to Pisa according to Wadding in his Annals and preaching there obtained many disciples among which was Agnello degli Agnelli, Nobile Pisano, who by his virtue and goodness was by the Saint himself made first Custode of France where in Paris he founded the first *convento* and then was given to him the *Ministerio* of England."[1]

noted that the text differs from that quoted by Wadding and Francesco a S. Clara, of whom the former had apparently seen an original document at St. Omer, or at any rate knew of its existence, and found therein the basis of his text. Perhaps there were two letters ; that of which we have a copy in the La Verna picture, dating from 1219, that we have in Wadding, the original of which was at St. Omer, dating from 1223. Upon the La Verna picture, see P. MARIOTTI, *Il Beato Agnello da Pisa ed i Frati Minori in Inghilterra* (Rome 1895), and P. GIO. GIACCHERINI, O·F·M·, in *La Verna : Ricordo del Settimo centenario* (Arezzo 1913), p. 374 *et seq*.

[1] TRONCI : *Annali di Pisa*(Livorno, 1682), p. 176.

Of Agnellus' early life we know little but that he was first professed at the Convento di S. Francesco in Pisa with others, and particularly Alberto, also a Pisan, who was given him for companion on his journey,[1] and who succeeded him in the *ministerio* of England and then was Provincial of Germany, then of Spain and finally Minister General of the Order.

In England, Agnellus was to have a great career, to become the friend of the King and of Grosseteste, whom he was successful in obtaining as the first master of the Minors. Friar Thomas tells us he was a man " especially endowed with natural prudence and foresight and conspicuous in every virtue." He died at last in Oxford crying continually upon Our Lord, " Veni, dulcissime Jesu," probably in the early months of 1235, and was buried there in the choir of the friar's church before the altar. That he was a man of most holy life is proved by the fact of his beatification. It is said that when the chapel in which he had first been buried was about to be destroyed in the course of building a larger church the friars came to remove his body by night and " they found both the sacred coffin in which he lay and the grave itself filled with the purest oil, but the body itself, and the garments in which it was clothed were incorrupt and gave forth a most sweet perfume."[2]

Blessed Agnellus of Pisa was, as I have said, but a deacon when he landed, and only later, and at the express command of the General Chapter, did he accept priests' orders. His first companion, Friar Richard

[1] Albert of Pisa did not, as stated by Bartholomew of Pisa and others, accompany Agnellus to England. We do not know when he first came to England. He reached England as Minister on Dec. 13, 1236, according to Friar Thomas.

[2] *De Adventu*, Coll. XIII.

of Ingworth, was not only a priest but an English-man. He was, too, older than Agnellus, had long been a friar before the landing of 1224 and " was the first of the brethren to preach to the people on this side the Alps." His career also was notable. It is probable that he was a Norfolk man. It was he who with three other friars established the Order in London, in Oxford, in Northampton, and at last he became custos in Cambridge. The facts that he was English, in priest's orders and a man of middle age probably explain why he was appointed so often as pioneer. In 1230, when Agnellus attended the General Chapter at Assisi, he was appointed Vicar of the English Province in his absence, and a little later was sent by the General John Parenti to Ireland as Provincial Minister. But about 1239, " having completed the term of his ministry in all things faithful and acceptable before God he was freed in General Chapter by Friar Albert of happy memory from all office amongst the brethren and burning with zeal for the faith he was sent to Palestine and there slept in peace."

The second companion of Blessed Agnellus was Friar Richard of Devon, a youthful Englishman in minor orders. He was noted for his stoutness of heart and his love of holy obedience. He was the chosen companion of Friar Richard of Ingworth when he set out to establish the Order in London, Oxford and Northampton. He was a great traveller, but at last was bidden to abide at Romehale (Romney), where he dwelt for fifteen years worn-out by frequent quartan fevers.

The third companion of Agnellus was William of Esseby, a novice " in the caperone of probation." He, too, was but a youth and English, probably of Ashby in Norfolk. Friar Thomas tells that he loved not only obedience, but also gentleness, and " by this most attractive and willing gentleness he gained the affection of many seculars for the Order. He led many worthy persons of different degrees of dignity, rank and age into the way of salvation." He was to become warden at Oxford, and when the English province was divided into custodies he became Custos of Oxford. Curiously enough it was he who founded the house at Cambridge. He died in London, " after many years."

Such were the four clerics. The five laymen were all foreigners. Friar Henry was by birth a Lombard. He was a very holy man, and because of his sanctity and discretion was made Guardian of London. " He returned after completing his labours in England into his own country." Brother Laurence was of Beauvais. He seems soon to have left England for Italy, to " go back to the blessed Francis," whom he frequently saw and was found worthy of the consolation of conversing with him. At length St. Francis gave him his own tunic and sent him back to England.[1] He was of the London house.

William of Florence, the third lay brother, quickly returned to France ; and of the fourth and fifth, Melioratus and James from beyond the Alps, a novice, we know nothing.

It is obvious that the four clerics, three of them Englishmen, were the heart and soul of the movement.

Such was the little band of Franciscans that set foot upon our shores in September, 1224. Whence had they come?

More than one reference in the Chronicle by Friar

---

[1] The actual habit of St. Francis was therefore at one time in England, and possibly preserved in London till the Spoliation.

Thomas confirms us in the obvious supposition that they came from Paris. The Franciscans had been established in Paris as early as 1219. Like our civilisation, the Franciscan movement came to us from Italy by way of France.

We know, for instance, that Blessed Agnellus himself had accompanied Friar Pacifico to Paris and was there when he was ordered to go into England. Friar Thomas, wishing to give us an example of Friar William of Esseby's love of holy obedience, tells us that " when Friar Gregory the Minister of France asked him whether he would be willing to go to England he replied that he did not know. At which reply the Minister wondered until Friar William said that the reason why he did not know was that his will was not his own but the Minister's and so whatever the Minister willed he willed." The same Chronicle also tells us of Friar William of Florence that he " quickly returned to France." Moreover, we know on the same authority that the nine were " charitably conveyed across to England by the monks of Fécamp." It was from Paris they came, and we know not with what doubts and fears they saw the white cliffs of Albion. All we know is that they had love in their hearts. On the day they landed St. Francis had just two years and twenty-three days to live.

II

TO CANTERBURY

THUS the nine " cordially provided for in their necessities " by the monks of Fécamp landed in England at Dover upon September 10, 1224. *Viri simplices et despicabiles* as they were regarded, not without derision and astonishment, upon landing they sought as mendicants the hospitality of a certain noble lord, who received them, we read,[1] as vagabonds (*ignobi*), shut them up in a strong chamber and in the morning went forth to consult his neighbours as to what should be done with them. The nine, meanwhile, weary as they were, slept till morning light ; when, rising to continue their journey, they found themselves prisoners. News of their arrival had spread, and a crowd gathered to see them, and they were at once pronounced spies and robbers. Then one of the friars took the cord of St. Francis, and offering it, s aid: " If indeed we be robbers here is a rope to hang us withal." And immediately the minds of those present were changed and the nine were allowed to continue their journey. Was it on account of this inhospitable greeting that no house of the Order was ever established in Dover ?

The nine went on to Canterbury, sixteen miles away. Doubtless they went by the Roman Watling Street through Ewell and Lydden and over Barham Down,

[1] *Chronicon de Lanercost* ad ann. MCCXXIV (1839).

crossing the Little Stour at Bridge and entering Canterbury at last by the old Riding or Reding Gate. This gate had been the chief entrance to the city from Roman times, the three great roads from Dover, Richborough and Lympne uniting there. The gate consisted of two circular arches of Roman brick flanked by a tower. All was unfortunately taken down in 1782 and even the street new made. The present Beer Cart lane continues the line of the ancient way.

So they came on that early autumn day, but into a very different Canterbury from that we know, different both without and within, materially and spiritually. Spiritually it was above all the city of St. Thomas, whose relics, amid rejoicings that have become famous and in the presence of many thousands of pilgrims, had been translated from the crypt of the cathedral to the chapel built for them but four years before. Materially, I suppose the most striking difference must be sought for in the cathedral which no angel steeple crowned, which still possessed its low Norman nave, and where high over all William of Sens' choir and sanctuary towered new made, scarce fifty years old.

On arriving at Canterbury the nine, bearing Pope Honorius' letter and probably an introduction from the monks of Fécamp, went to " the Priory of Holy Trinity,"[1] to the monks of Christ Church, that is, of the Benedictine Order, since the early days of the Porziuncula, the traditional friends of St. Francis and the Franciscans. There, Friar Thomas tells us, the nine sojourned for two days, when four of them set

---

[1] It is possible that the Priory of Christ Church was so known in the thirteenth century owing to the recent erection and dedication of the Chapel of the shrine of St. Thomas, dedicated in honour of the Holy Trinity, to which, as is well known, he had a special devotion.

off for London ; the other five—namely, Agnellus of
Pisa, William of Esseby, Laurence of Beauvais, William
of Florence and James from beyond the Alps—" went
to the Priests' Hospice where they dwelt till they were
provided with a place to live in, which happened soon
after when they were given a small chamber (*camera
parvula*) at the back of a school, where from day to
day they remained almost continually enclosed."

The Benedictines of Christ Church thus handed the
friars over to the Priests' Hospice, of which one Alexander was then master. This hospice was an appanage
of Christ Church and stood between Stour Street and
the river Stour, where its successor, endowed in 1240
by Archdeacon Simon Langton, brother of the famous
archbishop, still stands, though fallen from religious
uses, still showing, in spite of additions and mutilations,
much work of the late fourteenth century, when it was
rebuilt for the second time.

Of the small chamber at the back of a school whither
the friars went from the Priests' Hospice we know
nothing. Perhaps it occupied a part of the site of the
small plot of ground that " Sir Alexander " presently
granted them, but of this we cannot be sure. There
Friar Thomas tells us " when the scholars had gone
home in the evening the friars would go into the school
and make a fire and sit near it. And sometimes at their
evening conference (*colatio*) they would put on the fire
a small pot in which were the dregs of beer and they
would dip a cup into the pot and drink in turn each
speaking the while some word of edification. . . . One
who merited to be a companion and participator in
this unblemished simplicity and holy poverty," says the
Chronicle of Friar Thomas, " has testified that at times
the beer was so thick that when the pot was put upon

[21]

the fire it was necessary to add water ; and so they drank rejoicing."

Later Friar Thomas continues : " As the number of the brethren increased and their sanctity became known the devotion of the people towards them increased likewise so that they provided them eagerly with suitable dwellings." At Canterbury " Sir Alexander, Master of the Priests' Hospice made over to them a plot of ground and built them a chapel sufficiently spacious and becoming for the time ; and because the friars would receive nothing of their own, it was given to the city and the brethren were allowed to live there at the will of the citizens. Most especially, however, were the friars cared for by Sir Simon de Langton Archdeacon of Canterbury and Sir Henry de Sandwich and by the noble Countess, the Lady ' Inclusa ' de Baginton[1] who in all things cared for them as a mother for her sons, and by a wise use of her influence she moreover obtained for them in an astonishing manner the favour of princes and prelates."

The date of the gift of this plot of ground and its situation are alike unknown to us. It is possible that it consisted of the eastern and the smaller of the two islands, which the friars occupied from 1269. This, however, is no more than a guess. The first resting-place of the friars in Canterbury after their brief sojourn at the Priory of Holy Trinity was in the Poor Priests' Hospice. This, as I have said, stood upon the western side of Stour Street, between it and a branch of the

[1] So the York MS., but the Lamport MS. (Mon. Franc. II, p. 18) ed. Howlett reads Hackington, which is close to Canterbury. The lady in question was Lora, daughter of William de Braose, widow of the Earl of Leicester, lord of the Manor of Hackington. She is referred to as *inclusa* because she had retired from the world, taken vows and become a recluse.

river. From there they passed to the chamber behind
the school which may well have been close by, and it
is possible that from there they never removed, that
the land given them was the school site, and that the
buildings erected by Sir Alexander were the school
buildings new made with a chapel added.[1]

There, the land and buildings being held by the
city whose guests the friars thus were, they remained
till 1267, when, according to Leland, one of the
ancestors of Sir Dudley Digge, John Digge, Alderman
as early as 1258 and commonly called Digges, " purchased an island in Canterbury called Bynnewyght and
the place of a gate over Stonestreete for the use of the
Friars to which he translated them at a convenient
time." This at first sight would seem to mean that
the site thus acquired was totally different and apart
from that hitherto occupied by the friars ; but it does
not necessarily mean this. If the friars had till then
occupied the lesser of the two islands which lie in the
angle of St. Peter's Street and Lamb Lane, it may well
be that it was the larger and more western island that
was now purchased for them, upon which their chief
buildings were to be erected. At any rate, from 1269,
if not earlier, this was their home till the suppression
in 1534. The site they were then in possession of consisted of more than the two islands, for it stretched
westward as far as a large dyke adjoining Black Griffin
Lane. It had then two entries, one called Northgate

---

[1] This supposition is supported by a fifteenth century MS. in the
possession of the Dean and Chapter of Canterbury, where we read that
the friars in 1224 "were lodged in Canterbury in Wyht." Wyht was
at the end of the thirteenth century, the name of this island. Cf.
Collectanea Franciscana (Brit. Soc. Fran. Studies : Manchester), II, 9 ;
and C. Cotton : *The Grey Friars of Canterbury* (Manchester, 1924),
p. 10 *et seq.*

in St. Peter's Street, facing the entry of the Black-friars across the way; the other called Eastgate, stood at the head of a bridge over the eastern branch of the Stour, where Lamb Lane meets Stour Street.[1]

The property purchased for the friars by Sir John Digge, as well as that given them by Sir Alexander, was held for them by the city, for they might have nothing of their own. In 1294, however, a change was made. By then it seems many houses and much ground of the fee of the Christ Church monks lay within the precincts of the convent, which perhaps thus early included the land towards Black Griffin Lane. In that year it was agreed between the Prior and Convent of Christ Church in Canterbury and the Guardian and Convent of the Friars Minor that, whereas the Prior and Convent of Christ Church had divers tenements of their fee situate within the precincts of the said Friars Minor, and each of these tenements is named in the document printed by Battely,[2] they, the monks, freely remitted all arrearages of rent on condition that the friars caused to be paid for the tenements in full for all services and demands the yearly sum of three shillings.

Weever finds in that document a rod to beat the friars withal; but it is doubtful if it really means anything more than that the monks were not willing that more of their property should pass to the city, and that therefore the friars, hitherto the tenants of the Corporation, became instead or as well the tenants of the monks.

It is curious that really all that is left of the convent

[1] Cf. Coll. Franc. II, 9.
[2] See SOMNER's *Antiquities of Canterbury*, enlarged by Battely, 1703; App. XVI.

to-day beyond a few walls and foundations should date at latest from about that time. In the precinct wall towards Black Griffin Lane is a small thirteenth-century doorway leading now to the gardens of the houses on the south side of St. Peter's Street; there is part of the bridge over the Stour of 1309, but the great treasure of the place, one of the loveliest relics of old Canterbury still left to us, is the little house that stands right over the branch of the Stour that separates the two islands the one from the other, bridging the stream. This is perhaps as early as 1269, and certainly not later than 1294. In its grace and littleness it remains to us, though all the other buildings and the church are gone. Upheld in midstream by pointed arches supported by capitalled pillars set in the bed of the stream, it is a rare and beautiful example of the work of the time, and if only for its beauty worth any trouble to see.

It cannot, alas! have been to this house, so exquisite in its humility, that Brother Salamon came all through the snow, as Friar Thomas relates; but it was to its predecessor, perhaps that school chamber, for he was the first of all those in England " led by the spirit of Jesus to seek and to win admission into the Order. He used to tell Friar Thomas how when he was a novice he was appointed procurator of the community and how one day he came to the house of his sister to beg an alms. And she bringing him some bread turned away her face and said ' Cursed be the hour on which I first saw thee.' But he with joy received the bread and went his way. And so perfectly did he keep the rule of most strict poverty that when now and then for the sake of some sick brother he would bring in his *caperone* flour or salt or a few figs

or an armful of wood for the fire he took diligent care
not to accept or retain anything beyond the measure
of the uttermost need. . . . Now when he was to be
promoted to the order of acolytes he was sent to the
venerable Father the Archbishop Stephen of holy
memory and presented by one of the elder brethren.
The archbishop received him most graciously and
ordained him under this title : ' Let Brother Salamon
of the Order of the Apostles draw near.' And this
incident I have related that men might know, in what
reverence wise men held the spirituality of the brethren
in the first days. But when they had eaten at the Archbishop's table the brethren returned barefoot to Canterbury in snow exceeding deep and dreadful, and
because of the cold and the snow Brother Salamon got
an infirmity in one of his feet . . . and during this
time was found worthy to be visited by Brother Jordan
of holy memory, Master General of the whole Order
of Preachers (Dominicans), who said to him : ' Brother
be not ashamed if the Father of the Lord Jesus Christ
leads thee to Himself afoot.' "

III

TO LONDON

WE turn now to follow those friars, who, as Friar
Thomas records, after two days in Canterbury
set out for London. There were four of them, namely,
the priest and preacher Friar Richard of Ingworth, a
man of middle age who afterwards became the Vicar
of Agnellus in England; Friar Richard of Devon, a
mere youth in minor orders, an acolyte; Henry the
Lombard, the first guardian of London; and Friar
Melioratus, also a layman. Doubtless these four came
in those September days up through Kent by the
Watling Street; on their arrival in London they went
first to the Dominicans, who had been settled in
Holborn since 1221. "With them," Friar Thomas
tells us, "they remained for fifteen days eating and
drinking what these set before them as though they
were members of the family." Then they hired a
house in Cornhill in which they made for themselves
little cells, filling in the walls with dried grass, and in
this simplicity they abode till the following summer
(1225), "having not even a chapel of their own; for
they had not as yet the privilege of erecting altars and
celebrating the divine mysteries in their dwellings."[1]
Before the feast of All Saints (Nov. 1, 1224), however,

[1] The first custom was for unconsecrated buildings and portable
altars. After 1250 they changed this custom with the Pope's leave.

and before Agnellus came up to London from Canterbury, Friars Richard of Ingworth and Richard of Devon went on to Oxford, leaving Henry the Lombard and Melioratus, both laymen, in London.

It was Sir John Travers, Sheriff of London, who first received the brethren at Cornhill and let them a house there, the guardian being Henry of Treviso "who now began for the first time to learn letters, sitting up at night in the church of St. Peter in Cornhill." Later this Henry was named Vicar of the English Province while Agnellus was away at a General Chapter, his socius or coadjutor being Richard of Ingworth ; but he [Henry] was unable, we read, " to bear so much dignity." Demoralised by honours, he became a stranger unto himself, and at length miserably apostatised from the Order.

During the few months they were in Cornhill, we read, " the devotion of the citizens grew towards them and the multitude of the brethren," till the house in Cornhill was too small for their needs. Therefore in the summer of 1225 John Iwyn, citizen and mercer of London, made over to the commonalty of the City of London for their use, land and houses near Newgate in the parish of St. Nicholas in the Shambles, and soon entered the Order himself.[1] Here the friars were to

[1] See *Prima Fundatio Fratrum Minorum Londoniæ* in *Mon. Franc.*, I, pp. 493 *et seq.* Friar Thomas writes as follows (*De Adv. Min.*, coll. III): " At London the brethren were befriended by Sir John Iwyn, who bought them a plot of ground and gave it to the city, but piously assigned the use of it to the brethren at the will of the citizens. He himself afterwards entered the Order as a lay brother and led a most penitential and devout life. Sir Joyce Fitz-Piers added to the ground. His own son, a man of good parts, afterwards devoutly entered the Order, and still more devoutly persevered unto the end. The Chapel was built by Sir William Joyner at his own cost. He also gave at various times upwards of two hundred pounds towards other buildings, and until his death he continued unweariedly in spiritual relationship with the brethren bestowing upon

remain until the Suppression. It was, in the thirteenth century, a spot well suited to the Franciscan profession. Close to the city slaughter-ground, it bordered on and presently included a lane known as Stinking Lane, where Jocius Fitzpiers gave property for the use of the Order, which still increased, so that in 1243, twenty years after the first landing at Dover, the convent of London consisted of not less than eighty friars.

The land given by John Iwyn formed thus the nucleus of what was to be a large convent which came to occupy the greater part of the land covered till a few years ago by Christ's Hospital and Christ Church, Newgate Street.[1]

Of the church the friars now built, the first Franciscan church in London, we know only what the *Prima Fundatio* tells us. We are doubtful of its site, which if it were not that of the later and much larger church which Queen Margaret began to build for the friars in 1306, is unknown to us.

In the *Prima Fundatio*, under the heading, " The first foundation of the church of the Friars Minor in London," we read :—

" In the first place the Chapel which later became a great part of the choir was built for them by Sir

them frequent benefactions. For the building of the infirmary Sir Peter de Heyland left one hundred pounds at his death. The laying of the water-pipe was chiefly due to the donations of Sir Henry de Fowie and to a young man of good address, Salekin de Basing, increased, however, by the King's ample munificence. Many other and ever-increasing gifts have I seen in my own time in London, both as regards buildings and books and additions to the ground and for the relieving of other needs. . . ."

[1] A rather vague description of the lands acquired for the use of the Friars round about the first lands given by Iwyn is to be found in the *Prima Fundatio*. There are twenty gifts of land between 1226 and 1294, twelve of these being in Stinking Lane. Of these twelve, four were bounded by the city wall.

William Joyner." Now, Sir William Joyner was mayor in 1239.

" The nave of the church was built at great cost by Sir Henry le Waleys, mayor of London." Waleys was mayor for the first time in 1273–4, and died in 1302. He had close connections with France, and in 1275 was elected mayor of Bordeaux. He stood high in the royal favour and in his day was the most famous citizen London could boast. The *Prima Fundatio* goes on to tell us that he also gave the timber for the altars, which " extended lengthwise toward the south and were built out of various common alms."

The Chapter House was built by Sir Walter Potter, alderman of London, and the Dormitory by Gregory de Rokesley, the rival of Waleys. The Refectory was built by Bartholomew de Castro, and the Infirmary for the greater part by Peter de Heyland.

All this does not at all enlighten us as to the site or the extent of the church, which, however, seems to have been a fairly complete structure. It does, how-ever, inform us as to the patrons of the Order in the thirteenth century. They were the citizens of London, the merchants and magnates of the day. It was they who welcomed the friars to London ; it was they who founded, built and completed the first church and monastery. In the fourteenth century all this is changed. Queen Margaret in 1306 founded the " new Church," and kings and queens and great nobles were its benefactors and claimed burial within it. But it is to the glory of London that it was her citizens and not any king or queen who first made welcome the sons of St. Francis.

That the friars in these first days deserved as well as needed such assistance and welcome is obvious from the narrative of Friar Thomas. In those early days, he tells us, " so strictly did the brethren avoid contracting debt that hardly in extreme necessity would they become debtors. It happened once that Brother Agnellus with Brother Salamon, the guardian of London, wished to audit the accounts of the brethren of London to see what were their expenses during one term of the year, and he found that the expenses had largely increased in spite of their penury. Whereupon he threw from him the account books and bills and striking his face exclaimed : ' They have got the better of me ! ' and never again would he audit the accounts."

Friar Thomas or another continues : " Until the time when the Order was regularly established the brethren were accustomed to have an evening conference every day, at which they drank, those who wished, in common ; and after in due course they held the chapter. Nor were they restricted from taking various dishes nor even from wine. Nevertheless in many places they would not accept the portions of fish, or flesh meat which were offered them, except on three days in the week. In the convent of London itself in the time of the Minister Provincial Brother William of happy memory [1240–1251] and of Brother Hugh the Guardian I have seen the brethren drink beer of such sourness that some preferred to drink water and I have seen them eat bread which the people call *torta*. Nay for want of bread I have often eaten spelt, even in company with the said Minister-Provincial and guests in the hospice."

So far as I can find, this is the only mention extant of Brother Hugh the Guardian. He probably succeeded John de Kethene in that office about 1239. The first Guardian of London was Henry of Treviso, who could not read when he came to London, and afterwards miserably apostatised from the Order. The next guardian we have any record of was Brother Salamon or Solomon, the first English convert of the mission. "For a long time time," we read, "he lived in his cell on account of his frost-bitten foot and was unable to hear holy Mass since the brethren went to hear Mass said and to celebrate in the parish church"[1] (St. Peter's, Cornhill). "At length he became so desperately ill that in the opinion of the surgeons the foot had to be amputated ; but when the knife was brought and the foot was uncovered a corruption came out of it, so that it was hoped it might heal. Therefore the surgeon's knife was for a time put aside. Brother Salamon indeed hoped that if he were brought to the shrine of St. Eloi he would regain both the use of his foot and his health. So when Brother Agnellus arrived he commanded that somehow or other Brother Salamon should be brought to the shrine of St. Eloi overseas. And so it was, nor did the faith of Brother Salamon fail him ; for he afterwards so far recovered as to be able to walk without a stick, and to celebrate Mass and became Guardian of London and General Confessor to the whole city."

"Now it happened when he was Guardian of London after his sickness that the Lord Roger of holy memory, Bishop of London, demanded of him canonical obedience. But Brother Salamon in friendly fashion, for he had long known the Bishop, withstood him and besought a delay. And this Bishop held the Order in such respect that he would rise whenever a friar saluted him. But Brother Agnellus on this occasion sent at once to the Roman Curia and obtained the

[1] *De Adv. Min.*, coll. III.

decree which is styled *Nimis iniqua* for the brethren."[1]

"Now because Brother Salamon had so often besought the most sweet Jesus that he might be cleansed
from his sins in this present life, there was sent him
an infirmity of the spine and he became hunchbacked
and bent ; and the sweet Jesus sent him also the dropsy
and bleeding hæmorrhoids until his death. At last on
the day his soul went forth unto his Lord he was in
such sorrow of heart that all he had suffered till then
seemed as nothing in comparison of this agony ; nor
could he discover why he sorrowed. Then he called
to him three of the brethren whom he loved most and
telling them his agony besought them that they would
earnestly pray for him. And whilst they thus prayed
and persevered there appeared to Brother Salamon the
most sweet Jesus with the Holy apostle St. Peter, by
his bed looking upon him. And as soon as he knew
that it was the Saviour he cried out : ' Have mercy
upon me, O Lord ; have mercy upon me.' And the
Lord Jesus answered : ' Because thou didst ever be-
seech Me to afflict thee in this present life, and so
cleanse thee, I sent thee this agony ; the more so for
thou didst leave thy first charity and didst not as became thy vocation, bring forth fruits of penance and

[1] *De Adv. Min.*, coll. XI : Bishop Roger was Roger Niger ; consecrated
10 June, 1229 ; died 29 Sept., 1241. The Bull referred to, *Nimis iniqua*,
is dated 28 August, 1231. It is addressed to all prelates. There is to
be found the direction in regard to the oath demanded of the friars by
the Bishops. It appears again in the Bull, *Nimis prava*, of Innocent IV
(21 July, 1245). The Friars were thus, at any rate from 1231, in
England exempt from episcopal jurisdiction and free to hear confessions.
The decision is of the greatest importance ; without it the Friars would
have been largely disarmed in their missionary work. The passage which
follows seems to show that the earliest Friars were not always unin-
fluenced by riches in spite of their profession. For an exhaustive
account of this question of privilege see Little : *Studies in Eng. Franc.
Hist.*, pp. 92–132.

c

that thou didst spare the rich in enjoining them penance.' And the blessed Peter added : ' Moreover know that thou didst grievously sin in thy judgment of Brother John of Chichester who died of late. Pray now that the Lord give thee such a death as he had.' Then Brother Salamon cried out : ' Have mercy upon me, sweet Jesus ! ' Who smiling looked upon Brother Salamon with so gentle a countenance that all his preceding anguish immediately departed and with great joy he was filled with the most certain assurance of salvation. And quickly calling the brethren to him he told what he had seen whereat they were not a little consoled."[1]

Brother Salamon was the first convert. The second brother, according to Friar Thomas, to be received by Brother Agnellus, was William of London, a dumb man who recovered his speech at Barking through the merits of St. Ethelreda. " He also was admitted to the habit in London while still the brethren had neither chapel nor building ground.[2] He was of the household of the Lord Justiciary of England, Hubert de Burgh and though he was a layman knew Latin, and was very famous for his skill in carving at table."[3]

The third convert was Brother Joyce of Cornhill, a cleric. " He was born," Friar Thomas tells us, " in the city of London itself and was a man of the best parts, a noble and delicate youth. Exactly who he was we do not know, but it is perhaps possible that he was the son of Sir Joyce Fitz-Piers who added a gift of land to that which Sir John Iwyn had already given to the city for the use of the friars. At any rate Friar Thomas

[1] *De Adv. Min.*, coll. III.   [2] That is not later than 1225.
[3] *De Adv. Min.*, coll. III.

later speaks of the son of Sir Joyce as entering the
Order and ' persevering unto the end.' Brother Joyce
of Cornhill, whether the son of Sir Joyce or no, after
bearing many labours here, went to Spain and there
died happily."[1]

The fourth convert was Brother John, a cleric. " He
was about eighteen years old of good parts and the best
conversation, but he very soon finished the course of
this present life and went to the Lord Jesus Christ.
It was he who persuaded the priest Sir Philip who was
suffering from toothache to send bread and beer to the
Friars Minor promising that the Lord Jesus would cure
him ; and so it was. And shortly after both gave themselves and entered the Order."

The fifth convert was the Brother Philip. " He was
a Londoner by birth and as I have said a priest. Later
he became guardian of Brugensis (? Bridgenorth in
Shropshire) and by his preaching gained many ; and
at last he was sent to Ireland and there departed
happily to Our Lord."

Such were the first converts of the Order in London.
Their simplicity of life, even the buildings at this
time were of the rudest and plainest sort,[2] was
doubtless what appealed to the citizens of London and
explains the enthusiasm of the people's welcome, an
enthusiasm to which the number of the smaller gifts
testifies even more eloquently than the greater. They
had come to redeem the common people, and more
especially to the cities. They seized as by inspiration
upon the first need of the citizens—intellectual train-

[1] He was, perhaps, the Friar Jocelinus Anglicus who with Stephen
Anglicus met John of Parma at Tarascon in 1248 ; but this man died in
Rome. Cf. SALIMBENE : *Ed. Parma* (pp. 126 and 143), and LITTLE :
De Adventu Minorum (Paris, 1909), p. 19, *n.* B.

[2] Cf. *De Adv. Min.*, coll. IX.

The Franciscans in England

ing; and one of the first acts of Albert of Pisa, who succeeded Agnellus as Provincial of England *ca.* 1237, was to appoint lecturers at London and Canterbury. By then it was obvious that the Friars were succeeding beyond their hopes. In 1243 there were eighty friars in the London convent, and in 1255, according to Friar Thomas, there were in England not less than forty-nine houses of the Order, and as many as 1242 friars.[1] Nor was this marvellous success to begin to diminish until the great catastrophe of the middle of the fourteenth century.

[1] Cf. *Mon. Fran.*, I, 10.

IV

TO OXFORD

FRIAR THOMAS tells us that when the four brethren—Brother Richard of Ingworth, Brother Richard of Devon, Brother Henry and Brother Melioratus—came up to London from Canterbury in September, 1224, they remained together in London first at the Friars Preachers, and then after fifteen days at a house in Cornhill, till towards the end of October, when just before the feast of All Saints (Nov. 1), and before Brother Agnellus came up to London, Brother Richard of Ingworth and Brother Richard of Devon went on to Oxford, and it is possible that the adventure told by Bartholomew of Pisa befell upon this journey.[1] Wood, quoted by Dugdale,[2] gives the following version of Bartholomew of Pisa's story :—

" These two Friars being strangers mistook their way and night coming on and the rivers overflowing their banks from a great fall of rain they made into a certain manor house about six miles from Oxford, a grange belonging to the Benedictine monks of the Abbey of Abingdon which being said to be situated in a great solitude amongst the woods and between Baldon and Oxford must needs be either Great Milton about two miles from Baldon where heretofore stood

---

[1] LITTLE : *The Grey Friars in Oxford*, p. 2, appears to think it does, though B. of Pisa distinctly says that it befell Agnellus of Pisa and his four companions on their way to Oxford. *Lib. Conformitatum* (Milan, 1510), fol. 79.

[2] DUGDALE : *Monasticon* (1830), VI, Pt. III, p. 1524.

a Grange of the said monks on the south side of the church; or Culham within one mile of Abingdon, which conjecture I rather assent to because of its situation agreeing with the description of a place amongst woods and rivers more than the former; but wherever the said cell of Benedictines was these friars went to it being compelled by the approach of the night; and having gently knocked at the gate they humbly begged a lodging for the love of God, being ready to perish with hunger and cold. The porter to whom they made this earnest address viewing the distressed couple of friars and observing their beggarly dress, their mortified looks and their dialect somewhat foreign, and imagining them to be some masqueraders that made fools of themselves for the diversion of the spectators ran immediately to the prior to tell him the agreeable news; whereupon he with the sacristan, the spenser and two other younger monks made haste to the gate and readily invited the disguised strangers to come in, hoping to be diverted with morrice-dancing or other tricks of pastime. But when the friars with a composed grave look, assured them that they were mistaken and that they were no such fellows but were men who had chosen to serve God in an apostolic life, the monks being thus disappointed of their expected merriment began now to be severe upon the two men and thrust them out of doors with coarse treatment. And now the two poor disconsolate friars, destitute of any shelter, and not knowing which counsel to take wandered up and down and must have been forced to take what repose they could under some tree or other had not Almighty God inspired one of the said young monks to take some care of them now ready to perish. So this young religious prevailed with the porter (as

soon as the prior and the other monks were gone to
rest) to open the gate to these distressed creatures
whom he relieved with a refreshment as seasonable to
them as charitable in itself ; after which he laid them
in the hay-loft and having recommended himself to
their prayers (whom he now perceived, to be no
jesters) he returned to his own lodging. When this
young religious was fallen into a sleep he seemed to
himself as if he saw Christ our Lord sitting on a
tribunal and passing judgment and that he heard Him
command the Masters and Rulers of this place or
Grange to be brought before Him and then appeared
over against Him a certain person clothed in the habit
of a friar minor who received the Prior and his three
other monks after the following manner ;—O just
Judge ! Avenge the blood of Thy servants whom the
barbarous cruelty of these men has turned out of doors
to the dangers of cold and hunger and a most bitter
night. Remember O Lord that these persons have
refused the common reliefs of life to Thy servants, who
have abandoned all worldly pleasures to gain souls for
whom Thou hast suffered death ; reliefs which they
would have bestowed upon buffoons. Then Christ
turning towards the prior asked him with an angry
voice to what Order he belonged. And he replying
to St. Benedict's our Lord asked St. Benedict (who
stood near at hand) if this was true. And when he
answered that they were overthrowers of his Order
whereby he had given a command that his houses
should always be open to all strangers, the sentence
was immediately passed ; and (as it was represented in
this dream) the prior, the sacristan, and spenser were
hanged on a neighbouring elm tree. Then Christ
looked upon the monk by whose charitable assistance

the two poor Franciscans were relieved and asked him what Order he was of? But he fearing to be a partner in the punishment if he owned the Benedictines answered that he was of the Order of that Poor Man who stood there; and therefore our Blessed Saviour presently demanded of the said Poor Man (who had appeared to be St Francis) if that was true? And St Francis, running to the young monk cried out; He is mine Lord, He is mine and from this present moment I receive him into my arms and into my family; and saying this he so closely embraced this his new pupil that he suddenly awakened from his sleep and laying hold of his clothes in haste he ran half undressed to the prior and found him and the other monks in such a deplorable condition that they seemed to be as near being strangled as if they had in good earnest been expiring by a real hanging; but struggling as it were with death and with much ado awaking they were seized with a dreadful fear at the hearing of the young monk's dream. And when the young pious man made haste to look for his guests in the hayrick yard he found they were already gone off, thinking it not safe (it's likely) for them to be caught by the prior. In fine, from hence such an awful reverence and religious respect possessed men's minds towards the Franciscans that not only this young man, but also the Abbot himself of Abingdon having heard what passed at the aforesaid Grange went to Oxford some time after and there took upon him the humble habit of St. Francis and was a member of the Franciscan Community there as soon as they were provided with a house and church, as shall be said hereafter. Now 'tis high time to return to the two friars Richard of Ingworth and Richard of Devon who early in the morning

made the best of their way to Oxford praising the
divine goodness with their whole hearts and offering
up their prayers and vows to heaven for a favourable
reception from the inhabitants of the town. . . ."

Arrived in Oxford at last, Brother Richard of Ingworth and Brother Richard of Devon were received as
in London by the Dominicans, and Friar Thomas tells
us that " they ate in their refectory and slept in their
dormitory for eight days as though they belonged to
the community. At the end of this time they obtained
a house in the parish of St Ebbe and there they dwelt
without a chapel until the following summer. Here
the sweet Jesus sowed the grain of mustard seed which
was afterwards to become greatest among herbs."[1]

The house they obtained in St. Ebbe's parish seems
to have been let to them by Robert le Mercer, and
there " many learned bachelors and many nobles took
the habit." In this house they dwelt till the following
summer (1225), when Brother Richard of Devon and
Brother Richard of Ingworth went on to Northampton,
while in Oxford the brethren removed to a house
" they rented from Richard le Mulliner on the ground
where they now are, but within a year he gave the
ground and house to the city for the use of the
brethren. The ground was very narrow and of no
great length."[2]

The site of the first Franciscan house in Oxford, that
let to the friars by Robert le Mercer, is unknown to us.
It was in the parish of St. Ebbe's and probably near
that church within the city wall.[3] According to Wood,
it stood between St. Ebbe's church and the Watergate.
The house of Richard le Mulliner, the second Franciscan

---

[1] *De Adv. Min.*, coll. II. [2] *Ibid.*, coll. III.
[3] See LITTLE, *op. cit.*, p. 12.

house in Oxford and the site of their permanent convent, was, as Mr. Little has shown, between the city wall and what is now Church Street. Some light seems at first to be thrown on the site of the two houses by the fact that in 1244 Henry III permitted the friars to pull down the city wall in order to connect their new site with the old one,[1] but by then they had not only lost the house of Robert le Mercer, but had acquired many later possessions to which, indeed, the term " new site " certainly refers ; the " old site " being the house of Richard le Mulliner. For long before this the land occupied by the friars had been enlarged. Not later than 1229, " in the mayoralty of John Pady " (1227–29), the Oxford people had given forty-three marks to buy a house in St. Ebbe's " to house the Friars Minor for ever " ; and in 1236 Robert, son of Robert Owen, had given them a house adjoining the land they already occupied, this house being one of the " mural mansions," the occupiers of which had to keep the city wall in repair,[2] a duty now undertaken on behalf of the friars with the King's consent by the Mayor of Oxford.

Friar Thomas tells us that " during the lifetime of Brother Agnellus (*d.* 1236) there was a large increase both of houses and places but because of his love of poverty he would never permit any ground to be enlarged nor any house to be built except as inevitable necessity required. The infirmary at Oxford which he built is a clear evidence of this for he built it in such humble fashion that the height of the walls did not much exceed the height of a man, and even until the

[1] Cf. *Mon. Franc.*, I, 616–17, where the documents are printed.
[2] See LITTLE, *op. cit.*, p. 13, and PARKER : *Early History of Oxford*, p. 342.

time of Brother Albert (1237–38) this same house was without a guest room. . . . But under Brother Haymo (1238–9) the grounds were enlarged in various places for he said he would rather the brethren should have ample ground and should cultivate it and so supply themselves with the fruits of the earth, than that they should beg their bread of others."

It was thus not till the time of Haymo that the holdings of the friars began largely to increase, but from that time (1238) it seems that the whole spirit of the Order was gradually changing and that the old original idea of absolute poverty was more and more lost. Under William of Nottingham (1239–51) Friar Thomas notes, however, that the place at Oxford was " sufficiently large " already. This was probably before 1244, when a large increase of land is to be noted at Oxford. By a deed quoted by Little[1] and dated 22 December, 1244, the King gave the friars of Oxford leave " for the greater quiet and security of their habitation to enclose the street which extends under the wall of Oxford from the gate which is called Water-gate (Little Gate) in the parish of St Ebbe up to the postern in the same wall towards the Castle ; so that a crenellated wall like the rest of the wall of the same town be made round the aforesaid dwelling beginning from the west side of Watergate and reaching south-wards as far as the bank of the Thames, and extending along the bank westward as far as the fee of the Abbot of Bec in the parish of St Bodhoc and then turning again northwards till it joins the old wall of the afore-said borough on the east side of the small postern."

They threw down, then, the old wall, but in 1248[2]

---

[1] *Op. cit.*, p. 14, Pat., 29 Hen. III, m. 9; for text see *Mon. Franc.*, I, 616.   [2] *Mon. Franc.*, I, 617.

they had to rebuild it. Certainly by 1278 they were actually in possession of land without the wall, perhaps " the gift of Agnes widow of Guydo,"[1] and they had long been attempting to obtain possession of several plots in the south-west " suburb of Oxford."[2] Nor was this all. On April 22, 1245, the King gave the friars " our island in the Thames which we have bought from Henry son of Henry Simson,"[3] and gave them permission to make a bridge over that arm of the river which divided it from their houses and to wall it in. This, with other lands whose situation is unknown, completed their holdings in the thirteenth century.

As regards the buildings of the Franciscans in Oxford we know very little. Friar Thomas tells us that having come to Oxford in 1224, " they dwelt without a chapel until the following summer," that is, the summer of 1225, when presumably they had one. And we have already heard of the low built infirmary of Agnellus. Of these buildings, however, we know almost nothing. But we read that in 1232 the King gave them beams from Savernake for the fabric of the chapel.[4] And Friar Thomas speaks of its " choir,"[5] and we know that Agnellus was buried there[6] and that when the new church was built this chapel was pulled down.

But Agnellus built more than this chapel or church and the infirmary. Here in Oxford, " seeing how the place was increasing where the highest learning in England flourished and where scholars from all parts were accustomed to meet, he had a school of becoming dimensions built in the convent of the brethren and

---

[1] LITTLE, *op. cit.*, p. 14.   [2] *Ibid.*, p. 14.   [3] *Ibid.*, p. 16.
[4] Close Roll, 16 Hen. III, m. 9 (June 17) ; quoted by LITTLE, *op. cit.*, p. 21.
[5] *De Adv. Min.*, coll. IV.   [6] *De Adv. Min.*, coll. XIII.

besought Master Robert Grosseteste of holy memory to lecture to them."[1]

These buildings, such as they were, of which the last was probably the most important, were within the city wall. It was not, as we have seen, till after 1240 that the friars occupied land without, and their buildings, then begun, were not undertaken without serious opposition from some of the brethren. Friar Thomas relates that Friar Henry de Reresby, who was vicar of the Custos of Oxford, " after his death appeared to the Custos of Oxford and said that if the brethren were not damned for that they expended more than they should upon their buildings they would nevertheless be grievously punished."[2] In spite, however, of opposition from the more conservative element in the Order a splendid new convent began to rise[3] before 1240, and was still unfinished in 1272. The new church dedicated in honour of St. Francis was also begun, and was in course of erection in 1246 and 1248.

We know, alas! very little of the new priory and not very much of the new church, but it is probable that the latter stood due east and west, the west end being without the old wall, between the south end of Paradise Place and the north end of King's Terrace, where Church Place, which may very well take its name from the church of St. Francis, now stands. We have no description of the church till 1480, when William of Worcester[4] thus speaks of it : " The length of the choir of the church of St Francis at Oxford contains sixty-eight steps. The length from the door of the choir to the west window contains

---

[1] *De Adv. Min.*, coll. X. [2] *De Adv. Min.*, coll. V.
[3] Cf. LITTLE, *op. cit.*, p. 22, and Wood MS., F. xx, 29a ; f. 179a
[4] *Itinerarium*, p. 296. See LITTLE, *op. cit.*, p. 24.

ninety steps ; so in the whole length it contains one hundred and fifty (? 158) steps. The width of the nave of the said church *ab oriente parte* is with the aisle twenty-eight steps. The length of the nave from the south side to the north door contains forty steps only and there are ten chapels in the said north nave of the church. The width of the north nave of the church contains 20 steps. The width of each chapel contains twenty-six steps, and each chapel contains in length six steps, and each glass window of the ten chapels contains three dayes glazed."

This confused and inaccurate description of the church of St. Francis at Oxford helps us but little to picture it as it was. It makes no mention of the Cloister and Chapter House, which we know to have existed at the Dissolution, probably to the south of the church. It has been reckoned by Little, however, that the church measured 79 yards from east to west ; of this the choir occupied 34 yards and the nave 45 yards. At its widest the same authority reckons the church to have measured 20 yards, 10 yards of which were taken up by the north aisle. The choir, he thinks to have been aisleless, or the north aisle of the nave the only one in the church. This north aisle appears to have narrowed from 10 yards to 4 at the east end of the nave. The ten chapels in the north wall were probably for the most part sepulchral chantries, and were in all likelihood later additions. But it is probable that the church itself, as described to us in the end of the fifteenth century, is the church of the thirteenth century, the chief founder of which was Richard Plantagenet, Earl of Cornwall and King of the Romans (1209–72), a great patron of religious houses and the only Englishman who attempted to rule the Holy

Roman Empire. His heart was buried in the choir of St. Francis at Oxford, and in 1277 his third wife, the beautiful Beatrice of Falkenstein, was buried before the high altar. As in London and elsewhere, so here at Oxford, the Franciscan church became the most sought after burial-place in the city.

Of the first brethren and converts of the Order in Oxford we happily know more than of their buildings. Friar Thomas tells us that the first guardian of Oxford was Brother William of Esseby, " who being as yet a novice was now given the habit of profession." He was an Englishman and one of the original nine who had landed at Dover. Among the first converts of the Order were " certain Masters of the University who added to the fame of the brethren. One of these was Brother Walter de Burgh concerning whom a brother had a wonderful vision ; for he saw our Lord Jesus descending from heaven who offered to Brother Walter a scroll on which was written : ' Thy harvest is not here but elsewhere.' To this brother was revealed the deception of a certain religious woman who had deluded a certain prudent brother so far that he committed her visions to writing. Now Brother Agnellus did not believe in the visions and he enjoined the brethren to pray that God would make clear to him a certain matter about which he was much concerned, and behold that very night Brother Walter saw in vision a doe run quickly at the brow of a high mountain and two big dogs followed her and turned her down into the valley and there strangled her. Whereupon he ran to the place where he thought he would find the doe and found nothing but a small vessel full of blood. This vision he related to Brother Agnellus who judged that the woman was a hypocrite and he

[47]

sent unto her therefore two discreet brethren who at length brought her to a confession of the truth and she confessed that she had invented all she had told.

" Another Master was Brother Richard, a Norman who was once asked by the aforesaid Brother Walter for a word of edification ; and after long deliberation within himself, replied : Whosoever wishes to be at peace, let him hold his peace.

" Then came Master Vincent of Coventry and he not long after, by the grace of Jesus Christ, prevailed upon his brother, Master Henry, to enter also. They were received on the day of the conversion of St Paul (Jan. 25, probably 1227) together with the Master Adam of Oxford of holy memory and Sir William of York.

" Master Adam of Oxford was famous through the whole world. He had made a vow that whatsoever was asked of him for the love of the Blessed Virgin he would grant and this he told to a certain woman, a recluse who was a friend of his. She revealed his secret to her friends namely a monk of Reading and certain others of the order of the Cistercians and to a Friar Preacher, telling them that they should gain so great a man for their Orders ; for she did not wish the Friars Minor to have him. But the Blessed Virgin brought it to pass that none of them should ask anything, of Master Adam for love of her even when they got into his company, but always they deferred their request until another time. But one night Master Adam dreamt that he was crossing a bridge where certain men were setting snares to catch him. With great difficulty he escaped them and found himself in a most pleasant spot. But just as divine Providence had delivered him from the others he came by chance upon the Friars Minor ; and William de Colville the elder, a man of sanctity, spoke amongst other words, these : ' Beloved Master for the love of the Mother of God enter our Order and rouse up our simplicity,' and at once Master Adam gave way as though he had heard the Mother of God herself speak. He was at that time the companion of Master Adam de Marisco and in his service whom also by the grace of God he induced to enter the Order not long after. For one night Brother Adam de Marisco dreamt that he came to a castle and above the gates was an image of the Crucifix which all who passed in must kiss. Now Brother Adam of Oxford went through first after kissing the Crucifix and the other Brother Adam kissing the Crucifix followed him. But the first at once discovering the stairs in the tower ran up swiftly and was soon out of sight. The other following cried out : Not so fast ! But never was the first seen again. The meaning of this vision afterwards became clear to all the brethren in England. For Brother Adam of Oxford after entering the Order went to Pope Gregory (IX) and according to his own wish was sent by him to preach to the Saracens. He died at Barlete (? Barletta in Apulia in Italy) before the death of Brother Adam de Marisco, and it is said was renowned for miracles."

Of Brother Adam de Marisco I shall speak later when I deal with the Friars and the University. Friar Thomas thus continues : " After these came Master John of Reading, Abbot of Osney who left us an example of all perfection. Next after him Brother Rufus who was well known both in Paris and Oxford. There came also certain knights to wit Sir Richard Gobion, Sir Giles de Merk, Sir Thomas a Spaniard and Sir

Henry de Walpole. Concerning their entrance into the Order our lord the King afterwards said : ' If you friars had been discreet in receiving brethren, if you had not promised privileges to the injury of your fellows and especially had you not been unfortunate in questing, you might have ruled over princes.' "[1]

This rather cryptic saying ascribed to the King refers perhaps to a later time than that we have yet reached. In the beginning, at least, the brethren were filled with humility, and Friar Thomas devotes a whole collatio[2] to an exposition of the primitive piety of the brethren. With it I shall close this chapter.

" The brethren in those days having the first fruits of the Holy Spirit served Our Lord not so much by the observance of human institutions as by the free outpouring of their piety, being content with their Rule and the very few statutes which were made the same year that the Rule was confirmed. The first statute made by St Francis after the Rule was confirmed was this (as we are told by Brother Albert of holy memory) that the brethren when they eat with seculars should not take more than three mouthfuls of food continuously, that the holy Gospel might be observed, for a rumour had reached St Francis that the brethren ate greedily. They were accustomed to keep silence until the hour of Terce and so untiring were they in prayer that there was scarce an hour of the night when some one of them was not at prayer in the chapel. Moreover in the chief feasts they chanted with such fervour that their vigils sometimes lasted the whole night and although there might be but three or four brethren or at the most six they sang

[1] *De Adv. Min.*, coll. III.   [2] *De Adv. Min.*, coll. IV.

the office solemnly according to note. Such too was their simplicity and purity that did anyone of them unwittingly any shame he confessed it before all the brethren in the chapel. There grew up amongst them a most religious custom never to swear to anything but only to say ' know that it is so.' Were anyone accused by his superior or companion he at once answered ' Mea Culpa ! ' and often prostrated himself. Whereupon Brother Jordan of holy memory Master-General of the Friars-Preachers has related how the devil once appeared to him and said that this *mea culpa* snatched from his grasp whatever hope he had of getting the Friars Minor since whenever one offended against another he always acknowledged his fault to the other. Yet the brethren at all times were so joyful and merry amongst themselves that even when they were silent their countenances seemed to laugh. Whence it happened that at Oxford where the young brethren were frequently given to much laughter, it was enjoined on one of them to take the discipline as often as he laughed. Now one day he neither restrained his laughter nor took the discipline. The next night therefore he dreamt that the whole community was standing according to custom in the choir and as usual some of the brethren were laughing when, lo, the Crucifix which stood at the door of the choir turned to them as though it lived and said : ' They are the sons of Core who at the time of the Divine Office laugh and sleep.' It seemed to him also that the figure on the crucifix strove to free its hands as though wishing to come down and to go away, but the guardian himself immediately went up and made the nails fast so that the figure could not come down. When this dream was told to the brethren they were terrified and henceforth bore themselves more seriously and without overmuch laughter.

" So jealous were they for the truth that they would hardly permit themselves to speak in hyperbole nor would they conceal their faults even when they knew that they would be punished did they confess. When they were sent to new places or were told to abide in this place they were already in, they made no difficulty nor in regard to any matter or place whatever once they knew it was the superior's will. Whence it happened that brethren noble by birth or in other ways who were notable men in the world and most respected in the Order would without a murmur allow themselves to be sent to places which in those days were simple wildernesses. This only in the sweetness of their souls seemed to sadden them, that they should have to separate ; wherefore the brethren would often accompany those who were sent away unto a far distance and at parting tears of affection would show how they loved one another."

V

THE MOVEMENT THROUGH ENGLAND

HAVING established the Order in Oxford, Brother Richard of Ingworth and Brother Richard of Dover, according to Friar Thomas,[1] " went on to Northampton," near by which, at Kingsthorpe, it is possible the former was born. At Northampton they " were taken into the hospice." Afterwards they rented a house in the parish of St. Giles, where the first guardian was Brother Peter, a Spaniard, " who wore an iron breastplate next to his flesh and in other ways gave evidence of perfection." This was perhaps in 1225. Ten years later, in 1235, John of Reading, Abbot of Osney, entered the Order at Northampton Later, in the time of Brother Albert, that is 1237–8, according to Friar Thomas, " the place at North-ampton was changed, as also the places at Worcester and Hereford." It had first been outside the eastern walls and was then moved to a good site north-east of the town granted by the burgesses. Leland thus describes it : " The grey friars house was the best builded and largest house of all the places of the friars, and stood a little beyond the chief market-place almost by flat north. The site and ground that it stood on belonged to the city whereupon the citizens were taken for the founders of it."

We thus know the names in order, and perhaps also

[1] *De Adv. Min.*, coll. II.

the dates of the foundation, of the first four Franciscan convents in England : 1. Canterbury, September, 1224. 2. London, September, 1224. 3. Oxford, November, 1224. 4. Northampton, founded perhaps in the summer of 1225.[1] What was the fifth convent founded in England ? The next place mentioned by Friar Thomas is Cambridge, and there is reason to believe that the foundation of the Cambridge convent dates from 1225. Though it never attained the fame of the Oxford convent, nevertheless at the suppression its church was the finest in the town. The site was that of Sidney Sussex College. But at the first entry of the friars into Cambridge Friar Thomas tells us " the brethren were received at first by the burgesses who made over to them the old Synagogue near the Gaol. This was intolerable to the brethren for both they and the gaolers had to use the same entry ; so our lord the king gave them 10 marks with which to buy the lease from the court of Exchequer. Then they built a chapel so humble that one carpenter made in one day and in one day set up fourteen pairs of rafters. On the feast of St Laurence (Aug. 10) (? 1225) though there were as yet but three brethren namely Brother William of Esseby and Brother Hugh of Bugeton both clerics, and a novice named Brother Elias who was so lame that he had to be carried into the choir, they sang the office solemnly according to note and the novice wept so much that the tears ran freely down his face. Now this novice afterwards died a most holy death at York and he appeared to Brother

[1] *De Adv. Min.*, coll. II. We read there that the two Richards having obtained a house in the parish of St. Ebbe in Oxford, " dwelt there without a chapel, till the following summer." We are then told that they went on to Northampton. Whether " till the following summer " refers only to the clause " without a chapel " or not, I cannot determine

William of Esseby at Northampton and when Brother William asked him how he was, he answered, ' I am well, pray for me.' "

The name of Brother William of Esseby, who here appears as perhaps the founder of the Cambridge convent, suggests another mission separate from that which had founded the London, Oxford and Northampton convents. Indeed, the friars were by every means quickly spreading their Order through all England.

It was perhaps the entrance into the Order of Brother Haymo of Faversham that caused this to be so quickly achieved. This famous man in 1238–9, the third Minister Provincial in England, and later the fourth General of the whole Order, was born at Faversham in Kent. After studying in England he went to Paris, where he was known as the most Aristotelian of Aristotelians. There, already a priest and a famous preacher, he entered the Franciscan Order at St. Denys, on Good Friday, but the year of his reception is unknown.[1] Shortly after, he returned to England, and, as Friar Thomas asserts, " his entrance into the Order caused the number of preachers to be greatly increased and gave them influence and fame for he was a priest and a famous preacher at the time he entered the Order. . . .

" When Brother Haymo came to England there came also Brother William de Colville the elder, a man of great simplicity and exceeding charity. . . .

" And after these many other distinguished brethren came to England who were Englishmen but had entered the Order at Paris, whom whilst I was yet in

---

[1] That it was prior to 1224 the following extract from *De Adv. Min.*, coll. V, seems to show ; " and so, as I have said, after the brethren had come to England, Brother Haymo came also."

secular dress I myself saw. There was brother Nicholas Rufus a reader of great merit, who being zealous for the reformation of the Order went afterwards with Brother Haymo to represent France in the appeal against Brother Elias. . . . At that time also came Brother Ralph de Rosa who because of the delight of his preaching was received with great favour by our lord the King of England. . . . Then came Brother Henry de Burford . . . who was found worthy to be the special companion in England of four Ministers General and four Provincials. . . . About the same time came Brother Henry de Reresby who from being Vicar to the Custos of Oxford was appointed Minister of Scotland, but died before he could proceed thither. . . . There came also Brother Martin de Barton . . . and lastly Brother Peter the Spaniard who afterwards became guardian of Northampton."[1]

There might seem to be little doubt that the amazingly rapid growth of the Order in England was largely due to this reinforcement of preachers. That the increase of the Order was extraordinarily rapid is certain. In the *De Adventu Minorum* we read[2]: "Well worthy to be recorded is it that in the second year of the ministry of Brother Peter, the fifth Provincial Minister of England, that is to say in the thirty-second year since the coming of the brethren into England,[3] there were in the English Province forty-nine houses and the number of the brethren dwelling therein was one thousand two hundred and forty-two."

It is not, alas! possible for us to name all of those

---

[1] *De Adv. Min.*, coll. V.   [2] *De Adv. Min.*, coll. II.
[3] The second year of the ministry of Brother Peter cannot be earlier than 1252; the thirty-second year since the coming of the brethren into England was 1255.

forty-nine houses, but with some accuracy we can trace the establishment of most of them. In 1258, according to Wadding, St. Bonaventure held a General Chapter of the Order at Narbonne, and it there appeared that England was divided into the seven Custodies which Bartholomew of Pisa in 1399 enumerates with their sixty convents. But it is certain that long before 1258 the Province of England had been divided into Custodies, for Friar Thomas tells us[1] that " the brethren having increased from day to day both in merits and in numbers and their houses being consequently multiplied it seemed expedient that the Province should be divided into Custodies. This therefore was done at the first Provincial Chapter of London." He proceeds to enumerate these Custodies, making them six in number, namely, London, Oxford, Cambridge, York, Salisbury and Worcester. Unhappily the date of the first Provincial Chapter of London is uncertain, but it might seem impossible that it was later than the thirties of the thirteenth century.[2] That there was an earlier division than that of 1258 is supported, too, by this, that the Custodies there set up were not altogether the same as those which Friar Thomas names.

[1] *De Adv. Min.*, coll. VI.

[2] It was at this Chapter, perhaps that Agnellus was ordained priest (coll. XIII). The first Provincial Chapter of the Dominicans in England was held in Oxford in 1230. The first Provincial Chapter of London referred to may date as early as 1229. There were Visitatorial Chapters in London about that year, in 1230, and 1238; in 1241 there was a Provincial Chapter at Whitsuntide. Cf. Little in *Collectanea Franc.*, II, 145. According to an uncertain reading in the Phillipps MS. of Eccleston, the English Province at first consisted of four Custodies. Cf. Little: *Studies in English, Franc. Hist.* (1917), p. 235. Eccleston in naming six Custodies implies a seventh—Hereford, later in the Province of Bristol. Salisbury disappears as a Custody altogether by 1331. The seventh Custody, not mentioned by Eccleston, is Newcastle.

Thus Bristol, where the convent had been established before 1234, seems to take the place of Salisbury, and Newcastle is added to the number.

Of the six earlier Custodies Friar Thomas gives us the character; for each Custody, according to him, had its special mark of sanctity.

" Now each Custody," he writes, " was remarkable for some singular note of sanctity. Thus in the Custody of London governed by Brother Gilbert (c. 1230) to whom the Blessed Virgin appeared at the hour of death, there especially flourished the spirit of fervour, reverence and devotion in reciting the Divine Office.

" The Custody of Oxford, presided over by Brother William of Esseby, was noted for its learning.

" The Custody of Cambridge of which Brother Richard of Ingworth was the Custos was particularly remarkable for its want of temporal goods, so that at the time of his first visitation of England[1] Brother Albert of Pisa, as he himself related, found the brethren of this custody to be without cloaks.

" In the Custody of York over which presided Brother Martin de Barton there was a great zeal for poverty and it was not allowed that more brethren should dwell in any place than could be sustained there by begging without running into debt.

" The Custody of Salisbury under Brother Stephen was notable for brotherly love. Brother Stephen himself was a man of great sweetness of heart and cheerfulness, of great charity and compassion so that he would never allow anyone to be sad if he could by any means prevent him. Now when he came to die, and they brought him the Saving Host, he beheld in the

[1] 1237 or 1238.

Host the door by which he would enter into eternal life, and singing with a loud voice the *Salve Regina*, he died happily at Salisbury.

"In the Custody of Worcester over which Brother —— of Leicester presided there especially flourished the primitive simplicity; for this Brother, small of stature but large of heart, always studied to observe the greatest simplicity and brought many simple persons into the Order. At length with tears and a loud cry he gave up his simple and holy soul into the hands of the Lord, dying at Worcester."

Such was the first division of the Province[1] and such the character of the local centres, the Custodies. That the establishment of these Custodies was a further cause of the increase of houses is probable. That they did increase we know not only from the records of new foundations, but from Friar Thomas. "The number of the brethren having increased from day to day the houses and ground which sufficed for them when they were few could not contain them when they were a multitude. Moreover by the providence of God many persons entered the Order for whom it seemed but right to make more honourable provision. And, in some places the brethren had in their simplicity without thought for the future, so placed themselves that their holdings could not be enlarged and so they had to remove elsewhere. Hence it happened that even during the life-time of Brother Agnellus there was a large increase both of houses and places and yet because of his love of poverty he would never permit any ground to be enlarged nor any house to be built except as inevitable necessity required."

[1] It is possible that Newcastle was omitted by inadvertence in Eccleston.

To follow in detail the wonderful progress of the Order through England would perhaps be impossible. We may, however take a large view of it. We have seen in some detail at least the establishment of the Canterbury, London and Oxford houses; we have followed Richard of Ingworth and Richard of Devon from Oxford to Northampton; we have seen the erection of the Cambridge house. Such was the road of the Franciscans into England, and these houses, the milestones upon it, were probably set up—the first four of them certainly were—before the end of 1225. But it is impossible for us to pursue that road any further. We do not know what was the next house in order after Cambridge, nor if we did should we be able to continue thus, for each capital centre doubtless began to develop and to establish houses and this independently and simultaneously. If we would obtain some idea of the penetration of England by the Order we shall be wise to take the Custodies in order, for they are the framework upon which the Order built.

As we have seen, there were seven Custodies, viz. London, Oxford, Cambridge, York, Salisbury, Worcester and Hereford. In 1258, as I suppose, Bristol took the place of Hereford as the south-western Custody. In the same year Newcastle may have been erected as the head of a new Custody, that of the North. The Salisbury house has come into the Custody of London.

It is not, however, till about 1334, in the *Provinciale Vetustissimum*, that we have a complete list of the Franciscan houses of England under their Custodies, and it is by an examination of that catalogue that we shall best understand how swiftly and completely the

friars established themselves throughout England.[1]
And this I shall now undertake as briefly as possible.

1. THE CUSTODY OF LONDON

The Custody of London consisted of nine convents,
namely : London, Salisbury, Canterbury, Winchester,
Southampton, Lewes, Chichester, Winchelsea and
Ware. Of these, all save Winchelsea and Ware were
in existence in 1255–6, that is to say, in " the thirty-
second year since the coming of the brethren into
England," to which Friar Thomas refers when he says
that " there were then in the English Province forty-
nine houses."[2]

London.

The convent, the second founded in England, dates,
as we have seen, from September, 1224.

Salisbury.

This convent was founded before 1230,[3] when the
King made it a gift of fuel. It is probable that Richard
Poore, Bishop of Salisbury and founder of the Cathedral, was the founder here also ; at any rate, we read
under date 1228–9 that he " pro tunc Fratres Minores
Sarum constituit et eisdem aptum locum pro habita-
tione eorum dedit et confirmavit."[4] The King was
often their benefactor.[5] It was for a time the head
of a Custody, but before 1331 it had become a house
in the Custody of London.

[1] LITTLE : (*Studies in Eng. Franc. History*) prints the Perpignan List
of 1331.   [2] See *supra*, p. 56.   [3] Close, 14 Hen. III, m. 13.
[4] *Charters, etc., illustrating the History of Salisbury* (Rolls), p. 269.
[5] See Pipe Rolls, quoted by HOARE : *A. & M. Wilts*, Vol. 6, p. 57 ;
The dates are 1230, 1232 and 1239.

The house was situated, as Leland tells us, " within the town of Saresbyri."[1]

Canterbury.

The house here, the first founded in England, dates from September, 1224.

Winchester.

This convent was founded in 1237, in which year the friars were given a place by the King.[2] According to Friar Thomas, it was Albert of Pisa who placed brethren here, " in spite of great difficulties,"[3] which, if we are to judge by what occurred at other great monastic towns,[4] were due to the opposition of the monks. The house was situated by the East Gate, but it is difficult to-day to find even its site. It was, according to Leland, " hard within the gate on the right hand."

Southampton.

The convent here was founded before 1235,[5] in which year the King made the friars a gift. The founder is said to have been Isabel de Chekebull, who died in 1253 ; while Walter le Flemyng, bailiff of the town in 1237, was one of the benefactors. The convent was situated to the south-east of the town in the poorest part close by " God's House," the Hospital of St. Julian, founded for the poor by Gervase le Riche in 1197. The burgesses of Southampton soon built the friars a cloister of stone, to the

[1] Cf. Wilts Arch. Mag., XVII, 165.   [2] Lib., 21 Hen. III, m. 5.
[3] *De Adv. Min.*, coll. XIII.
[4] See *infra*, Reading, Bury St. Edmunds, etc., pp. 66–7, 72–3.
[5] Close, 19 Hen. III, Pt. I, m. 10 and cf. MADOX : *Formulare Anglicanum*, and DAVIES : *Hist. of Southampton*, 444 *et seq.*

scandal of Albert of Pisa, and this, Friar Thomas tells us, "he pulled down though with much trouble because of the opposition of the townsfolk."[1] It is not till towards the end of the thirteenth century that we hear of a stone chapel being built. The first stone of this was laid on July 8, 1280, and it was first used on July 16, 1287. It was dedicated in honour of St. Francis and was of some size, for Bishop Sandale held a great ordination there in February, 1317. At Christmas, 1291, the friars went into the new convent, and in the same year the Chapter House was completed. Nothing at all is left of chapel or convent. Leland says : " There was a college of Grey Freres on the est-south-est part of the towne, touching the towne waulle betwixt the est and the south-est gates."

Lewes.

This convent was founded before 1241, in which year the King gave the friars ten marks for vestments.[2] The date of the foundation is unknown. In 1253 the house, like that at Chichester, received 20 shillings and a book of the gospels of St. Luke and St. John by the will of St. Richard.[3] And in 1299 King Edward was at Lewes and paid them 24 shillings for three days' food, there being then twenty-four brethren in the convent.[4]

The Friary of Lewes was situated near the church of All Saints, where the street is still called the Friars' Walk. After the Suppression its site was occupied by a house in which in 1830 King William and his queen

---

[1] *De Adv. Min.*, coll. XIII (*ca.* 1236).
[2] Lib., 26 Hen. III, m. 18 (Oct. 31, 1241).
[3] *Suss. Arch. Coll.*, I, 167.   [4] *Suss. Arch. Coll.*, II, 146.

were entertained. It is now occupied by the Railway
Goods Station.

Chichester.

This convent was founded here before 1253,[1] when
the King granted the friars money to pay their debts,
and a little later in the same month ordered the Sheriff
of Sussex to give to the minister of the Friars Minor
of Chichester " twenty-six tunics " (*xxvi tunicas com-
petentes distribuendas*). The date of the foundation
of the convent is unknown, but it was probably early,
as Friar Thomas tells us that Brother William de
Coleville the elder, " a man of great simplicity and
exceeding charity," had relations at Chichester. He
goes on to relate how William de Coleville's sister " was
afterwards cruelly murdered in the Cathedral of
Chichester because of her chastity. For a certain
youth taken with her beauty had long desired to meet
her alone and seduce her ; and when he could by no
means lead her astray he proved how wicked carnal
love may be, by killing her in the church."[2]

One of the founders of the convent here was apparently Richard, Earl of Cornwall, whose grant of land
adjoining the house was confirmed by Henry III in the
same year in which he made his own gifts to the friars.
And again in this same year St. Richard of Chichester
bequeathed them 20 shillings and a psalter.[3] They
were then settled on the site occupied after 1269 by
St. Mary's Hospital, a short distance east of North
Street. In 1269 the friars removed by leave of the
King to the vacant site of the Castle.[4] There they

[1] Lib., 37 Hen. III, m. 1 (July 8, 1253).
[2] *De Adv. Min.*, coll. V.
[3] *Suss. Arch. Coll.*, I, 167.   [4] Pat. ,53 Hen. III, m. 2.

built the beautiful church, a part of which still happily
remains to us. It is Early English in style, has a fine
east window of five lancets and very beautiful sedilia,
now hidden by the magistrates' benches, for it is now
used as the Guildhall. In this chapel Archbishop
Peckham held an ordination in 1282.[1]

Winchelsea.

A convent was founded here before 1253, in which
year it appears in the will of St. Richard.[2] The date
of the foundation is not known. When old Winchelsea
was destroyed by the storm of 1267 and the new town
built on the hill by the King, it was agreed that no
monastery or friary should be built there save only a
house for the Friars Minor.[3] This was erected where
now the modern mansion called " The Friary " stands,
the old convent having been pulled down so lately as
1819. A part of the ruined chapel of the Blessed Virgin
remains, however, the choir and the apsidal east end.
The chancel arch is especially lovely, the style, Decorated, and thus contemporary with the re-foundation
of the house.

Ware.

A convent was founded 1338 by Thomas, second
Lord Wake of Liddell.[4] The house stood between the
High Street and the Lea. There are no remains, but
the old rectory probably marks the site of the Priory.
This convent is added to the Custody by Bar-
tholomew of Pisa.

[1] Reg. Epist. Peckham (Rolls Ser.), III, 1029.
[2] *Sussex Arch. Coll.*, I, 170.
[3] Parl. Proc., 2, No. 6.
[4] Cal. Pat., 1338–40, p. 14.

The Franciscans in England

The Custody of Oxford consisted of eight convents, namely : Oxford, Northampton, Reading, Bedford, Stamford, Nottingham, Leicester and Grantham. Of these eight, all save Grantham were in existence in 1255–6.

Oxford.

The convent, the third founded in England, dates, as we have seen, from November, 1224.

Northampton.

The convent, the fourth founded in England, dates, as we have seen, from 1225.

Reading.

This convent was founded in 1233,[1] when by a deed dated July 14 the abbot Adam de Lathbury and the monastery granted to the friars a plot of waste ground by the highway leading to Caversham Bridge, with leave to build and dwell there so long as they should be verily mendicant and should hold no property of their own and did not encroach upon the rights of the Abbey, nor seek to extend their holding. There, as Friar Thomas tells us, the King built the friars a chapel. When Albert of Pisa was minister (*ca.* 1236), who was so eager to keep the whole rule of St. Francis he would have liked to pull down this chapel, but would not " for that the king had built it, but he earnestly prayed that heaven would destroy it." It was he who " returned to the monks of Reading the

[1] Cart., 17 Hen. III, m. i.

writing whereby they had bound themselves not to
expel the brethren at their own will and he offered,
if the monks wished, himself to remove the brethren."[1]
It is obvious that here, as elsewhere, the friars were
very jealously opposed by the monks.[2] In 1282 Archbishop Peckham, who was himself a friar, wrote to the
abbot in a very different tone. He asked for leave to
enlarge the site of their house, which they had promised
not to do, and his excuse was that the convent was
often under water in the winter.[3] In 1285 we find
that this had been allowed ; at any rate, in that year
the Archbishop wrote to the Minister-General of the
Order to ask him to confirm the change of site of the
house at Reading, and he speaks there of the simplicity
of the friars who had accepted a swamp for a convent
site, and one some distance from the town. In consequence of his representations and those of others the
monks were obliged to allow the friars a better site on
high ground within the town, but they were subject
to every sort of restriction, which the Archbishop had
accepted in the hope that royal benevolence or his own
power might in time do away with it.[4] These restric-
tions were the old ones over again, with the right con-
served to the monks to expel the friars without appeal
if they transgressed them in any particular. In 1288,
however, Robert Fulco bequeathed them certain pieces
of land adjoining the grant of the Abbey in New Street.

The church of the Grey Friars, of which much
still remains, was at the Spoliation granted to the

[1] *De Adv. Min.*, coll. XIII.
[2] For this and other examples of the disputes between the friars and
the monks, see LITTLE : *Studies in Eng. Franc. Hist.* (Manchester),
p. 1 *et seq.*
[3] Reg. Epist. Peckham (Rolls), II, 415–16.
[4] Reg. Epist. Peckham (Rolls), III, 211–12.

Corporation, which converted it into a town hall (1543). In 1560 it was a workhouse and in 1613 a prison, as it remained till 1863. In the year following an (Anglican) ecclesiastical parish of " Grey Friars " was formed out of the parishes of St. Mary and St. Laurence, and the old church of the friars standing at the corner of the Caversham road was appointed as the mother church. It now consists of a wide nave of five bays, aisles and transepts. The north transept and south and west aisles of the south transept are entirely new. There is no chancel. The arcades consist of pointed arches borne by clustered columns of the Decorated style of the early fourteenth century.

Bedford.

The convent here was founded before 1242,[1] in which year the King gave three marks to buy wood for building purposes. According to Leland, the house was founded by Lady Mabel de Pattishall ; but in the Valor Ecclesiasticus we find that John St. John was the founder.[2] The church was finished and dedicated on November 3rd, 1295.[3] The house was in St. Paul's parish in the north-west of the town, and its site is still remembered as the modern " Grey Friars' Walk " and Priory Street. The old convent or part of it, then a farm, still existed till 1889.[4]

Stamford.

This convent was founded before 1230,[5] when the

1 Lib., 26 Hen. III, m. 7.
2 Valor Eccles. (Rec. Com.), IV, 190.
3 Linc. Epis. Reg. Memo.   Sutton, 127.
4 V.C H., *Bedford*, Vol. 3, p. 22.
5 Close, 14 Hen. III, Part I, m. 18.

King made it a grant of fuel, and in 1235 we find that he gave the friars timber for their stalls.[1] In September, 1239, a Provincial Chapter was held in the house, and the King bade the sheriff of Lincoln give the friars 100 shillings for one day's expenses.[2] At a later Chapter here, according to Mr. Little in 1247 or 1249, the friars welcomed the Austin Friars to England.[3] In 1244 the King had given them 100 shillings for their church from the revenues of the bishopric of Chester.[4] In 1293, and again in 1300, the Provincial Chapter was held here. Mr. Little argues that at the end of the century the convent had between thirty-nine and forty-six friars.[5]

We know nothing of the founder.

The house was in the eastern suburb of the town by St. Paul's Gate, and the walls were still standing in 1727, as Peck tells us in his *Antiquarian Annals of Stamford*. He says, " it appears that the church, monastery and gardens took in a great compass of ground," and adds, " out of the ruins have been frequently dug many fine pieces of carving . . . and in the outgoing wall down from St Paul's to St George's gate is yet to be seen part of a figure of a woman with dishevelled hair which was dug up here." This he engraved. Nothing now remains.

Nottingham.

This convent was founded here before 1230,[6] in which year the King made it a gift of timber for the building of the chapel. Further gifts of a similar

[1] Close, 19 Hen. III, Pt. I, m. 4.   [2] Lib., 23 Hen. III, m. 7.
[3] *De Adv. Min.*, coll. XIV.   [4] Lib., 28 Hen. III, m. 6.
[5] V.C.H., *Lincolnshire*, Vol. 2, p. 228.
[6] Close, 14 Hen. III, Pt. I, m. 14.

nature were made the convent by the King in 1232, 1234, 1236, 1242, 1247.[1] When the friars began to build a chapel of stone the King gave them leave to take stone from his quarry at Nottingham.[2] This church was dedicated in 1303,[3] and appears to have been finished about 1310.[4]

The house was situated in the south-west part of the town in Broadmarsh, not far from the Castle.

Nothing remains.

Leicester.

This convent was founded before 1230, as Friar Thomas tells us when he writes, " Now came Brother John Naverius who for the first time brought over the explanation of the Rule according to the Lord Pope Gregory IX. On account of the Visitation therefore he assembled the brethren, even the novices, in great numbers under Brother Agnellus at London, Leicester and Bristol."[5] This explanation of the rule by Gregory IX (*Quo elongati*) is dated 28 September, 1230.

In 1255 we have a gift of timber to the convent from the King.[6]

It is traditional that the convent at Leicester was founded by the second Simon de Montfort. The house stood on the south side of St. Martin's churchyard, where when Nichols wrote his *History of Leicestershire* a gate remained, but all the rest had been demolished. In the church the body of Richard III was buried after the battle of Bosworth. It was carried from the field " trussed across a horse's back behind a pursuivant and with a halter round the neck."

---

[1] See V.C.H., *Nottingham*, II, p. 144.   [2] Close, Hen. III, m. 11d.
[3] *Relig. Inst. of Old Notts*, I, 68.   [4] Harl. MS., 6970, fol. 238.
[5] *De Adv. Min.*, coll. VII.   [6] Close, 40 Hen. III, m. 20.

Some years later Henry VII built a fine tomb for him with an effigy in alabaster, all destroyed at the Spoliation. The church was dedicated in honour of the Holy Trinity.

Grantham.

The convent here was founded before 1290,[1] when the Pope granted an indulgence of one year and forty days to all those penitents who should visit the church of the friars at Grantham on the four greater feasts of the B.V.M. and on the feasts of St. Francis, St. Clare and St. Anthony of Padua. There were twenty-one friars here at the end of the thirteenth century.[2] We know nothing of the date of foundation or the founder or the buildings, though a new church was certainly founded here in the first third of the fourteenth century. Nothing remains.

3. THE CUSTODY OF CAMBRIDGE

The Custody of Cambridge consisted of eight or, with Walsingham, nine convents, namely : Cambridge, Norwich, Bury St. Edmunds, King's Lynn, Ipswich, Colchester, Yarmouth, Dunwich, Walsingham. Of the nine, all save the last four were in existence in 1255-6.

Cambridge.

The convent, the fifth founded in England, was established probably in 1225, as we have seen. It was

---

[1] *Bull. Franc.*, IV, 194. Cal. Papal Lett., I, 521.
[2] Brit. Mus. Add. MS. 7966a., f. 23b.

a disused synagogue situated next the gaol, given the friars by the burgesses.

Norwich.

This convent was founded in 1226[1] on land given for the use of the friars by John de Hastingford between the churches of St. Cuthbert and St. Vedast in Conisford. In 1285 we find them enlarging the site,[2] and in the following year building a large church.[3] Further extension of land in 1292, 1297 and 1299 enabled them to complete what they had begun.

Bury St. Edmunds.

In the *Annales de Dunstaplia* we read ad. ann 1233 : " *Eodem anno fratres minores volentes habitare in burgo Sancti Edmundi. . . .*"[4] But they were not successful till 1257. We have an account of their efforts from the monks' point of view.[5] We are there told that the friars had long tried in vain to establish themselves in Bury ; till at last they obtained a Bull in their favour from Alexander IV, relying on which they entered Bury June 22, 1257, and hastily established themselves on a farm at the north end of the town. The monks, however, remonstrated with them and at last ignominiously expelled them. The friars naturally appealed to Rome. The Pope wrote severely to the monastery and enjoined the primate and the dean of Lincoln to induct

[1] BARTH. DE COTTON : *Hist. Anglicana* (R.S., p. 113) ; BLUMEFIELD : *Hist. of Norfolk*, IV, 106 *et seq.*, and KIRKPATRICK : *Relig. Ord. of Norwich*, 104 *et seq.*

[2] Pat., 13 Edw. I, m. 27.

[3] W. DE WORCESTER : *Itin.* (Rolls), 306 and 308.

[4] *Ann. Monast.* (Rolls), III, 134.

[5] *Memorials of S. Edmund's Abbey* (Rolls), II, 263 *et seq.*

the friars into another house in Bury. The delegates invested the friars in new premises, and again the monks indignantly drove them away. The friars then turned to the King, Henry III, who in spite of the resistance of the monks, caused the friars to be put in possession of this second site. There they built and there they remained for seven years. But Alexander IV then being dead, the monks laid their cause before his successor, Urban IV, who ordered the friars to pull down their buildings and abandon the ground. The friars obeyed and were reconciled with the monastery, and in 1262–3 quitted Bury, the monks granting them land at Babwell outside the town, beyond the north gate. There they remained till the Dissolution.

Now, that record is typical of what appears to have occurred wherever the friars tried to enter a monastic stronghold. It was the same at Reading, at Durham, at Exeter and at Winchester.[1]

We know little of the history of the buildings ; only parts of the walls of the precincts remain.

King's Lynn.

This convent was probably founded about 1230, for Friar Thomas speaks of it[2] as remarkable as possessing a man of extraordinary sanctity, " Brother Galfrid of Salisbury, who because of the austerity of his life was said to be a second Francis and because of his sweetness and simplicity was called a second Anthony. When he was hearing confessions such was his gentleness and

---

[1] For an account of this quarrel as of others, see LITTLE. *Studies,* p. 1 *et seq.*

[2] *De Adv. Min.,* coll. XI. In 1264 " brother John Stamford, eighth Minister Provincial of the English Franciscan, died and was buried at Lyene."

the pity he felt towards his penitents that if these did not show befitting signs of sorrow he would weep and groan until they too began to weep as happened to a certain nobleman, Sir Alexander de Bissingbourne. He had confessed his sins as though he were telling a tale but Brother Galfrid wept so sore that at last the nobleman wept too. Then listening to the brother's salutary advice and assisted by his merits he formed the purpose of entering the Order in which purpose he died in holy fashion. . . ." Perhaps it was this nobleman who founded the convent of the friars in Lynn ; at any rate, he must be considered a benefactor. Blomefield[1] tells us that the convent here was founded by Thomas Feltham or de Folsham. It stood, according to the same authority, in Fuller's Road.

The only fragment left to us of the house is " the Grey Friars Steeple," consisting of a lantern tower 90 feet high, supported on an arch of red brick. This is well engraved in Dugdale. The whole seems to date from the fifteenth century.

Ipswich.

This convent was founded before 1236, about which time we have a document which speaks of the enlargement of the house.[2] Tanner tells us that the house was in the west part of the town in the parish of St. Nicholas, and asserts that the friars were placed there in the time of Edward I by the charity of Sir Robert Tippot of Nettlested, who died 1298, and Una his wife, who, Weever tells us, were the founders and were buried there in the church.

Nothing remains of the house.

---

[1] *Hist. of Norfolk*, VIII, 526.
[2] D.C. of Ancient Deeds (P.R.O.), A.3292.

Colchester.

This convent was founded before 1237,[1] in which year the King granted it land to extend its premises. The founder, like the year of foundation, is unknown. The house was situated just within the north-east corner of the wall of the East Gate and almost opposite St. James' Church.

Nothing remains of the buildings.

Yarmouth.

This convent was founded here before 1271,[2] in which year the King gave the friars permission to enclose a "venella." In that year, 1271, William Gerbrigge, whom Speed asserts to be the founder of this house, was one of the bailiffs of Yarmouth.[3] The convent, however, is almost certainly older than that, and if William Gerbrigge founded it he was probably the father of the bailiff. According to Palmer,[4] the site of this house was in the middle of the town where Queen Street now runs. In 1285 the friars extended their premises, as they did again in 1290.[5] We know nothing of the church, and there are no remains.

Dunwich.

This house was probably first founded early, Weever says by Richard Fitzjohn and his wife Alice. Afterwards, he says, it was refounded by Henry III. When this was we do not know, but in 1289 we know that the site was changed and the house refounded further

---

[1] Close, 21 Hen. III, m. 14.   [2] Pat., 55 Hen. III, m. 17.
[3] BLOMFIELD, *Hist. of Norfolk*, XI, 322.
[4] *Hist. of Yarmouth*, I, 419.
[5] Cal. Pat., 13 Edw. I, m. 18, and Cal. Pat., 18 Edw. I, m. 28.

inland away from the sea.[1] We know nothing of the buildings. Only the vast precinct wall and a few other ruins remain there on the edge of the cliff over the sea.

Walsingham.

This convent, which does not of course appear in the list of the *Provinciale Vetustissimum*, dates from 1347, when it was founded by Elizabeth de Burgh, Countess of Clare, by license of Edward III[2] (Feb. 1), in spite of opposition from the Augustinian friars.

The ruins of it remain in the south end of the town. They are all in the Perpendicular style, and there are many of them, but they are without much interest. The church has entirely disappeared.

4. THE CUSTODY OF YORK

The Custody of York consisted of seven convents, namely: York, Lincoln, Grimsby, Scarborough, Beverley, Doncaster, Boston. Of these, all but the last three existed in 1255–6.[3]

York.

This convent was founded before 1236, when the King gave the friars twenty oaks for building, as he did forty in the following year.[4] But before then certainly it was in existence, and the head of a Custody, for it is named as such by Friar Thomas.[5] Its first Guardian was Brother Martin de Barton. It was distinguished for poverty.

---

[1] Pat., 18 Edw. I, m. 11.
[2] Pat., 21 Edw. III, Pt. I, m. 28 ; 22 Edw., Pt. I, m. 48.
[3] See *supra*, 9.
[4] Close, 20 Hen. III, m. 20 ; 21 Hen. III, m. 2.
[5] *De Adv. Min.*, coll. VI.

Adam of York before 1233 was sent to lecture at Lynn. Thomas of York in 1253 was lecturer to the friars at Oxford and later at Cambridge.

About 1243, according to Little, at any rate, under Brother William, the friars removed to a large place[1] between the Ouse and the north-west moat of the castle, and the King gave them 40 marks for new buildings.[2] In 1288 he gave the friars a moat to the east of their land, and this they were to enclose with an earthen wall 12 feet high, and the place was to be used for open-air preaching.[3]

Nothing remains. We have a memory of the house, however, in the name Friars' Walls.

Lincoln.

This convent was founded about 1230,[4] when William de Beningworth, sub-dean of Lincoln, granted the citizens of Lincoln a place near the Guildhall for the use of the friars. In the following year the city gave them part of the ground on which the Guildhall then stood and all was confirmed by the King[5]; and in 1237, at the King's request, the burgesses of Lincoln gave to the friars the whole of the old Guildhall in exchange for another place in the town granted by the king.[6] Later in 1258 Henry allowed the friars to block up a postern gate in the city wall and to enclose a lane leading to the postern and on the north of their property.[7] In 1268 we find them building,[8] and they were still at work on their church in 1284, when Edward I gave them timber. It is the choir of this

---

[1] *De Adv. Min.*, coll. IX.   [2] Lib., 28 Hen. III, m. 14.
[3] Pat., 52 Hen. III, m. 4.   [4] *Ibid.*, 15 Hen. III, m. 4.   [5] *Ibid.*
[6] Close, 21 Hen. III, m. 3 and m. 2.   [7] Pat., 42 Hen. III, m. 2.
[8] Close, 52 Hen. III, m. 3.   [9] *Ibid.*, 12 Edw. I, m. 9.

church which still remains to us. The friary stood on the south-east of the city, was bounded on the east by Broadgate, on the north by Silver Street, on the south by the old Roman wall and the river, and on the west by what is now Free School Lane. What remains stands to the north of St. Swithin's church in Sheep Square and consists of a large vaulted chamber east and west, with a chamber over it. This upper chamber, till lately divided into two, is about 120 feet long and some 20 feet high. To the north is a doorway with blocked pointed arch, an inserted fireplace, and on the south, not far from the east wall, a beautiful double piscina. The east window has three lights, to the north of it and below it is a lancet. An oval window is over this, and over the gable end is a lovely pierced cross. The original roof still for the most part exists. This was the chancel of the church. The undercroft is later.

Grimsby.

This convent was founded before 1240,[1] for Friar Thomas tells us that in the time of Brother William (1240–54) this place was " sufficiently large." We know nothing of the founder. In 1255 the friars were building, and Henry III granted them in that year twenty oaks from Sherwood Forest.[2] The site, according to Oliver,[3] was " on or near a field by the present haven known by the name of Kiln Garth."

Scarborough.

This convent was founded before 1240, when Henry III bade the sheriff of Yorkshire provide food

---

[1] *De Adv. Min.*, coll. VIII.   [2] Close, 39 Hen. III, m. 3.
[3] OLIVER : *Monumental Antiq. of Great Grimsby*, 108.

for the friars there once a week.[1] But the Cistercians of Citeaux, who had property in Scarborough and to whom the church of St. Mary was appropriated, here, as elsewhere, resisted the entry of the friars, appealed to the Pope, who wrote to the Bishop of Lincoln to have the friary demolished. The friars through their proctor pleaded the privilege granted to the friars by Gregory IX with some success before Grosseteste, but withdrew on the third day of the hearing, when one of the friars, on behalf of the community, waived every right and claim in the name of the Gospel which said, "If any man sue thee at law and take away thy coat let him have thy cloak also." He declared they would give up the place, and, falling on his knees before the monks, prayed for pardon. The effect of this was such that the monks asked for leave to appeal to Citeaux.[2] Citeaux decided that the monks should insist, and in consequence we find that in 1245 the King gave the friars " who used to dwell at Scarborough " leave to build " in the area lying between Cukewaldhull " and the watercourse called Milwebre on the east side, which William, son of Robert de Morpath, has surrendered and quit-claimed to the King, of the land which he held in chief in " Haterberg " in the parish of Scalby.[3] On August 12 the bailiffs assisted the friars to remove their buildings.[4] The new site contained about 1½ acres.[5] However, about twenty-five years later the friars returned to Scarborough " and settled in the old town near the

[1] Lib., 24 Hen. III, m. 19.
[2] Grosseteste *Epist.* (Rolls), 321 ; *Mon. Franc.* (Rolls), 1406, and V.C.H., *Yorkshire*, III, p. 274.
[3] Pat., 29 Hen. III, m. 2, and V.C.H., *u.s.*
[4] Close, 29 Hen. III, m. 4.
[5] Pat., 32 Edw. I, m. 1, and V.C.H., *u.s.*

The Franciscans in England

cemetery of St Sepulchre,"[1] probably on land granted by Reginald the Miller, who was known as their founder, and buried in the choir of their church before the high altar.[2] But the monks were not done with. In 1281 the abbot of St. Albans, "conservator of the rights of the Franciscans," excommunicated all who performed or heard divine Office in the church, and Archbishop Peckham in consequence, after in vain requesting the abbot to withdraw his order, publicly had it declared null and void on pain of excommunication. And he informed the mayor and burgesses of Scarborough that the Cistercians had no power at all over the Franciscans, "whom the Pope permitted to build churches and oratories wherever it seemed expedient to them."[3] The friars remained, but not without further protest by the monks.

Nothing remains of the church.

Beverley.

This convent was founded before 1267, when, according to the *Lanercost Chronicle*, a friar of this house on the feast of St. John not only preached at Beverley, but after heard the confession of "a woman possessed by the devil."[4] We know, too, that John of Beverley was a Franciscan at Oxford about 1250,[5] and that in 1274 a number of friars belonging to the house were ordained.[6] Mr. Little says that the house at this time was probably within the walls and considers that the founder may have been John de Hightmede.[7] " In

[1] Pat., 9 Edw. II, Pt. I, m. 2.   [2] *Coll. Top. et Gen.*, n. 132.
[3] PECKHAM : *Reg.* (Rolls), 214 *et seq.*, 246 *et seq.*
[4] *Lanercost Chron.*, 83.   [5] *Mon. Franc.* (Rolls), I, 317.
[6] Giffard's Reg. (Surtees Soc.), 197.
[7] V.C.H. ,*Yorks.*, III, p. 265.

1297," we read,[1] "William Luketon and Henry Wygthin bought certain lands near Beverley about the chapel of St. Elene and granted them to the brethren of the Order of St. Francis for to build their house. And also they conferred upon them many other good things." This was no doubt the granting of a new site, and that near Westwood. The house flagged, we learn from the same source, and was rescued by Sir John Hotham, who rebuilt it.

Doncaster.

This convent was founded before 1290, when Nicholas IV granted an indulgence to such as should visit the church of St. Francis at Doncaster.[2] We know nothing of the date of foundation or the founder.

The house was established on an island formed by the rivers Cheswold and Don at the bottom of Francis Gate at the north end of the Friars' Bridge.[3] Nothing remains.

Boston.

This convent was founded before 1268,[4] when a certain Luke de Batenturt charged the friars with theft. The founder is unknown, as is the date of foundation ; but Leland affirms that " merchants of the steelyard were wont greatly to haunt Boston and the Grey Friars took them in a manner for founders of their house and many Esterlings were buried there." Among these was Wisselus de Sinalenberg of Munster, part of whose

---

[1] *Coll. Top. et Gen.*, IV, 129, from a MS. preserved in Coll. of Arms.
[2] *Cal. of Pap. Letters*, I, 516.
[3] See Fairbank : *The Grey Friars of Doncaster* (Yorks. Arch. Journal), XII, 481.
[4] P.R.O., Abbreviatio Placitorum, p. 176.

tomb (1340) is now in the parish church of St. Botolph. Mr. Little tells us that at the end of the thirteenth century there were some thirty friars in this convent.[1] The friary was in the south-east part of the town. Nothing remains of it.

5. THE CUSTODY OF BRISTOL

The Custody of Bristol consisted of nine convents, namely : Bristol, Hereford, Bridgwater, Exeter, Gloucester, Dorchester, Bodmin, Carmarthen, Cardiff. Of these, all but the last four were in existence in 1255–6.

We have seen that the original head of this, the south-western Custody, was Salisbury. The successor of Salisbury was not necessarily Bristol ; indeed, it would appear to have been Hereford, which in its turn gave way to Bristol.[2]

Bristol.

This convent was founded before 1234,[3] when the king made it a small gift, as he did again, this time giving fifteen oaks, in 1236.[4] In the time of Brother William (1240–54), according to Friar Thomas, " the place at Bristol was changed." Leland found the convent " on the right site of From Water not far from Saint Barptolemes Hospitale " in St. James' parish in the street called Lewenesmede. William of Worcester reckons the church as follows : " Longitudo Ecclesiæ Fratrum Minorum Bristolliæ continet 4454 steppys. Latitudo continet 52 steppys." Nothing remains.[5]

---

[1] V.C.H., *Lincolnshire*, vol. II, p. 215.   [2] See *supra*, p. 60.
[3] Close, 19 Hen. III, Pt. I, m. 26. Cf. *De Adv. Min.*, coll. VII, which points to a foundation before 1230.   [4] Close, 20 Hen. III, m. 9.
[5] See WEARE : *The Friars Minor of Bristol* (1893).

The Movement through England

Hereford.

This convent was founded before 1228.[1] It was perhaps in the time of Albert of Pisa (*ca.* 1236), when, as Friar Thomas tells us, the place at Hereford was changed,[2] that it gave way as the head of the Custody to Bristol.

The house stood, as Leland bears witness, without Friars' Gate on the west of the city. " Frere Gate standith west, caullid of the Grey Freres house standinge without it." Nothing remains of it.

Bridgwater.

This convent was founded before 1245,[3] when the gift of land made by the bailiffs of Bridgwater was ratified by the King. According to Leland, the founder of the house was William Briwere, son of that William who founded in Bridgwater the Hospital of St. John Baptist (1214) and " one of the Lords Botreaux and his wife were especial benefactors to this house. Thereupon his hert and hys wife's body were buryed there." It is probable that the house founded by William Briwere was quickly abandoned and that the land given by the bailiffs of Bridgwater, which gift was ratified by the King in 1245, was in a different place. At any rate, Friar Thomas records[4] that " under Brother William (1240–54) the place at Bridgwater was changed." It was in this new place that the friars set about building a chapel and convent, for which the King made them gifts of timber in 1278 and 1284.[5] The convent was situated in the west part of the town

---

[1] Close, 12 Hen. III, m. 3.   [2] *De Adv. Min.*, coll. IX.
[3] Pat., 30 Hen. III, m. 8.   [4] *De Adv. Min.*, coll. IX.
[5] Cal. Close, 1279–88 and 1272–79.

not far from the parish church. Nothing certainly belonging to it remains, though an arched doorway in Silver Street may have been part of this house.

Exeter.

This convent was founded before 1240.[1] Leland speaks of the house now standing " betwixt the north and west gate neere the towne waulle now a plain vacant ground caulled Frerenhay." He adds that " Bytten Bishop of Excester de remevid thens the Grey Freres and buildid them an house a litle without the South Gate." Nothing remains.

Gloucester.

This convent was founded before 1231,[2] in which year the King made it a small gift. The founder is unknown, as is the date of foundation. The first we hear of the convent from Friar Thomas is that " the windows in the chapel at Gloucester caused the visitor to act with great severity against the friars." Presumably they were decorated, as was the pulpit, with painted pictures, for permitting which the guardian of Gloucester lost his hood, as did the friar artist.[3] Friar Thomas also tells us that the ground at Gloucester was presently enlarged, and it was on this occasion that Brother Haymo (1239) said " he would rather the brethren should have ample ground and cultivate it and so supply themselves with messes when they were at home than that they should beg their food from others." It appears, according to Friar Thomas, that the brethren at Gloucester " had formerly by the decision of Brother Agnellus parted with a large plot

[1] OLIVER : *Monast. Dioces. Exon.*, 330.
[2] Close, 15 Hen. III, m. 17.   [3] *De Adv. Min.*, coll. VII.

of ground which was later with great difficulty again
acquired from Sir Thomas Berkeley through the sagacity and devotion of his wife."[1] Some have thought
that this points to the first founder as Sir Thomas
Berkeley.[2] This must have been about 1239. In that
year, moreover, Ralph of Maidstone, Bishop of Hereford, resigned his Bishopric and entered the Order at
Gloucester. He was given the habit by Haymo of
Faversham. This befell, according to Friar Thomas,
"in accordance with a vision concerning Brother
Haymo which the Bishop had whilst he was yet Archdeacon of Chester ; for it seemed to him that he was
sitting and arranging his clergy in their places at a
synod when a boy came and threw water in his face,
whereat he himself was immediately changed into a
sickly and wretched youth ; and he came to the bed
on which Brother Haymo lay and besought that he
might lie there too. Accordingly he had a happy end
in the Order."[3]

That the friars were in good favour here is certain.
In 1246 we find the King allowed them to set up a
school of Theology in a tower of the town wall.[4] But
they had one enemy, and that a powerful one, in the
abbot and monastery of Gloucester, who in 1285 refused them permission to extend their site and
quarrelled with them over the body of a man who
had desired to be buried in their church, but the
monks had seized his corpse. The friars appealed to
Archbishop Peckham, himself a friar who bade the
abbot satisfy the friars.

The house was in the parish of St. Mary le Crypt in
Southgate Street.

[1] *De Adv. Min.*, coll. IX.   [2] V.C.H., *Gloucester*, II, p. 111.
[3] *De Adv. Min.*, coll. XIII.   [4] Close, 30 Hen. III., m. 6.

The Franciscans in England

I find the following in Fosbrooke[1] : " It is probable
that little alteration had been made in the buildings
(of the friary) after the dissolution except the conversion of them into dwelling houses till the time of the
siege when considerable damage was done by the King's
artillery. The choir was till some late alterations so
perfect in its exterior as to exhibit a very fine specimen
of the architecture of the XV century ; the tracery
of all the windows was rich but the east window in
particular was large and beautiful covering the whole
end of the building. The other building of the same
size and length running parallel with it was probably
the south aisle ; and the Prior's lodgings to the south
of that connected by a gateway over which a com-
munication might be kept up with the church. . . .
The building is now converted into dwelling houses
and manufacturies. . . ."

Dorchester.

This convent was founded before 1267,[2] in which
year the friars were charged with encroaching on the
road by the erection of a wall. The date of the foundation is unknown, but, according to Speed,[3] the
founders were the ancestors of Sir John Chideok ; but
it is to be noted that Richard III claimed it as of royal
foundation,[4] and at the dissolution there was still a
chamber in the friary known as " the king's chamber."
In 1296 there were thirty-two friars in the house when
Edward I gave them 32 shillings for three days' food.[5]
The convent stood to the north of the town on the

[1] FOSBROOKE : *Hist. of Gloucester* (1819).
[2] P.R.O., Assize Roll, 202.   [3] SPEED : *Hist.*, 1055.
[4] *L. and P., Hen. VIII :* XIII (2), 474 (2).
[5] B.M., Add. MS., 7965, fol. 7.

bank of the river to the east of the Castle, out of the ruins of which, according to Dugdale, it had been built. Priory Lane still preserves its memory, but nothing is left of the buildings. Tradition asserts that monuments in St. Peter's Church are the tombs of the Chideocks removed from the friars' church ; but I can find no record to support this.

Bodmin.

We have no document earlier than the notes of William of Worcester's *Itinerarium* upon this convent, so that we cannot certainly date it before 1280. But it is highly probable that William of Worcester is right in asserting that it was founded 1239. It perhaps owed its being to John de London and was under the patronage of Edmund, Earl of Cornwall. William of Worcester asserts that its original founder was John, son of Ralph, Lord of Kayryshays. According to the same authority, the church was consecrated by Bishop Grandison in 1352.

Part of the Refectory is still standing and is divided into a corn market and schoolroom. On the gable is preserved one of the piers of the crypt, and another has been erected in the churchyard. Mountfolly, in front of the Assize Hall, was the burying-ground. The old workhouse, built by Sir W. Irby in 1769 and now divided into a hospital or dispensary and a Literary Institution, occupies a part of the site of the convent.

Carmarthen.

This convent was founded before 1284.[1]

[1] Cf. *Mon. Franc.* (Rolls), II, 387.

Cardiff.

This convent was founded before 1304.[1]

6. CUSTODY OF WORCESTER

The Custody of Worcester consisted of nine convents, namely : Worcester, Coventry, Lichfield, Shrewsbury, Chester, Llanfaes, Bridgenorth, Stafford and Preston. Of these, all but the last two were in existence in 1255–6.[2]

Worcester.

This convent was founded before 1226,[3] in which year Peter of Eport, victor of Stoke Prior, was received into the Order.[4] There certainly Adam de Marisco was received not later than 1230.[5] The site of this first house is not known, for in the time of Albert of Pisa the friars moved to a new place,[6] and in 1298 William Beauchamp, Earl of Warwick, was buried in the new church in the choir " in a place where no one had yet been interred, in which in the winter time he will be said to be " drowned rather than buried where I have seen herbs growing." [7] Leland describes the house as in a suburb without St. Martin's Gate, where " in a loose marish ground was a place of Grey Freres." Nothing remains.

Coventry.

This convent was founded before 1241,[8] in which

---

[1] Brit. Mus., Cott. Charter, xxx, 40.   [2] See *supra*, p. 56.
[3] Mr. Little (V.C.H., *Worcester*, q. p. 169) says between 1225 and 1230.   [4] *Ann. Mon.* (Rolls), IV, 419.   [5] See *supra*, p. 49.
[6] *De Adv. Min.*, coll. XIII.   [7] *Ann. Mon.* (Rolls), IV, 537.
[8] Lib., 25 Hen. II, m. 5.

year the King made it a gift; but the convent is certainly earlier. Dr. Cox[1] states that "The Pipe Rolls of 1234 show that at that time Henry III was allowing it timber out of the woods of Kenilworth to use for shingles to cover their oratory or church."

The founder appears to have been Ralph Blundeville, Earl of Chester; and Roger de Montalt and Cicely his wife, niece of the Earl, were benefactors, and both were buried in the choir of the friary church.[2] Here, too, there seems to have been opposition on the part of the monks of Coventry.[3]

Nothing remains of the house.

The Grey Friars of Coventry were chiefly famous for the Mystery play they performed upon Corpus Christi.

Lichfield.

This convent was founded about 1237,[4] when Henry III gave the friars wood for building of their house and for their chapel. According to William of Worcester, the convent was burned down in 1291. Leland tells us " there was a house of Grey Friars in Lichfield on the south-west part of the towne." " The Friary," in Bird Street, is a part of the convent, now a private house. Built into the wall is the tombstone of Richard the Merchant, its reputed founder.

Shrewsbury.

This convent was founded in 1245–6 by the King.[5]

[1] V.C.H., *Warwick*, II, p. 103.
[2] *Memo. of the Franciscans of Coventry* (Birm. and Midland Institute) (1882), and Pat., 17 Edw. I, m. 11.
[3] Reg. Epist. Peckham (Rolls), III, 963.
[4] Close, 21 Hen. III, m. 2.
[5] Close, 30 Hen. III, m. 25, and Lib., 30 Hen. III, m. 18, m. 3.

The site then given was outside the town wall between the Wyle Cop and the river, a marshy place liable to flood, on the south-east of the city. A part of the convent remains in what are now cottages near the foot-bridge across the Severn ; but this remnant is of much later date than the foundation, and indeed cannot be much older than the dissolution. The Jesse window now in St. Mary's church was originally, so it is said, in that of the Grey Friars.

Friar Thomas tells us that, just as at Salisbury, with " merriment and joy at the hour of conference around the kitchen fire the brethren would drink the dregs of beer for want of better liquor, so it was the same at Shrewsbury at their first coming, as Brother Barton an old man who began the house there would tell you with glee."[1]

Chester.

This convent was founded about 1238.[2] In 1240 the King gave the friars here leave to build a house.[3] Friar Thomas tells us that it was Albert of Pisa who placed the friars here, and that only with great difficulty, presumably because of the monks.[4] The house stood near the Watergate upon the site now occupied by Stanley Place. Nothing remains.

Llanfaes.

This convent was founded in 1245.[5]

Bridgenorth.

This convent was founded in 1244.[6] The church

---

[1] *De Adv. Min.*, coll. I.
[2] Grosseteste *Epistolæ*, p. 120.
[3] Close, 24 Hen. III, m. 17.
[4] *De Adv. Mon.*, coll. XIII.
[5] Pat., 29 Hen. III, m. 2.
[6] Lib., 28 Hen. III, m. 6.

was dedicated in honour of St. Francis and was standing in 1272. The house stood to the west of Severn, under the church of St. Leonard. Adjoining vaults are still known as " Friars' Caves," and the Great Hall or Refectory is still in tolerable condition.

Stafford.

This convent was founded before 1282.[1] The house stood in the south part of the town.

Preston.

This convent was founded before 1260,[2] in which year the King granted the friars five oaks from Sydwood for building. The founder, according to Leland, was " a member of the local family of Preston an Irish representative of which became Lord Hormanston in 1390."[3] The great builder here, however, as Leland allows, was Edmund, Earl of Lancaster, younger son of Henry III. Nothing remains.

7. Custody of Newcastle

The Custody of Newcastle consisted of nine convents or, with Durham, ten, namely : Newcastle, Hartlepool, Carlisle, Roxburgh, Haddington, Durham, Richmond, Berwick, Dundee, Dumfries. Of these, all but the last four existed in 1255–6.[4]

Newcastle.

This convent was founded before 1239,[5] when

[1] Pat., 10 Edw. I, m. 10.   [2] Close, 44 Hen. III, m. 1.
[3] Cf. V.C.H., *Lancashire*, II, 162.   [4] See *supra*, p. 56.
[5] Lib., 23 Hen. III, m. 11.

The Franciscans in England

Henry III made it a gift of ten pounds. We know nothing of the founder. The convent was near or upon the site of Anderson Place, " a princely house built out of the ruins of the friars," and stood in the street called High Friar Chare, according to Brand.[1] The most notable thing about the convent was that it was there Duns Scotus entered the Order. This house was one of those which in the fifteenth century was given to the Observant Friars of the Order. Leland notes it thus : " The Observant Frires House stode by Pandon Gate. It was a very fayre thinge." Nothing remains.

Hartlepool.

This convent was founded before 1240,[2] in which year the King made the friars a grant for a tunic. According to Layton, one of the infamous visitors of Henry VIII, the " friarage of Hartlepool was founded by Robert de Brus," who had founded Gisburn.[3] This is not possible, but it may have been founded by one of his descendants of the same name. Nothing at all remains of the friary or church, the site being now occupied by the Hartlepool Hospital called the Friarage. According to Surtees, " there is an excellent well belonging to the friary, 43 feet deep and six feet square of hewn stone." The garden of old was said to produce " the best reputed Ribstone pippins in the country."

Carlisle.

This convent was founded in 1233,[4] when " about the feast of the Assumption (Aug. 15) the Friars Minor

---

[1] Cf. SYKES : *Local Records*, Vol. I, p. 28.
[2] Lib., 25 Hen. III, m. 23.   [3] MS. Treas. Dur., 2a, 16.
[4] *Lanercost Chronicle*, p. 42.

came to the city of Carlisle and received a house within the walls." In July, 1235, the King granted them wood for the building of their chapel. A further grant was made by the King in the following November, and again in 1280.[1] In 1292, however, the whole city with all its religious houses was burnt down, only the Friars Preachers escaping. The convent, then rebuilt, was situated on the south-east side of the city. Nothing at all remains of it.

Roxburgh.

This convent was founded before 1235.[2]

Haddington.

This convent was founded before 1242.[3]

Richmond.

Mr. Little, following Clarkson, notes that " the foundation of this friary is attributed to Ralph Fitz Randal, lord of Middleham in 1258, whose heart was buried in the choir in 1270."[4] We know nothing of it in the thirteenth century, save that in 1291, at the request of Archbishop Romanus, one of the friars preached the Crusade at Richmond and another else-where.

The house was to the north of the town just without the walls, as Leland says, and there still remains of it a noble great Perpendicular tower, the central tower of the church which tradition says was never finished.

---

[1] Close, 19 Hen. III, Pt. I, and 20 Hen. III, m. 24 ; 8 Edw. I, m. 2.
[2] *Liber de Calchon* (Bannatyne Chib), p. 321.
[3] *Lanercost Chron.*, pp. 49–50, 68.
[4] V.C.H., *Yorkshire*, III, p. 273.

The Franciscans in England

Berwick.

This convent was founded before 1231.[1]

Dundee.

This convent was founded before 1296.[2]

Dumfries.

This convent was founded before 1264.[3]

Durham.

The convent, which only existed for a short time in the thirteenth century and does not properly make one of the nine convents of the Newcastle Custody, was founded in 1239,[4] in which year the King made it a grant.

Such were the houses of the friars in England in 1334. In 1255-6, Friar Thomas tells us, there were 49 convents established in the English Province, and of these we have traced by far the greater number. In these 49 convents there were, according to the same authority, 1242 friars, which gives an average of 25 friars to each convent. We know, however, as we might suppose, that the convents varied greatly in

[1] Chron. de Maitros, p. 142. Here was the first entry of the Friars into Scotland (1231).

[2] STEVENSON : *Doc.* (Rolls), II, n. 484.

[3] Exchequer Rolls of Scot., I, p. 17.   [4] Lib., 24 Hen. III, m. 2.

size, the head house of each Custody being certainly larger than its sub-houses. Thus, in 1243 the London house had 80 friars,[1] and Oxford, according to Mr. Little, boasted about the same number ; but at Winchester in 1243 there were but 33,[2] at Reading in 1239 but 13, and at Chichester in 1253 but 26.[3]

[1] Lib., 28 Hen. III, m. 18. [2] Lib., 27 Hen. III, m. 2.
[3] Lib., 23 Hen. III, m. 3, and Lib., 37 Hen. III, m. 1.

VI

THE MINORESSES

THE Second Order of Franciscans was that for
women, which S. Chiara, or as we say St.
Clare, founded in 1212 and called the *Ordo Dominarum
pauperum* of Poor Ladies, which soon came to be called
the *Ordo Sanctæ Claræ*, while in England the nuns
were known as Minoresses. St. Clare at the bidding
of St. Francis first lived under the Rule of St. Benedict,
and for that reason Franciscan nunneries were and are
called abbeys and the Superior the Mother Abbess ;
but in 1224, the very year in which the Friars came to
England, St. Francis at St. Clare's earnest desire gave
her a Rule which was confirmed in 1246. This Rule,
which consists of twelve chapters, is harder than the
Rule of the Friars. All possessions are to be given away
in alms before entering the convent ; the nuns fast
all the year round save on Christmas Day whereas the
friars only fast on Friday. The novitiate lasts a year ;
the divine office is recited as by the friars. No nun
may speak with those outside the convent during Lent
or from All Saints to Christmas, and at all times she
must be accompanied to a curtained *grille* by two
sisters. She is not seen by, nor does she see, the person
to whom she speaks.

Of this Order of Poor Ladies, or Minoresses, there
were twelve houses in the English province in

1316,[1] but of these I can trace but four. Perhaps these houses which could by strict Rule neither receive nor hold anything as property, but subsisted entirely on alms, were for the most part too poor to be thought worthy of record.

London.

The Minoresses seem to have arrived in England about 1290. At any rate, in 1291 we find a house of Minoresses, the house of the Grace of the Blessed Mary, in existence outside Aldgate in the parish of St. Botolph, London, and in 1293 its foundation was confirmed by the King.[2] There can be little doubt that this was the first house of the Order in England, nor that it was founded by the brother of the King, Edmund, Earl of Lancaster, whose wife Blanche, Queen of Navarre, first brought the Sisters to England from France, perhaps from the nunnery of the Humility of the Blessed Mary at St. Cloud where the Rule Boniface VIII prescribed for them was followed.[3] The house enjoyed very special privileges. It was endowed by the Earl of Lancaster and by the Mayor Henry le Galeys, who was buried in the conventual church in a chantry built by him,[4] and both the King and the Pope granted special exemptions, among these being a complete freedom from the jurisdiction of the Archbishop and the Bishop of London.

[1] Cf. Cod. Vindobon. Palatino, n. 4349, f. 11v–12 r., quoted in *Archivum Franciscanum Historicum.* An. I (1908), p. 18. A volume on the Minoresses is in preparation by Miss C. Bourdillon for the British Society of Franciscan Studies.

[2] Pat., 21 Edw. I, m. 11, quoted by Dugdale.

[3] V.C.H., *London,* I, 517, and authorities there quoted.

[4] *Ibid.*

Denney.

In 1293 the Lady Dimysia de Mountchensey built at Waterbeche in Cambridgeshire a convent for the Minoresses in honour of the Piety of the B.V.M. and St. Clare. In 1348 Mary de St. Pol, widow of the Earl of Pembroke, came into possession of the manor of Denney, also in Cambridgeshire, and first wished to bestow it on the nuns of Waterbeche ; but she changed her mind and in the same year founded in Denney a convent of Minoresses to the honour of the B.V.M. and of St. Clare, to which a few years later the nuns of Waterbeche were removed.

Bruisyard.

In 1346 a college or chantry of four chaplains and a warden was founded in the chapel of the Annunciation in the church of the Austin nuns of Campsey in Suffolk. In 1354 this college was removed to the manor of Rokeshall in Bruisyard, where a chapel of the Annunciation was erected and a house provided for the warden and four priests. They seem to have been moved chiefly because it was inconvenient to have them in the same place as the nuns.[1] In 1364, however, the college was suppressed and the buildings were surrendered for the use of the Minoresses[2] who entered on 4 October, 1366. The Hall, now a farmhouse, occupies the site of the buildings.

Northampton.

There was for a time a house of Minoresses in Northampton of which we know nothing more than that it received a grant of clothes.[3]

---

[1] Pat., 30 Edw. III, Pt. III, m. 5.   [2] Pat., 38 Edw. III, Pt. I, m. 5.
[3] Lib., 36 Hen. III, m. 2.

VII

THE ORGANISATION OF THE ORDER

THE Franciscan movement had thus spread, long
before the end of the thirteenth century,
through all England. If, indeed, we take a map and
mark it out into seven areas to correspond with the
seven Franciscan Custodies, we shall find that every
part of the country is covered, except the highlands of
Wales, and those hills, still so barren and lonely, which
divide to-day with their silence the industry of the
Yorkshire towns from that of the Lancashire and
Cheshire plain, the Pennines. For the mission, it was
just that—as is obvious at once, especially to the
townsfolk, the more wretched of whom, neglected by
the secular priest, and outside the power, economic
and spiritual, of the monasteries—the one uncertain
and unaccountable element in the society of that time,
which the Crusades had exposed to more than one new
peril. The direct experience of the Orient, indeed,
was responsible not only for new ideas and new tastes,
but for new diseases. While indirectly the Crusades
which had enormously increased the commerce of the
Italian maritime republics, and especially of Venice
and Genoa, undoubtedly stimulated the mercantile
communities even of our far island ; it was in the
towns that these influences were chiefly felt, the
towns which alone harboured the returned adventurer,
the broken crusader, the wretched refuse of the Holy

Wars. Half Saracen or wholly skeptic, corrupted by strange experiences heaped on ignorance, rotten with disease or broken with misery, such an one returned to infect his fellows, and in the comparative freedom of the town, for the most part out of reach of the strong arm of the monastery, he spread his heresy or his indifference, with his disease. In the town there was nothing to fill the place the monastery occupied in the country. The evidence we have of the condition of the secular clergy of the time is altogether as horrible as it is unimpeachable. It is no heresiarch, but Bishop Grosseteste himself, who speaks of the clergy as haunting taverns, gambling, drinking, rioting and debauching. It is Grosseteste who declares that the clergy corrupt the people.

Into these confined, unstable and unspeakably filthy towns of Europe the friars came like saviours. To the corruption and debauchery of the town clergy they opposed their purity, to the wealth of the plural-ists their poverty, to the scandalous living of canons and great ecclesiastics their humility. It was not less than a revolution. Everywhere the welcome of the people, of the burgesses, was enthusiastic, while it is only the clergy and especially the monks who are found in opposition. And yet even the monkish historians, such as Roger of Wendover and Matthew Paris, strict contemporaries of the early Franciscan movement through England, almost in spite of themselves, bear witness to the friars' success and, without meaning to do so, show us the necessity for it.

" About this time," writes the former, " there sprang up under the auspices of Pope Innocent a sect of preachers called Minorites who filled the earth, dwelling in cities and towns, by tens and sevens,

14968

possessing no property at all, living according to the Gospel, making a show of the greatest poverty, walking with naked feet and setting a great example of humility to all classes. On Sundays and feast days they went forth from their habitations preaching the word of the Gospel in the parish churches, eating and drinking whatever they found amongst them to whom they preached ; and they were the more remarkable for their regard to the business of heaven the more they proved themselves unconnected with the matters of this life and with the pleasures of the flesh. No sort of food in their possession was kept for the morrow's use that their poverty of spirit which reigned in their minds might show itself to all in their dress and actions."

The strangeness of the Franciscan ideal surprises even this monkish historian by its beauty and its simplicity. Matthew Paris is less astonished and more resentful. " Some folk," he asserts, " refused to confess to their proper priest because he was a drunkard and for some other secret reason, but flew with confidence to make their confessions under the shelter of the wings of consolation and counsel spread out to them by passing Preachers the Dominicans and Minors."

But the work of the Franciscans had another than a spiritual purpose ; it was physical also. The founder of the Order, St. Francis himself, was not a priest, nor was his apostle to England the Blessed Agnellus.

The increase of the populations in the towns, rapid as it was at this time, contributed to make them the fever traps they were. Plague and leprosy were but the more terrible diseases which flourished in the wretched hovels of the time, and not least in the

LINCOLN BIBLE INSTITUTE

suburb without, and it was there in the worst plague spots that the Franciscans were wont to establish themselves, as their founder had suggested. At London, as we have seen, their house was in the shambles of Newgate, at Oxford, at Lynn, at York, at Bristol, at Norwich, at Shrewsbury in the swamps between the town wall and the river. There they built first their huts of wattle, stuffed the walls with mud and straw and built their wooden chapel, and so made their friaries. As they went through the land the monks took them for tumblers and minstrels, and when they found they were mistaken imprisoned and buffeted them ; the people knew them for disciples of Our Lord. Their amazing success was due in the first instance to a popular recognition of their holiness and charity, and to the swift patronage of the richer burgesses. They had, however, two very powerful patrons from the first, namely, Grosseteste of Lincoln and the King. Grosseteste it was who set them up at Oxford, and as early as 1224 was their first rector there, and it is recorded of him in the *Liber de Adventu Minorum* that he " would sometimes say that unless the brethren fostered their studies and gave themselves diligently to the learning of the divine law, it would most assuredly happen to us as it had happened to other religious whom we see (oh, the misery of it !) walking in the darkness of ignorance." This was scarcely Franciscan doctrine, but Grosseteste had his way as we shall see, and his patronage was not less valuable than that of the King which was certainly not more Franciscan.

For if Grosseteste imposed learning upon the Friars Minor in despite of St. Francis, the King was not less pressing with gifts, the acceptance of which was not less contrary to the intention of the founder. There was, indeed, scarcely a friary in England that was not the King's debtor. At Reading he had built the friars such a chapel that Albert of Pisa, who dared not pull it down " for that the king had built it, earnestly prayed that Heaven would destroy it." Indeed, it was not sumptuous stone chapels or stone cloisters such as the burgesses of Southampton built for the friars, and Albert of Pisa pulled down, that were needed for the conquest of England, but places such as St. Francis loved and praised as Friar Thomas relates. " Here Brother Robert of Slapton told me that it once happened that the brethren were in a certain place which was lent them for they had not yet acquired ground there and it seemed to the brother who was guardian that Saint Francis came to the place and the brethren went to him and led him into the Solarium and there the Saint sat for a long time in silence looking about him. And the brethren being astonished, the Guardian asked : ' Father, of what art thou thinking ? ' St. Francis answered : ' Look around this house.' And the Guardian looked and saw that the whole house was built of wattles and mud and refuse. And St. Francis said, ' Such ought to be the houses of the Friars Minor.' " Well might Brother William of Nottingham exclaim, "' I will tell the Minister-General I did not become a friar in order to build walls.' "

But the true Franciscan spirit could not endure the patronage of the King, of Grosseteste and the rich burgesses of the time ; still less was it able to withstand the later patronage of the nobles. Little by little the more wretched places were improved and transformed or exchanged, as at Northampton,

Worcester, Hereford, York, Bristol, Bridgwater and elsewhere, for better and larger sites. Before the end of the century the fears of the monks and clergy, the only opponents of the friars, had been justified, and we see the Order quickly enriching itself and already erecting sumptuous and noble buildings and churches.

Alas, of these earlier medieval buildings, but four even in part remain to us ; the exquisite fragments I have already described at Canterbury,[1] Chichester,[2] and Lincoln,[3] and the ruins of Winchelsea.[4]

That the buildings of the friars soon became splendid, and that this did not come to pass without a long and bitter opposition, we are assured at once by the briefest examination of the history of the province.

After the division of the Province of England into the first six custodies, special Visitors, that is to say, representatives of the Minister-General of the Order, coming in his name, were sent to England, we read, and there held chapters concerning the matters of their visitation. Brother William de Colville the elder had, however, already been visitor to England and had held his chapter at London during the ministry of Brother Agnellus (1234–36), and we read that at that time " a chapel had been built for the brethren in London at the expense of Sir William Joyner and Bishop William seized the occasion of this chapter to celebrate the opening with a splendour to be remembered."[5]

The next visitor, the first after the establishment of the Custodies, was Brother John Naverius, who for the first time brought over the exposition of the Rule according to the Lord Pope Gregory IX (1230). " On

[1] *Supra*, p. 25.   [2] *Supra*, p. 65.   [3] *Supra*, p. 78.
[4] *Supra*, p. 65.   [5] *De Adv. Mon.*, coll. VII.

account of this visitation," we read,[1] " the brethren,
even the novices, he assembled in great numbers under
Brother Agnellus in London, Leicester and Bristol.[2]
At that time the brethren had so strict a conscience
regarding the building of houses and the possession
of pictures that the visitor acted with great severity
because of the windows in the chapel at Gloucester ;
moreover he deprived a brother of his hood because
he had decorated a pulpit with pictures and inflicted
the same penance upon the Guardian of the place,
because he had allowed the pictures to be painted."

The third visitor, we read in the same place, " came
as the delegate of Brother Elias the Minister-General
(1232–39) during the ministry of Brother Albert
(1237–38).[3] He was Brother Wygmund a German very
famous for his knowledge of Law and known for the
strictness of his conduct. He was moreover very
familiar with the Lord Cardinal Otto at that time
legate in England."[4] This visitation caused the
greatest confusion on account of the " very strict
and cunning instructions from the Minister-General,
Brother Elias." It was apparently an exhaustive
inquiry into the whole attitude and inclinations of
the friars in England in the grave matter, that, as we
shall see, was then dividing the Order in which Elias
was the militant head of one party and in possession
as Minister-General of the whole machinery of govern-

[1] *De Adv. Mon.*, coll. VII.

[2] As to the dates of these visitations ; both took place in the lifetime
of Agnellus, and the second not later than 1231, for the date of the
exposition of the Rule of Gregory IX (Quo elongati) is Sept. 28, 1230.

[3] The third visitor, Brother Wygmund, must have come in 1237–38
therefore. In 1239 Brother Albert of Pisa succeeded Brother Elias as
Minister-General.

[4] Cardinal Otto came to England in the summer of 1237.

ment. The chapters held at London (May, 1238), Southampton, Gloucester and Oxford (June, 1238) met in confusion, and " the whole province was caught in an intolerable tempest."

The friars of Scotland, which since the election of Elias had been a separate province from England, refused to receive the visitor, asserting that they had already been invited by the Minister of Ireland. In the confusion Brother Wygmund returned to Germany with his report, and Brother William of Esseby, who had been sent by him to Ireland to make a visitation there, joined him at Cologne. Meantime, an appeal was sent to Rome, that " in future the Visitation of the Provinces should be made only by authority of the General Chapter in accordance with the constitution concerning visitors."[1]

Much of this trouble seems to have been caused by the monetary demands of the visitor on behalf of the Minister-General,[2] who was then engaged in building and decorating the church of St. Francis at Assisi. It is interesting to note as comment upon this, that it was the demands of Tetzel on behalf of the Pope then engaged in building St. Peter's church, and his sale of indulgences for the same end, that gave so much cause for offence at the time of the Reformation.

That visitation of Brother Wygmund in 1238 shows us the Province of England already divided into two parts, the Province of England and the Province of Scotland. This was the work according to Friar Thomas,[3] of Brother Elias as Minister-General, and

---

[1] *De Adv. Mon.*, coll. VII.

[2] Cf. Salimbene (ed. Holder-Egger), p. 107. "Mettebat visitatores ... qui sollicitarent provincias et ministros ad tributa solvenda et munera largienda."

[3] *De Adv. Mon.*, coll. VIII.

if he is right did not take place before 1232.[1] This division, according to Friar Thomas, was made because Elias wished " that as the order of Preachers had twelve Priors-Provincial scattered through the world after the manner of the twelve apostles, so in like fashion he might have under his authority seventy-two Ministers after the manner of the seventy-two disciples."

Brother Henry of Reresby, who was then vicar to the Guardian of Oxford,[2] was appointed Minister of Scotland, but he died before he could proceed thither, and after his death he appeared to his friend, the Guardian of Oxford, and declared that " if the friars were not damned for excess in buildings they would at least be severely punished."

In his place Brother John de Kethene, then Guardian of London, was appointed, " and he caused all the houses beyond York to be included in his province." In other words, I take it, he incorporated into the Province of Scotland the whole Custody of Newcastle with its southern outpost in the North Riding of Yorkshire at Richmond, if, indeed, that house was yet founded. Brother John de Kethene was, according to Friar Thomas, a model Franciscan, " full of piety and most zealous for the divine office. It was he who received with reverence our venerable father, Brother Albert (of Pisa), at our house in Leicester and humbly besought him to expound the statutes to the brethren. Now when he had laudably governed the Province of Scotland for many years and that Province was again

---

[1] Little notes, cf. his edition of Eccleston (Paris, 1909), p. 50, n. 6, that Germany was divided into two provinces at the Chapter-General of 1230. He thinks it is possible that England was divided at the same time.

[2] *De Adv. Min.*, coll. V.

united to England Brother John was sent by Brother Albert then Minister-General to be Minister in Ireland." This must have been in 1238, for in 1239 the Chapter which deposed Brother Elias elected Brother Haymo of Faversham Minister to the whole English Province, and made Brother John de Kethene, who had been Minister of Scotland, Minister of Ireland. Thus was the work of Elias, even in this matter, undone by the English Province, in all things one of his most determined opponents as we shall see. Indeed, we may note here that Friar Thomas particularly reminds us that John of Kethene, himself the nominee of Elias, is especially to be remembered, because with Brother Gregory da Bossellis " he faithfully stood by Brother William of Nottingham of happy memory, the Minister of England (1239–51) and in opposition to almost the entire chapter[1] fortunately brought it to pass that the privilege granted by Our Lord the Pope to receive money through procurators be altogether abolished, and that moreover the interpretation of the Rule of the Lord Pope Innocent (1245) in those matters in which it was more lax than the interpretation of Pope Gregory (1230) be put aside."

The Province of England thus torn asunder and restored, both in its government and in opinion, was especially fortunate in these early years in its great Ministers. The first of these, as we have seen, was the Franciscan Apostle of England the Blessed Agnellus of Pisa. He ruled from 1224 to 1236 when he died. Friar Thomas gives him the character of " a man highly

[1] Friar Thomas speaks of the Chapter of Genoa (1234), probably in error for the Chapter of Metz (see *De Adv. Min.*, coll. VIII and coll. XIV). The Declaration of Innocent IV was promulgated November, 1245. William of Nottingham was Minister of England, 1239–51.

endowed with natural prudence and conspicuous for
virtue, observance of the Rule and honesty of life."
He had been chosen by St. Francis himself. One of
his first difficulties was with the English Bishops
concerning the claims of the friars to hear confessions.
He appealed to the Roman Court with success in this
matter.[1] He was not always so fortunate. In 1233 he
was chosen by the King to negotiate with the rebel
Simon de Montfort after the slaughter at the Castle of
Monmouth, and to bring him back to his allegiance.
Roger of Wendover gives a very full account of the
interview and the arguments that took place in the
abbey of Morgan in Glamorganshire. It was the worry
and hard labour of this embassy, " as well as his
frequent journeys through the province," that killed
him at last in 1236. So long as he lived the English
Province departed not from the Rule and the ideal of
St. Francis, and though, as Friar Thomas tells us,
chiefly owing to the increase in converts and the
impossibility of enlarging the first sites occupied in
many places, " there was a large increase even during
the lifetime of Brother Agnellus both of houses and
places, yet because of his love of poverty he would
never permit any ground to be enlarged nor any house
to be built except as inevitable necessity required."
And to this the infirmary he built at Oxford is no con-
tradiction, for " he built it in such humble fashion
that the height of the walls did not much exceed the
height of a man and even until the time of Brother
Albert this same house was without a guest chamber.

---

[1] Surely this refers to the Bull *Nimis iniqua* (Aug., 1231), although
Brother Salamon and not Peter of Tewkesbury (*De Adv. Mon.*, coll. XIII)
was then Guardian of London. Cf. on this whole question LITTLE:
Studies, p. 92 *et seq.*

In London indeed he had the walls of the dormitory rebuilt of stone in place of mud but left the roof as it was."[1] We find him also praying " to the blessed Francis that he would destroy " the " house at Paris," which was so spacious and lofty that many of the brethren considered it contrary to the poverty of the Order. " And behold when the brethren were about to enter it, by divine intervention not one was able to take up his abode there for the walls collapsed even to the very basement."[2] Yet it was Agnellus who at Oxford " had a school of proper dimensions built in the convent of the brethren ; "[3] and better still, " besought Master Robert Grosseteste of holy memory to lecture to them." In that convent Grosseteste " preached at a chapter of the brethren on poverty and in his sermon put the beggar's estate as the degree of poverty most high for the attainment of heavenly things." And this he did, perhaps, chiefly to please Agnellus, for " afterwards he said to Brother William of Nottingham that there was yet a higher degree of poverty namely that of living by one's own labour." When Agnellus came to die, " he advised," Friar Thomas tells us, " that Brother Hugh of Wells be sent to Brother Elias with a petition from all the brethren that one of these three be appointed minister, to wit, Brother Albert of Pisa, Brother Haymo and Brother Ralph of Rheims. And in so far as it was in his power he named Brother Peter of Tewkesbury his vicar. . . . But when Brother Elias heard from the messenger that Brother Agnellus was dead he immediately caused the Provincial seal to be broken, which bore the figure of a lamb with a cross for he was angry that the brethren of England should ask for Provincial

[1] *De Adv. Min.*, coll. IX.   [2] *Ibid.*   [3] *Ibid.*, coll. X.

Minister one they themselves nominated. Wherefore he refused to send them any Minister till nearly a year had gone by. At length recalling one whom he had already sent hither he commanded Brother Albert of Pisa to go to England and minister to the Brethren. . . . He arrived in England therefore on the feast of St. Lucy (Dec. 13) (? 1237) and on the following festival of the Purification (Feb. 2) held a Provincial Chapter at Oxford."[1]

Albert of Pisa (1237–8) had, like Agnellus, known St. Francis, and was apparently, for all Elias's appointment, as loyal to the Rule of Poverty as his predecessor. He had a vast experience of the Order and had been Provincial in Hungary, Germany and Spain, as well as in the March of Ancona, the March of Treviso and Tuscany. He was, we learn, " always cheerful and merry in the company of the brethren." For all that, however, Friar Thomas does not approve him. " He did unto the brethren in all things according to his own will, he greatly tried the humility and the meekness, the simplicity and the zeal, the charity and the patience of the brethren in England." He seems to have had to meet the provincialism, not to say the nationalism, of the English friars. And his first sermon in England was preached from the text, " Look unto the rock whence you were hewn and to the hole of the pit from which you are dug out."[2]

In time, however, he and the English friars " were drawn towards each other so that at last he so far approved of the brethren in England that he gave his

[1] *De Adv. Min.*, coll. XIII.
[2] *Ibid.*, coll. XIII. Have we here an obscure reference to the rock of Assisi, upon which the church of S. Francesco had been built by Elias, and to the hidden tomb within it?

heart to them entirely and bound them in an attach-
ment beyond words." His love of the English Province was, indeed, so great, that he " died commending
the English above all nations in zeal for the Order."[1]

That he was a man after Agnellus' heart[2] we see by
his acts. He it was who "pulled down the stone
cloister at Southampton though with much trouble
because of the opposition of the burgesses." He
wished to pull down the chapel at Reading and did
humble the friars there before the monks. He insisted
on silence at table in the refectories, and that the
brethren should wear old tunics over their new ones
both for the sake of humility and that the new tunics
might last longer. He it was who with great difficulty
established the friars at Winchester and Chester. The
two formidable problems which he appears to have
solved in England were the interior indiscipline of
the friaries, not, perhaps, so much wilfully, as noisily
unruly and democratic, and the quarrel with the
Dominicans. Friar Thomas gives us two parables
which he spoke concerning the former trouble, and an
account and an epigram concerning the latter. The
Dominicians it seems used to lay all and sundry under
an obligation not to enter any other Order than their
own, and, to put a stop to this, Albert of Pisa obtained
a decree from Pope Gregory, which Innocent IV
afterwards acknowledged, and so, " having nobly
governed the English Province for two years and a half
he went with many others elected for that purpose to
the Chapter which was held against Brother Elias "
(1239). Then, having been elected Minister-General
of the Order in succession to Elias, he died happily

---

[1] *De Adv. Min.*, coll. XII.
[2] Had Agnellus known him in Pisa?

in Rome amongst the English brethren he had so loved.

He was succeeded by Haymo of Faversham (1239–40), whom Agnellus had named with Albert of Pisa to be his successor. It was, however, under Haymo of Faversham that an ideal, the very opposite to that of St. Francis and Blessed Agnellus, began to inform the English Province. He seems to have agreed with Grosseteste rather than with St. Francis. For him, too, the highest degree of poverty was that of living by one's own labour. He preferred, as Friar Thomas tells us, that "the brethren should have ample ground and cultivate it and so supply themselves with the fruits of the earth at home rather than that they should beg them of others. This he said on the occasion of the enlargement of the ground at Gloucester where the brethren had formerly by the decision of Brother Agnellus parted with a large piece of ground which was afterwards with great difficulty acquired again from Sir Thomas Berkeley through the sagacity and devotion of his wife."[1]

Haymo's career in England as Provincial had endured but for a year, during which he had received the Bishop of Hereford into the Order, when he was elected Minister-General in 1240, the second Minister-General England had given to the Order. He was a man of even greater experience than Albert of Pisa, an Aristotelian, a Theologian and a diplomatist. In 1233 he had been one of Gregory IX's envoys to bring about a union of the Greek and Latin Churches, and in 1238 he played no small part in the deposition of Elias. He was now an old man.

He was succeeded as Provincial in England by his

[1] *De Adv. Min.*, coll. IX.

vicar, Brother William of Nottingham, who appears to have been as inexperienced as his predecessor had been experienced in government. Friar Thomas tells us that he was " altogether without experience of the lesser offices such as those of Guardian or Custos ; nevertheless so strenuous was his government that he was famous through all the provinces." That he was a born Franciscan, as we might say, we know. " He told me," writes Friar Thomas, " that when he was living in his father's house and some poor boys came begging alms he gave them of his bread and received the crust from them because it seemed to him that hard bread, which was asked for the love of God, was sweeter than the delicate bread which he ate and his companions ; and so to make their bread sweet like his the little boys went and begged in their turn for the love of God." He used also to say " that it behoved us to consider the mind of St. Francis and his intention in giving us the Rule, else we should gather superfluities into the Order as insensibly as one's beard grows upon one's face." He was learned in the Holy Scriptures, and was the author of the famous Commentary on the Gospels called *De Concordia Evangelistarum*, and his piety was such that it was his custom " to sit long in meditation especially after Matins when he would not hear confessions nor give counsel as his predecessors had done. He used to say that as it was a greater evil to lay down false principles of action than to do such actions themselves so wrong opinions concerning the state of the Order are worse than imperfect observances." At Oxford he had attended the lectures of Grosseteste, and as Provincial he energetically supported the study of theology and especially the educational functions of the friars. Before the end of his ministry there were in England "thirty readers who held solemn disputations and three or four who read without disputations, for he placed students in the universities for each Readership who were to succeed the actual Readers when these died or were removed."[1] About 1248 he was deposed, we do not know why, but the English friars in the Chapter at Oxford (1248?) refused to admit his deposition, and, in fact, re-elected him. We have a letter from Adam Marsh congratulating him upon this and urging him not to decline the office.[2] But he was already dead. Friar Thomas says: "Now when he had governed the province of England for about nine years he was relieved of the ministry at the Chapter of Metz and was sent as delegate of the Chapter to the Pope. But when he had come with the Minister-General as far as Genoa his companion Brother Richard was struck down by the plague and all the others taking flight Brother William remained to console his companion until he himself was struck down in like manner and died. Now the brethren hearing that he had been relieved of the ministry but not knowing of his death held a chapter and re-elected him Minister-Provincial which when the Minister-General heard of it, moved rather by feeling than by reason, he convoked the chapter again through the vicar Brother Gregory de Bossellis and commanded that no Friar who had been dismissed from office by the General Chapter should be re-elected in the Provincial Chapter; but he left the confirmation of the Minister-Elect to Brothers John de Kethene, Adam de Marisco and John of Stamford. And thus Brother Peter of Tewkesbury was elected and at the same time confirmed."

[1] *De Adv. Min.*, coll. X.　　　[2] *Mon. Franc.*, I, 373.

The Franciscans in England

In considering the influence of this pious and lovable man upon the Order in England, we must note that though the places and buildings of the friars increased in his day, he was still, as Friar Thomas has it, " zealous for poverty." Thus, he " ordered the stone walls in the dormitory at Shrewsbury to be removed and mud walls put in their stead which was done by the brethren with admirable meekness and at great cost."[1] He also asserted roundly that "he did not become a friar for the purpose of building walls." He unroofed the chapel in London and "ordered the embossments on the cloister should be scratched away. Yet he sometimes said that it was well that our houses should be large enough lest the brethren who came after should make them exceeding large."[2]

We seem to have here a man eager to follow the Franciscan ideal, but foreseeing the future in which it would be but a tale that is told. He had, too, as I have said, stood out most manfully against the exactions of the procurators.[3] Indeed, this struggle, the struggle with Elias and all that it meant for the Order in those first years after the death of St. Francis, was felt not less in England than elsewhere. And though Elias was condemned and deposed largely through the efforts of the English Friars, and afterwards excommunicated, it is his ideal and his genius which more and more inform the Order till they provoke the reaction which divides the Order even to this day.

The attitude of the English friars to Elias is well shown by Friar Thomas.[4] They were utterly opposed to him. The tragedy of Elias was that he was

[1] *De Adv. Min.*, coll. III.   [2] *Ibid.*, coll. IX.
[3] *Ibid.*, coll. VIII.   [4] *Ibid.*, coll. XII.

Franciscan. A man of genius, a great organiser, he would have understood St. Ignatius Loyola; he only loved St. Francis. In his mind, the quick superficial mind of the *parvenu*, of the politician, of the "self-made man," with whom success must outweigh almost every other consideration, the Franciscan Order was an army to be organised above all for success, for triumph. If anything hitherto inherent in the Order stood in the way of this success, it must go; he certainly would neither spare nor regret it. Well, what stood in the way of this success, this triumph, was Poverty, the ultimate Poverty that was St. Francis' bride, a doctrine as mystical as that of the "Equality of Man," as difficult for certain minds to seize, to appreciate at its full value, but as practical as a military command, a command above all to be obeyed. It might seem that St. Francis had taught Elias only to love, not to obey; yet it was Elias who saw him—with what astonishment we may imagine—turn even the sick out of a house at Bologna which was said to "belong to" the friars. And so when Elias became Minister-General his mind was set on organising the Order for success, not in obeying and administering the Rule—a thing to be obeyed. Above all other things he wanted money, money for the great church we owe to him, money for himself that he might live with and influence, and, if possible, control Popes and Princes and Lords, and maintain himself, not as the *Poverello* had done, but as a great Abbot.

If the Benedictine and the Jesuit ideals are noble, if success in great and splendid schemes is admirable, then we may not curse Elias. Only he was not a Franciscan. The Francis he loved, all unconsciously he betrayed. To many, to the English certainly, it seemed as though Christ had been succeeded by Judas Iscariot. Elias was overthrown. In that vital struggle the English Province played a great and even perhaps a predominant part; at any rate, it was Brother Haymo of Faversham who bore the brunt of the attack, and it was the English Minister-Provincial, Albert of Pisa, who succeeded the deposed Elias with Haymo of Faversham to follow him as we have seen.

Apart from the genius of Elias, we must ascribe his influence in the Order to the fact that his ideas were not only more in accordance with tradition than those of St. Francis, but appealed far more both to the ordinary man and to authority : and then, his position within the Order was due to the action of St. Francis himself. In the year 1220 St. Francis had resigned the office of General of the Order, and had appointed Peter of Cattaneo, but he died in March, 1221, and St. Francis gave his office to Elias. Elias was thus General by the choice of St. Francis himself when the Saint came to die in 1226, and it was he who summoned the Chapters at Pentecost in the following year when Giovanni Parenti was chosen as the first Minister-General. Elias thereupon had devoted himself to the building of the great church at Assisi, to be dedicated in honour of St. Francis whom the Pope Gregory IX had canonized on July 16, 1228. Here the body of St. Francis was destined to lie, but so jealous was Elias and so fearful for the future of his ideas, that on May 22, 1230, three days before the time duly arranged, he seized the body of St. Francis which lay in San Giorgio, with the connivance of the municipal powers of Assisi, and secretly buried it in the new church where it was not discovered till 1818.

This extraordinary act naturally enraged his opponents, and Elias was censured and punished by the Pope less than a month later, on June 16, 1230. But the publication of the Bull, *Quo elongati*, in September of that year, did not altogether discourage him, indeed it decided in his favour, putting aside the testament of St. Francis as not binding on the friars, and evading by a pious trick the fundamental precept of St. Francis which forbade the friars to receive money. Elias continued to build and adorn the church whose foundation was in a very real sense an infringement of the Rule, and in 1232 he was elected Minister-General. It is now the real trouble begins. He governed without reference to the Rule, and like a tyrant. But it was not the Italian friars who most keenly opposed him : his most formidable enemies were in Paris, in England and in Germany. This opposition was soon so strong that in 1239, with Gregory's approval, the Chapters of Rome deposed him. Of all this Friar Thomas gives an excellent account from which I take the following :

" When at the Chapter of Rieti (1232) Brother John Parenti was dismissed, the Pope permitted Brother Elias to be again appointed Minister-General, chiefly because of his intimacy with St. Francis.

" After this Brother Elias by reason of his unholiness and cruelty again threw the Order into a turmoil, and now Brother Haymo of Paris moved an appeal against him ; and notwithstanding the opposition of Brother Elias, Brother Arnuleph, Vicar of the Order and penitentiary of the Lord Pope Gregory IX convoked a General Chapter at which many of the Ministers-Provincial and upright brethren of the Cismontane

Provinces of the Order were elected who were to take measures for the reformation of the Order : which being done an account thereof was rendered in General Chapter before the Pope and at this Chapter seven Cardinals were present.

" Now when the Pope had preached—and his sermon was upon the golden statue that Nebuchadnezzar saw in his dream, and his text was : ' Thou, O King, didst begin to think what should come to pass '—then did Brother Elias begin to excuse himself alleging that the brethren when they elected him Minister-General did say that they wished him to eat gold and ride a horse if such his weakness required, whereas now they turned against him, and were scandalized, and when Brother Haymo desired leave to reply the Pope would not permit him till the Lord Cardinal Robert de Sumercote pleaded : ' My Lord Pope, this old man is a good man, and it is well you should hear him especially as he is sparing of his words.' "

Brother Haymo therefore rose up timid and trembling, but Elias sat to all appearance fearless and undisturbed. Thereupon, Brother Haymo began by briefly commending the words of Brother Elias as those of a revered father, but urged against him, that although the brethren might have wished him to eat gold, yet they had not asked him to amass it. Moreover, they might have asked him to ride a horse, but had never requested him to keep a palfrey or a charger. At this Brother Elias, unable to contain his rage, called out that Brother Haymo lied, and the partisans of Brother Elias began to insult Brother Haymo in like manner, and to make a tumult. Then did others of the opposite party cry out against these. But the Pope, greatly moved, commanded silence, saying :

" These are not the manners of religious," and for a long while he sat silent and pondering till they were all filled with shame.

" Meanwhile the Lord Cardinal Reginald protector of the Order, openly admonished Brother Elias to put his resignation into the hands of the Pope, but Brother Elias publicly declared he would not. Thereupon the Pope, having commended the personal character of Brother Elias and spoken of his intimacy with St. Francis concluded by saying that he had believed his ministry to be acceptable to the brethren, but that now since it was shown to be no longer acceptable his decree was that Brother Elias be dismissed, and at once he removed him from the office of Minister-General. Thereat did the brethren rejoice with an unmeasurable and unspeakable joy such as they had never before seen who merited to be present.

" The Pope thereupon entered to one of the cells and called to him the Ministers-Provincial and the Custodes for the election and before they gave their votes in writing he heard them orally. When therefore Brother Albert of Pisa Minister of England was canonically elected Brother Arnulph the penitentiary who more than anyone else had managed their affairs, announced the election and intoned the *Te Deum Laudamus.*"

What we have here, told so discretely, is not only the vanquishment of Elias, but the victory, temporary as it proved to be, of the idea of St. Francis over the opposition of the Papacy. The Papacy had stood behind Elias, the Bull *Quo elongati* proves this, until it perceived that that was too dangerous a way of achieving its end—the abrogation of the Rule of Poverty. Elias, who had not only known St. Francis but had been appointed General by him, secured to the Papacy a perfect instrument. Two things seem to have spoiled the plan, the sincerity and violence of Elias and the loyalty and enthusiasm of the Provinces, and especially of the English Province, from which came Haymo of Faversham and Alexander of Hales, Elias's chief opponents, and whose Minister-General was his successor, to be succeeded in his turn by Haymo.

The apostasy and fate of Elias are moving, but scarcely concern us here. What does concern us is the briefness of the victory which seemed so over-whelming. Crescenzio Guzzi of Jesi, who succeeded Haymo as Minister-General in 1245, was succeeded in his turn by John of Parma in 1247. He ruled for ten years, and with him the movement which had pro-cured the fall of Elias comes full circle. With his deposition in 1257 and the election of St. Bonaventura, the Papal idea begins to move forward again within the Order, and it was the *Constitutiones Marbonenses* of 1260 which decided what after all the future of the Order was to be. But the Bull *Exiit qui seminat* of August, 1279, shows us how slowly this idea was making headway. Therein the full renunciation of property by the Order is still maintained, but all property given to the Brethren is now vested in the Holy See save in cases where the donor wishes to retain his title : while all moneys are to be held in trust by *nuntii*, friends duly appointed, for the friars. Such was the beginning of reaction. It seems certainly harmless enough, and in a world where the practical questions of life and livelihood had to be faced both by the friars and the Papacy, which was responsible for them, little fault can be found with such a decision.

But we shall see later how from behind that Bull of 1279 the reaction was able to emerge, to overwhelm the Order and to impress upon it ideas which, from the beginning, the Papacy had been anxious to see victorious over the idealism of St. Francis.

VIII

OXFORD AND THE FRIARS

IT would seem to be an example of the irony of
things that though St. Francis had opposed and
even denounced learning for his friars, and had
certainly praised action above thought,[1] yet the chief
centres of Franciscan influence in the West, in France
and England that is, were destined to be the Univer-
ties of Paris and Oxford.

In Oxford, where the friars settled in November,
1224, the Blessed Agnellus himself, as we have seen,
built "a school of convenient dimensions," and
though later, according to Bartholomew of Pisa,[2] he
seems to have regretted what he had done, yet it was
from this school that the immense influence of the
Order in the England of the thirteenth and fourteenth
centuries was to come. Here it was that Agnellus first
"besought Master Robert Grosseteste of holy memory
to lecture to the friars. Under him they made exceeding
progress in a short time both as to their sermons and

[1] *Speculum Perfectionis*, cap. LXIX–LXXII, and esp. cap. IV.

[2] "Afterwards," says Bartholomew of Pisa, "he had reason for regret
when he saw the friars bestowing their time in frivolities and neglecting
needful things; for one day when he wished to see what proficiency
they were making he entered the schools whilst a disputation was going
on and hearing them wrangling and questioning *Utrum sit Deus* he cried:
'Woe is me, woe is me! Simple brothers enter Heaven and learned
brothers dispute whether there is a God at all!' Then he sent ten pounds
sterling to the Court to buy the Decretals that the friars might study
them and give over frivolities." *Lib. Conf.*, fol. 796, quoted by LITTLE:
Grey Friars in Oxford (1892), p. 30.

as to those refinements of manners which are suitable for preaching." By thus persuading Grosseteste, the best English scholar of that time, and, as Little asserts, the most influential man at Oxford, Agnellus rendered the greatest possible service to his Order. The date of Grosseteste's appointment is uncertain, but it is possible that he began to lecture to the friars in 1225–26, and if so, they had the inestimable benefit of his learning and protection for ten years, for it was only " when he by divine Providence was translated from the lecture hall to the Episcopate," [1] that is, when in 1235 he became Bishop of Lincoln, that he gave up his post.

To him, according to Friar Thomas, succeeded Master Peter, " who was afterwards promoted to be Bishop in Scotland." Of this man we know nothing. But he was succeeded by two friends of Grosseteste. The first of these was Master Roger de Wesham, who about 1239 became Dean of Lincoln, and in 1245 Bishop of Coventry, and the second was Master Thomas Wallensis, " who after laudably lecturing to the brethren in the same place was taken away (in 1247) to be Bishop of St. David's in Wales." These four lectors were all seculars, and since, as Friar Thomas tells us, " these Masters continued favourable unto the brethren, the deeds and fame of the brethren went forth into many places so much so that the good report of the English brethren and their progress in studies was spoken of in the other provinces of the Order."

Now this had a great and definite effect, according to Friar Thomas, for it was this fame and good report which caused " the Minister-General Brother Elias to

[1] *De Adv. Mon.*, coll. X.

[125]

send Brother Philip Wallensis and Brother Adam of York to read divinity at Lyons and at length caused Brother Albert of Pisa when he came to England to institute Brother Vincent of Coventry to be lector at London and Brother Henry (brother-german to Brother Vincent) to be lector at Canterbury, and in a little while to appoint other lectors in various other places,"[1] and last of all Brother Adam de Marisco was appointed lector at Oxford.

" Thus the gift of wisdom flowed out over the English Province, so that before Brother William of Nottingham had completed his ministry (1251) there were in England 30 lectors who held solemn disputations and three or four who read without disputations. For he placed students in the Universities for each lectorship who were to succeed the actual lectors when these died or were removed."

What we see here is the success of the secular lectors leading to the appointment of the friars themselves as lectors. And just as the first three lectors stand apart as seculars, so do the second three, who though friars were also graduates of the University ; they were Brother Adam de Marisco, Brother Ralph de Colebruge and Brother Eustace de Normaneville. With the fourth " regular " lector, Thomas of York, we come to a friar pure and simple, and his appointment, as we shall see, led to a similar, though far less bitter, quarrel in the University of Oxford, to that which had long been raging in the University of Paris.

These lectors had no real status as such in the University, and their position, apart from that which

[1] Brother William of Leicester at Hereford, Brother Gregory de Bossellis at Leicester, Brother Gilbert de Cranford at Bristol, Brother John of Weston at Cambridge.

belonged personally to such men as Grosseteste and
Adam de Marisco, is perhaps at first sight difficult to
understand.

Mr. Little[1] likens their position to that of a college
tutor, but one must not forget that all these first five
lectors were men for the most part already famous,
and that to the friars they were very much more than
readers in theology, they were their protectors and
friends. The *Lanercost Chronicle*[2] seems, indeed, to
put the matter beyond doubt when it describes " the
friars going to Robert (Grosseteste) as to a pedagogue
telling him what had happened and begging for his
advice "; and if this was so with Grosseteste, a
secular, it was even more so with Adam de Marisco,
a friar.

The entry of this remarkable and famous man into
the Order at Worcester has already been described.[3]
He had been educated at Oxford under Grosseteste,
who was a friend of his family, and after entering the
Order is said to have been appointed *socius*, that is
companion, or secretary, to St. Anthony of Padua,
and to have gone with him to study theology at
Vercelli, where they both remained for five years. He
came to Oxford as lector in 1247 already famous, and
one of the most influential men in the kingdom. We
see him as the friend of the King, of Earl Simon, of
the Archbishops, and, as papal commissioner, immersed in all sorts of affairs, directing events, a man of
European reputation. Oxford, through the influence
of Grosseteste, had only just succeeded in winning his
services from the University of Paris, where it was
decreed he should succeed Alexander of Hales. He

[1] Cf. LITTLE, *op. cit.*, p. 31.   [2] *Lanercost Chron.*, p. 130.
[3] *Supra*, p. 49.

assists the Archbishop of Canterbury, goes with Grosseteste to the Council of Lyons ; his presence is required by the Parliament in Westminster ; the Queen desires his advice ; he rebukes the King, yet the King cannot do without his counsel and calls him father. To the wife of de Montfort, the King's sister, he gives counsel on her duties as wife and mother, to Earl Simon he preaches patience and self-control. That he admired and sympathised with Earl Simon in his great struggle is certain if inexplicable. His Oxford friars, and indeed the Order generally, were the champions of the movement ; the Earl was buried by the friars at Evesham, and at Oxford he was regarded by them as a saint for all his excommunication, and they bore witness to the miracles he performed.[1] Yet with all this Brother Adam was a true Franciscan, he served the poor continually.[2] Grosseteste so loved him that he bequeathed his library to the Oxford Franciscans for the sake of Adam. Under his too many and too various duties his health broke down, and in 1258 he died, worn-out by work, and was buried next his friend, the great Bishop, at Lincoln, leaving to the world a pupil to be more famous than himself, Roger Bacon.

Such was the first " regular " lector of the Franciscans at Oxford. He had of course his *socius*, or secretary, and the work of this younger friar, under Brother Adam, can have been no light task.

Adam de Marisco was succeeded as lector by

---

[1] Cf. WRIGHT : *Political Songs*, pp. 72 *et seq.* Also YORK POWELL : *Hist. of England*, 148 *et seq.* Also see *Miracula Symonis de Montfort* in RISHANGER's *Chron.* (Camden Soc.), pp. 87, 95 *et seq.* Cf. LITTLE, *op. cit.*, Pt. 33 and 137.

[2] *Mon. Franc.*, I, 137, 244 and 398.

Brother Ralph of Colebridge, who had been lector at Paris, but he did not really fill his place.

The position of the first five lectors at Oxford was, as I have said, extraordinary, in that of the sixth Brother Ralph we at once see a change. The Franciscans, as Mr. Little says, " assimilated their system of teaching to the system in vogue in the University generally," and Brother Ralph and his successors were the first Regent Masters in Theology belonging to the Order, and after Brother Ralph, who was appointed by the Minister-General, they were appointed by the Minister-Provincial on the advice, it seems, of the friars at Oxford.[1]

The system obtaining at Oxford from the beginning allowed no friar to take any degree until he had received permission to do so by papal ordinance (*statuta papalia*) or by election of his Order.[2] Later, in 1336, it was enacted by the Constitutions of Pope Benedict XII that no friar could become a Bachelor unless " he had first lectured on the four books of the Sentences with writings of the approved doctors in other *studia*, which are in the same Order called *Generalia*," or in one of the following convents in England : London, York, Newcastle, Exeter, or Stramforicensis (Stamford ?). Later still the English friars were especially favoured in this that when it was decreed in the General Chapter in Rome in 1411 that no friar should proceed to the degree of master unless he had been at Paris the English Province was especially excepted.[3]

It must be noted that the friars were confined to the faculty of Theology as the Middle Age understood

---

[1] *De Adv. Min.*, coll. X.   *Mon. Franc.*, I, 335 and 357.
[2] Cf. LITTLE, *op. cit.*, p. 35.   [3] *Ibid.*

that term, and to the study of the Canon Law; the Order forbade them to take a degree in Arts,[1] and it is here their long quarrel with the University began, for the University required the student to graduate in Arts before proceeding to Theology.

The quarrel came to a head in 1253. In February of that year the University was formally asked to permit Friar Thomas of York " to ascend the chair of ordinary regent in Holy Scripture." It immediately raised the objection that he had not graduated in Arts, and a committee of seven was appointed to report on the matter. On March 8 the report was considered. It proved to be to the effect that Friar Thomas should incept as an exception, but that a statute should be made whereby no one in future should incept in Theology " unless he had graduated in Arts in some University and read one book of the Canon or of the Sentences and publicly preached in the University." The University reserved the right to grant dispensations, which, at any rate, till 1314, it did very freely; but such was to be the rule, and if any attempt should be made " to extort grace of the University through the influence of any magnate he should *ipso facto* be expelled from the University." This Statute Adam de Marisco was asked to sign. He refused, offering all sorts of excuses, and, fundamentally this, that he did not approve it. He had then for three years retired from the office of lecturing in the University; and when the matter was pressed he withdrew his opposition and left the assembly and Oxford, saying that " dangerous as the measure seemed and distasteful to him it did not appear to be conceived in a spirit of wilful injustice."

[1] Cf. BACON : *Op. Ined.*, I, 426, and LITTLE, *op. cit.*, p. 37.

Thus the University had its way, as in Paris, where the quarrel was a much more serious affair. That the friars were wrong might seem to have been the opinion of one of the greatest among them, Roger Bacon. Writing in 1271, he says : " During the last forty years there have arisen some in the Universities (*in studio*) who have made themselves doctors and masters of theology and philosophy, though they never learnt anything of real value (*dignum*) and are neither willing nor able to do so on account of their status. . . . They are boys inexperienced in themselves, in the world, in the learned languages, Greek and Hebrew . . . they are ignorant of all parts and sciences of mundane philosophy, when they venture on the study of theology which demands all known wisdom . . . they are the boys of the two Orders, like Albert and Thomas and others, who enter the Orders when they are twenty years old or less. Many thousands enter who cannot read the Psalter and Donatus, and immediately after making their profession they are set to study Theology . . ."[1]

The quarrel was renewed in the fourteenth century, but concerned the Franciscans less than the Dominicans ; the friars finally submitting to the University in 1320.

In considering the manner of life of the friars in Oxford in the thirteenth and early fourteenth centuries Mr. Little quotes a document showing that apart from the lectors they had little or no privacy. *Nullus frater cameram habeat clausam vel a dormitorio sequestratam, ministris exceptis et lectoribus in generalibus studiis constitutis.*[2] Yet this was the period of

[1] BACON : *Op. Ined.*, I, lv., and 399. Cf. LITTLE, *op. cit.*, p. 42.
[2] LITTLE, *op. cit.*, p. 55.

their greatest literary activity. Privacy indeed, in our sense of the term, scarcely existed in the Middle Age. No doubt a part of their work consisted in copying manuscripts, and it was probably for this that Adam de Marisco needed the vellum for which he asked the Custodian of Cambridge.[1] It seems likely that it was from Adam de Marisco that the friars received their first books, for Richard, his uncle, bequeathed him his library in 1226, while we know from Bartholomew of Pisa that Agnellus presented them with a copy of the Decretals, and then in 1253 Grosseteste for love of Adam de Marisco bequeathed all his books to the Oxford House.[2] Of this last bequest indeed one work still remains in Oxford, St. Augustine's *De Civitate Dei*, with Grosseteste's notes, now in the Bodleian. Besides this Caius College possesses a copy of the Gospels in Greek and a Psalter in Greek, which, perhaps, came from the Franciscan convent, and a few other MSS. at the Bodleian and at Lambeth may also be among the relics of the library Dr. Thomas Gascoigne was allowed to consult in the fifteenth century and which Leland found in complete ruin.[3]

It was round this convent and this library that little by little, and with a rapidity as astonishing as the spreading of their Order through England, the Franciscans erected an educational organisation that in fact covered the whole country, of which the convent at Oxford was the head. We have seen how lecturers were established by Brother Albert of Pisa at London, Canterbury, Hereford, Leicester, Bristol and Cambridge, as well as at Oxford,[4] and " thus," as

---

[1] *Mon. Franc.*, I, 391.   [2] Nic. Trivet : *Annales*, 243.
[3] Gascoigne : *Loci e libro veritatum ;* ed. Rogers *passim*, and Leland : *Collect.*, III, 60.   [4] *De Adv. Min.*, coll. X.

Oxford and the Friars

Friar Thomas says, " the gift of wisdom flowed out over the English Province." And he proceeds to give us a picture of the Oxford lecture-room as he himself had seen it; the only contemporary picture of it we possess. " There was," says Friar Thomas, " a certain eminent Reader who studied with me at Oxford, and he was accustomed as a student during the Master's lecture on disputations to give his attention to other matters rather than to the lecture. He would even compile original notes of his own. But when he himself was appointed Lector his own students were so inattentive that he declared he would as willingly each day close his book and leave them as stay and give his lecture. Then struck with remorse, he exclaimed, ' By a just judgment of God none of these will now listen to me who would never listen to my own teacher.' Moreover, he was too frequently in the company of secular friends, and for this reason was now seldom found with the brethren. Wherefore he was made an example to the other brethren to show how words of wisdom can be learned only in silence and quiet, and how the love of God, as the Saints tell us, can be understood only by the mind." This was he who too " frequently went to visit a devout matron in order to comfort her when he ought to have been busy with lectures. . . . But after he reformed and gave himself to quiet study, and made such progress that the Bishop of Lincoln would declare that he could hardly believe his lectures to be his own. So the fame of his good life increased until he was called by the Minister-General to the parts of Lombardy and in the very court of the Pope was held to be a great man. . . ."

He does not stand alone, the fame of the Oxford

The Franciscans in England

Franciscan school spread through Europe; friars came to it even from France, Italy, Spain, Portugal and Germany, and it supplied many teachers to the Franciscan schools of the Continent. We see Paris itself contend for Adam de Marisco, who is hardly saved to Oxford by Grosseteste. Nor was this all, for the school produced men whose names will never be forgotten, names among the greatest in medieval thought, which shed a never-fading lustre upon the Franciscan convent and school at Oxford.

IX

ROGER BACON

THE " most astonishing phenomenon of the mediæval schools," Roger Bacon, is at first sight certainly almost inexplicably the disciple of St. Francis ; that he was Franciscan at all, however discontentedly, might seem but to show indeed what the Franciscan Order had already become within a generation of the death of St. Francis. And yet a more thoughtful consideration would perhaps find that after all the two men had much in common, and might come at last to think of them as rather lonely friends, almost in spite of themselves, in an Order already utterly transformed for the sake of success, in which—this at least they had in common—the one would have been as great a stranger as the other proved to be. St. Francis, one might think, would have had as little patience with the logomachy of the Schools as Roger Bacon. And there is this, too : if St. Francis attempted to restore religion and to save the Church, as in the Pope's vision, by a return to the Gospel ; Roger Bacon no less tried to save scholasticism by a return to Nature and to Experience. He failed ; he was indeed too far away from his age to have much influence upon it. His life is a tragedy, and failing where St. Francis could not fail, in love, he dies at last with these words in his heart if not on his tongue : " I repent me of this, that I have given myself so much trouble to destroy ignorance."

Roger Bacon was born, according to Rous,[1] at Ilchester, in Somerset, in or about the year 1214.[2] His family, if we may judge from casual references in his works, was of some wealth and perhaps of some nobility, but it sided with the King in the Barons' Wars and thereby lost its property and suffered other penalties. He speaks of his brother as a ruined man.

Where Roger received his early education we do not know, but when he went up to Oxford he came immediately under the influence of Grosseteste who, as we have seen, from 1224 to 1235 was Franciscan Lector ; there, also, he met Adam de Marisco, and for these two men he had never anything but the most generous praise.

The influence of Grosseteste, perhaps the earliest of his life and certainly the most profound, is fundamental for Bacon in two respects : it confirmed once and for all the bent of his mind towards scientific, experimental, and linguistic studies, and, finally, when he had later, and under the influence of another man, to make up his mind as to whether he would enter the Order of St. Francis or no, it was probably the early influence of Grosseteste which at last decided him to do so. For Bacon had come to Oxford not only at a time when it was the second arena of the West, but at a moment when Grosseteste was there at the height of his fame, and perhaps the greatest achievement of the older man was thus to have formed the young Bacon.

The originality of Grosseteste lies in this, that his

---

[1] JOHN ROUS : *Hist. Regum Angl.*, 29, 82.

[2] In 1267 Bacon tells us that " it is now 40 years since I first learnt the alphabet . . . and except for 2 of those 40 I have always been *in studio*." *Op. Ined.*, I, 65.

mind was not absorbed in the syllogistic treatment of philosophical and theological questions which was the profound and beautiful work of the legitimate princes of thirteenth-century thought. He was interested chiefly in the study of languages, was in some sort a Greek scholar, had studied physics and optics, had a theory even of light as a constitutive principle of matter, of the principle of change in the universe, and above all perhaps was devoted to the study of mathematics. In pure philosophy, however, he was content with the Augustinian-Aristotelean system to which the Franciscan schools adhered until the advent of Duns Scotus. The chief impression then of the young Roger in an Oxford, almost wholly undisturbed as yet by the Parisian controversy, was this scientific curiosity confirmed by the study of languages and mathematics which he received from Grosseteste. Such an impression upon such a spirit informed with the genius not only to receive it, but to transform what it received and to endow it with a passionate life, could never be effaced. And if this was so, it was not the least of Roger's misfortunes that about the year 1240 he left Oxford to go to Paris.

If we ask why did Bacon leave Oxford for Paris, we can only reply that Grosseteste, and indeed all his masters, had studied there, and that Paris was then undoubtedly the first University in the world. There William of Auvergne and Alexander of Hales, the Franciscan, were lecturing, were busy destroying the Augustinian method and doctrine, rescuing Aristotle from the Arabians, and establishing his philosophy as the basis of a systematic exposition of Christian dogma ; there Albert the Great, the latinizer of Aristotle, was soon to arrive in triumph ; there the future princes, the young Aquinas and Bonaventura, were presently to gain their titles of *sacræ theologiæ magister*.

The whole atmosphere, as we might say, the whole intellectual conditions of the University of Paris bored and soon enraged Bacon. How far in this world of unreal words wholly philosophical-theological was he from Oxford and the methods and interest of his master, interests real enough, language, physics, optics, things to be governed and proved by observation and experiment ! He heard William of Auvergne dispute before the whole University on the *Intellectus Agens* of which the venerable Bishop was more terrified than Bacon was weary. " He proved that everyone was wrong," says Roger sententiously, wearily. He saw Alexander of Hales, the great English Franciscan, and found his *Summa Theologica* " heavier than a cart-horse," " vain " and " false." Albert the Great, whom all the world ranked with Aristotle, Avicenna and Averroës he dismisses as a diffuse and vain fool whose philosophy omits everything that is beautiful or useful and is therefore valueless. As for St. Thomas, he calls him a boy, and ranks him with Albert as " inexperienced in himself, in the world, and in the learned languages Greek and Hebrew . . ." [1]

But there was after all one man at Paris whom Bacon found wholly sympathetic and who was to have a great influence upon the course of his life. This was Petrus Peregrinus, Peter de Maricourt, a man, according to Bacon, unambitious, modest, but of such genius and learning that he could, had he wished, have wholly dominated that strangely unruly world, absorbed in words which he despised as heartily as

[1] *Op. Ined.*, I, 399.

did Roger himself. When Bacon speaks of this man it is as though we already heard, here in Paris, in the middle of the thirteenth century, the voice of Leonardo da Vinci. " He knows everything relating to the art of war," he writes in the *Opus Tertium*, " to the making of weapons and the chase ; he has looked closely into agriculture, mensuration, and farming work ; he he has even taken note of the remedies, lot-casting and charms, used by old women and by wizards and magicians, and of the deceptions and devices of conjurers. . . . It is impossible that philosophy should be carried to its perfection or handled with utility or certainty without his aid."

As it happened, this man was a Franciscan.

We have then this position. Here is Bacon, miserable, bored and enraged amid the scholasticism of Paris, looking back to Oxford with a bitter longing, remembering the interests of his first master, Grosseteste, the patron and Lector of the Friars Minor. Suddenly, in the desert of words that Paris seemed to him, he meets a kindred spirit as enraged as himself at the logomachy of the Paris schools, and this man is a Franciscan. Is it not here we may find the otherwise almost inexplicable reason of Roger's entry into the Franciscan Order ? In his disgust at the world in which he lived, in his enthusiasm for his memory of Grosseteste, of Adam de Marisco too perhaps, and certainly of Peter de Maricourt, he thinks it but a little thing to forego it all, to sacrifice everything and to enter an Order, which, if it were vowed to the renunciation of all possessions could yet attract and produce such men as these to whom in his eagerness the future seemed to belong ? And he was right : it was to the system and the method of these men that the future did belong ; but a future more than three hundred years away.

We do not know the year in which Bacon actually entered the Order of St. Francis, but it must have been in one of the twelve years between 1245 and 1257. He had already sacrificed everything but his liberty of action and thought, to his ideas ; he tells us himself in 1267 that he had spent more than two thousand *libræ* " on secret books and various experiments and languages and instruments and tables."[1] and his labour had been such that " before I became a friar men used to wonder that I lived owing to such excessive labour." Now as a friar he sacrificed even his liberty of action and thought, he was under the authority of his superiors, he had to work as they ordered ; could he think also as they desired ? That they permitted him to continue his experiments and his method of thought he tells us himself ; then suddenly he became ill, and this illness lasted two years. It was another turning-point in his life.

Without the memory of Grosseteste, the influence of Peter de Maricourt, it is impossible to explain Bacon's entry into the Order of Friars Minor. That it was a misfortune for him it is hard to deny. Perhaps his illness was the result of the impossible struggle between him and authority, at any rate it is upon his recovery from this long illness and when he is about to resume his work that he finds himself no longer free to pursue his way unmolested. Between 1245 and 1257 he seems to have spent his time between Oxford and Paris, where he took his degree, that of Master of Divinity, according to the *Analecta Franciscana*, that of Master of Arts rather, as the best modern opinion

[1] *Op. Ined.*, I, 59.

assures us. In Paris, and in exile under strict super-
vision, he was certainly in the year 1257, when St.
Thomas and St. Bonaventura there took their degrees.
Much had happened perhaps while he had been ill.
The Order had been greatly troubled by the un-
authorised publication of a commentary upon the
work of the famous Joachim da Fiore. A sect of
Joachists had arisen among the " spiritual " party
within the Franciscan Order, many of whom saw
Antichrist already in the world in the person of
Frederick II, nor was their faith shaken by his death
in 1250. One of these " spirituals," Fra Gherardo da
Borgo San Donnino, wrote a treatise entitled " Intro-
ductorium in Evangelium Æternum," which was
examined by the Church in 1255, and was condemned
by Alexander IV in 1256.[1] Now John of Parma, the
Franciscan General, 1247–57, was himself accused of
Joachism, and was acquitted by St. Bonaventura, his
real crime being probably a literal observance of the
rule of St. Francis. Nevertheless, the Order was involved in the condemnation of Alexander IV by
reason of the publication of Fra Gherardo's book, and
in consequence a general rule was promulgated for
the whole Order, in effect establishing a strict censor-
ship by the Order over the writings of the friars.
Owing partly to fear, partly to ignorance, this rule
doubtless hit Roger very hard. He felt it, it would

[1] The central doctrine of Joachim computed by St. Thomas in his
Summa Theologica is that there are three states of the world corresponding
to the three persons of the Trinity. The first age is of the Father, that
is the Old Testament dispensation ; the second of the Son, that is the
New Testament dispensation ; the third of the Spirit, a new Kingdom of
universal love proceeding from the Gospel of Christ but transcending the
letter of it. This third period Joachim was said to have held would begin
with a great cataclysm about 1260.

seem, as something personal to himself, which strictly speaking it was not, though in the application of it, it almost certainly was. No doubt this was a staggering blow, perhaps it brought his work to a standstill, though of course not his thought and preparation. Suddenly, in 1266, he seemed to be delivered.

In 1261 Guy de Foulques, who in 1259 had been consecrated Archbishop of Narbonne, was made Cardinal Bishop of Sabina, and it would seem that about 1263 Roger's name was brought to his notice by a clerk named Raymond of Laon, who roused the Cardinal's interest with regard to his discoveries. The great man wrote to him ; Bacon replied. Then, in 1265, the Cardinal Bishop of Sabina became Pope Clement IV. In the following year, as Pope, he wrote again to Roger bidding him send him a fair copy of the work which Raymond had spoken of, and to do this in spite of any constitution of his Order to the contrary, secretly, and without delay. The Pope seems to have thought that the work he desired to see was already written. But Roger writes : " Whilst I was in a different state of life I wrote nothing on science ; nor in my present condition had I ever been required to do so by my superiors ; nay a strict prohibition has been passed to the contrary under penalty of forfeiture of the book and many days fasting on bread and water, if any book written by us should be communicated to strangers."

Notwithstanding these difficulties, the jealousies of his superiors, the lack of money, of instruments and the enjoined secrecy, within eighteen months Roger wrote the *Opus Majus*, the *Opus Minus* and the *Opus Tertium*, all together a vast encyclopædia of know-ledge, and sent them to the Pope. Well may Brewer say that such an achievement is unparalleled in the history of literature!

The most modern opinion would seem to hold that the *Opus Minus* and the *Opus Tertium* were written before the *Opus Majus*. There can be no greater contrast than these offer to other works of the time. The whole scholastic method and system is discarded, and instead of almost unreadable treatises in philosophy and theology we have in the *Opus Majus* a great and passionate work of literature, a long and persuasive letter upon the whole realm of knowledge and thought of the time. Everything here is clear and violent and absolutely modern in its sane common sense.

He condemns utterly the teaching of the time and its methods—the endless commentaries which distort the work of Aristotle, the bad translations. Every sort of study needs reform. As for theology and ecclesiastical studies, there is too much poor philosophy in them and an absolute ignorance of those sciences so necessary to them. The *Liber Sententiarum* is more valued than Holy Scripture, and the text of the Bible is at the same time so corrupt, and the theologians so utterly ignorant of Greek and Hebrew, that all sorts of errors pass for truth. That Theology is the Queen of sciences he admits, but he maintains that it, with Philosophy and Canon Law, the whole realm of knowledge, in fact, are but the handmaids of that divine wisdom which is contained altogether and wholly in Holy Writ, that they have but an interpretative value and duty in regard to the Scriptures. Philosophy, the passion of the schools, is not indeed alien from the divine wisdom, but it is only its handmaiden and has no value in itself. In that opinion, violently expressed as it was and as violently opposed, we seem to see already in the thirteenth century a prophecy of the Reformation. And all this was very English, too; superficially, absurd, obvious or even common; but profoundly subtle, and if not a truth absolute, extraordinarily clairvoyant of the mind of the future.

Nor was Roger less antagonistic to the mind of his own time or even less English when he dealt, as he did, most faithfully with all those things he loved best, wherein indeed he is greatest, with the experimental sciences. He is most English in this, that everywhere he maintains that theory must be subordinate to life, to experience; must everywhere and at every moment be judged by it and modified accordingly. It is here he is least at one with the Latin mind. As an experimentalist he is absolutely alone in all the Middle Age: he had neither forerunner nor successor. He made himself a skilled mechanic, he constructed scientific instruments, and all his mind and heart, his insatiable curiosity, his clarity of vision, his violent desire for knowledge and for achievement he put into the works written with immense speed, in less than eighteen months, for the Pope. Upon them and their success with Clement his heart must have been fixed. Well, Clement IV was never to open them. He died shortly after they came to him.

There follows in Roger's life an interval of ten years during which we are in complete ignorance of what befell him. That interval was full of the triumph of St. Thomas and the antagonism which it roused in the Franciscan Order. Aristotle had ever been claimed alike by the friends and the enemies of the Christian Faith, and now at last it seemed as though St. Thomas with his new *Summa* had once and for all created a system of thought founded upon Aristotle before which not only the enemies of the Faith but its friends also must bow. But with this Aristotelian revival had come, too, an ever-increasing interest in the Arabian commentators, and especially in Averroës, whose teaching was, of course, antagonistic to Christianity, and who indeed had expounded the Koran according to Aristotle. The Averroist movement was led by Siges of Brabant, who in 1272 was famous in the University as the great enemy of the Scholasticism of St. Thomas. It was necessary to condemn him, and this was done in 1277, a few propositions of St. Thomas being also included in the condemnation. But Roger, profound Arabic scholar as he was, astrologer too, and by no means a friend to Scholasticism, least of all to the system of St. Thomas, found more than one of his opinions expressed in his works condemned also. Perhaps he considered, and, in view of all that has happened since, not unreasonably, that his whole experimental system was in danger. At any rate, he most bravely and violently, though imprudently, replied with the *Speculum Astronomiæ* in defence of his position. This he put forward anonymously. Therein he accuses, and rightly, his judges of ignorance. But he was unfortunate both in the moment of such a defence and in the man Etienne Tempier, Bishop of Paris, a bully, whom he defied. The moment was particularly unfortunate, because in that very year a *rapprochement* had been made between the two Orders of St. Francis and St. Dominic, which had long been rivals in thought as in action. The publication of the *Speculum* brought Roger violently to mind. It was remembered not only that he was a tireless enemy of the Thomist system, that he had poured contempt upon Albert the Great, but also that a few years before

K   [145]

in his *Compendium* he had attacked the Church from Pope to priest and friars, in all its officers, accusing all of corruption, and especially the Curia. In all this he was but repeating, though with a new force, what Grosseteste had said before him, what St. Catherine herself was to repeat after him. Grosseteste had told Innocent IV that the Curia was the source of all that vileness which rendered the priesthood a reproach to Christianity. Alexander IV himself had described the corruption of the people as proceeding from the clergy. What Roger had violently asserted in past years was remembered now that he had ventured to attack the Bishop of Paris. The Franciscan Minister-General Jerome condemned Roger and his teaching on account of suspicious novelties ; Roger himself was imprisoned, and that is all we know of the end of this great Englishman. He died about 1294, some eighty years old, and was buried in the Franciscan church at Oxford.

The chief merit of Roger Bacon's work was, as it appears to us, really a recent discovery, that he for the first time questions the authority of Aristotle and substitutes for it experience. He was, however, so far in advance of his time that he was scarcely able to influence it at all. Only a certain tradition remained concerning him which impersonally in men's minds surely bore fruit later at the Reformation, if not before. He was before all things English in the character and atmosphere of his mind, which refused to wander far from useful practical knowledge and experiment. He was Franciscan chiefly, one may think, by accident and perhaps because he seemed to see in that Order, influenced as he was by Grosseteste and Peter de Maricourt, something of that future for which he

sacrificed everything and to which his last gesture was
a passionate greeting.

Thus it was perhaps the experimentalism of St.
Francis, the actual testing of the teaching of the
Gospel by experience, which attracted him to the
Order. For in the thirteenth century he, with St.
Francis, represents above all the tendency to experiment. He had a contempt for the metaphysical
quarrels that everywhere surrounded him and criticised
them, let us admit it, with something less than charity
and with more ardour than justice. He had an in-
stinctive dislike and mistrust of the syllogism of the
schools, the scholastic method, its verbiage and arti-
ficial precision were repugnant to him. He attempted
to show that in the science of reason one ought not to
follow authority. Perhaps he did not fully understand,
he certainly did not appreciate, the questions which
were convulsing the universities of his day. In this,
too, he is a forerunner of the modern world. For he,
too, lonely though he was, isolated as he seemed, would
one day have disciples, a whole world of them, so that
we are his children over near seven hundred years.

X

JOHN DUNS SCOTUS

IN Roger Bacon we might seem to have the least typical Franciscan of any in the Order ; and though a somewhat closer view will fundamentally modify that opinion, we shall always regard that lonely figure rather as a great Englishman than as a great Franciscan.

The English Franciscan at his greatest and best was not Roger Bacon. Such a position belongs of right to a man less original and less amazing than Roger, but a very great man for all that : I mean Duns Scotus.

John Duns Scotus was perhaps the greatest, certainly the most famous, schoolman Oxford ever produced. What St. Thomas was to the Dominicans, Duns was to the Franciscans, and for centuries schoolmen were divided into Thomists and Scotists. Both these men, the one the glory of Paris and the other of Oxford, were famous scholastic philosophers, and before passing to some consideration of Duns Scotus' life we may very briefly consider what, after all, this Scholasticism was with which almost all the best minds of that day were so passionately concerned, but which Roger Bacon violently condemned and despised.

Scholasticism, the scholastic philosophy, was the creation of the Universities, above all of Paris. It was the rule that during Lent the would-be Bachelor " determined," as he said, that is, he put forward propositions and defended them ; and thus he went on from Bachelor, disputing his way to Licentiate till finally, still disputing, he became a Master. The "determinations" consisted of propositions, as : The rational soul is (or is not) the only form of man. Fiercely such a proposition would have been disputed, and though to us it has little or no meaning, for modern thought makes light, for instance, of the distinction between matter and form, we must convince ourselves that, in spite of Bacon and the Renaissance, these disputations were something more than a war of words ; that indeed in Scholasticism at its best we see in perfect action the sane and vigorous mind of Europe.

But if we are to grasp at all what Scholasticism was, we must, first of all, seize however loosely those distinctions it made between Matter and Form and Substance and Accident which we have almost lost sight of. The Schoolmen asserted that Substance alone really is, Accident having only a diminished being inherent in Substance. Substance was something determinate, definitely *this* (hoc aliquid), and in Substance they distinguished two constituents, matter, the determinable, and form, the determinant. Thus the substantial form of a thing makes that thing what it is, without it it would not exist ; accidental form, however, can be removed without the thing perishing. Take gold, for instance ; what its substantial form was the Schoolmen would not say, nor could the alchemists discover it ; but an accidental form of it was, let us say, lustre ; for when gold has grown dim and lost its lustre it yet remains gold. A thing may have any number of accidental forms corresponding to its various accidental qualities, but can a thing have more than one substantial form ? The most perfect type of form was, said the Schoolmen, the human soul. The soul informs the body which is its matter, not the mere prime mover of the body, but its prime constituent, soul and body making one entity. " Body and soul," said St. Thomas, " are not two actually existing substances but out of the two of them is made one substance actually existing ; for a man's body is not the same when the soul is present as when it is absent ; it is the soul that gives actual being."

So we ask are there other substantial forms in the human body beside the soul ? And St. Thomas answers. No—and wins. His doctrine of the Unity of form being established after much opposition and even ecclesiastical condemnation at Paris and Oxford.

There was then the question of Materia Prima, or primordial matter, out of which the universe was created by God. This the Schoolmen held was simply matter devoid of substantial form, and since matter cannot be isolated from form, as St. Thomas asserts it could not exist. But if matter cannot exist without form, neither can form without matter except in the angel, perhaps. Such were the contentions of St. Thomas. Augustinianism, the earlier Scholasticism, contended that primordial matter was not formless ; it had certain radical predispositions to become this rather than that.

The Schoolmen, and especially the later Schoolmen, were always more and more eager to distinguish ; thus we have the debate whether any real distinction can be made between the soul and its faculties, and St. Thomas answered : Yes. There was also the question of the principle of individuation, that whereby a thing is itself and not the species to which it belongs.

Such were the propositions and such the debates

that enraged Bacon and engrossed the Universities of Paris and Oxford at that day. Their beauty is not more easily discerned by a man of the modern world than is the beauty of a work by Duccio of Siena, but that both are of an incredible beauty there are every day more voices to testify. It was in a world debating such things as these, with a conventional method that was in its own way complete and perfect, that Duns Scotus appeared as a new hope for the Franciscans ; against the Thomists he erected the Scotists.

It is unfortunate that we know very little about John Duns. According to one tradition he was born in 1265, but another gives us the date of his birth as 1274, and the date of his death, which is placed in 1308, is almost as uncertain. Nor can we be sure of his nationality and birthplace. The Irish Franciscans of the end of the fifteenth century claim him as an Irishman, as does Hugh MacCaghwell, Archbishop of Armagh, who claims him for Ulster, and Luke Wadding, editor of his works in the seventeenth century, follows MacCaghwell. An earlier writer, however, a disciple of Duns in the fourteenth century and the author of a commentary on the " Metaphysics of Aristotle," describes his master as " natione Scotus," in accordance with his surname ; and what that means we know from Friar Thomas, who describes the whole Franciscan Province north of York as Scotia, while the Irish Province he invariably calls Hibernia. It is practically certain, then, that John Duns was a North Briton, but it does not necessarily follow that he was born north of the Cheviots. Indeed, Leland declares that in a manuscript in Merton College, Oxford, Duns was said to have been born in the village of Dunstown in Northumberland. There is, however, no evidence that Duns was ever at Merton, and in fact it is practically certain that he was not.[1] The probabilities are that Duns was a native of Duns in Berwickshire, as the Scotch maintain. The question, however, must still be considered unsettled.

That Duns entered the Franciscan Order in his youth is probably true, but the date of his entry is unknown ; it was perhaps about 1290. That he lived and taught at Oxford we know, for in July, 1300, the Minister-Provincial of the English Province asked the Bishop of Lincoln to license twenty-two friars to hear confessions. Among these friars was Johannes Douns, to whom the Bishop refused the licence. Not much later Duns lectured on the five books of the Sentences as B.D. at Oxford,[2] and at the end of 1304 he was called to Paris to incept as D.D.[3] At Paris he seems to have remained till 1307 or 1308, when he was sent to Cologne and was enthusiastically welcomed by the University there, where he had scarcely arrived before he died, and was buried in the church of the Friars Minor.

Tradition has it that he succeeded William of Ware in the chair of Divinity at Oxford in 1301, and great multitudes came to hear him lecture, but his name is not to be found in the list of Oxford readers in divinity given in the *Monumenta Franciscana*. On the other hand, his great theological treatise is known as

[1] The Statutes of the College excluded religious. The entry is under date 1455 and as such is beside the argument. In the catalogue of the library of S. Francesco at Assisi, under date 1381, we find Master John Scotus of the Franciscan Order known as the Subtle Doctor spoken of as from the Province of Ireland. The entry, however, is too late to settle the question.

[2] See LITTLE, *op. cit.*, p. 220.

[3] WADDING, VI, 48, v. LITTLE, *op. cit.*, p. 220, who cites and rightly interprets the letters which Wadding misunderstood.

the *Opus Oxoniense*. Again, tradition has it that he was regent of the University of Paris, where he maintained the proposition of the Immaculate Conception of the Blessed Virgin, and this with such ingenuity that he won the title of *Doctor Subtilis*. This may well be true. But all we know is that in 1513 a monument was erected to him in the Franciscan church in Cologne, where on a wooden tablet might be read—

> Scotia me genuit,
> Anglia me suscepit,
> Gallia me docuit,
> Colonia me tenet.

The position of Duns in the Scholastic world of his day, and especially in the Franciscan Order, is easy to understand. The Franciscans had been the more conservative in thought of the two Mendicant Orders. The advent of Aquinas found them decided in their allegiance to the Realist Alexander of Hales and the contemporary mystic Bonaventura. In fact, they were still Augustinian and in opposition to the Aristotelian innovations of St. Thomas, which soon acquired so overwhelming an authority in the Dominican Order. The real quarrel soon showed itself to be concerned with the Thomist views as to the principle of individuation and the unity of Form; and if the centre of the Dominican Thomism was to be found in Paris, the centre of the Franciscan opposition was Oxford. The tendency towards an independent study of Nature, to an independence of Aristotle too, was the very core of Roger Bacon's effort. It failed, and in the beginning of the fourteenth century we see Oxford as eagerly Scholastic as Paris, and ready to dispute that field with her. Of this revival, a revival, as it proved to be, of Realism in a wholly new form, Duns Scotus is the prince and leader. His philosophy is contained principally in his Commentaries on the *De Anima* and the *Metaphysic* of Aristotle, in the *Quæstiones Quodlibetales*, in his Commentaries on the Sentences of Peter Lombard, the *Opus Oxoniense*. Let us take what is perhaps the chief proposition in dispute : the Unity of Form. That Thomist doctrine had been attacked by Bacon and by Peckham ; it was met by Duns Scotus with the essential doctrine of his system, that of the plurality of forms in the same individual. St. Thomas, as we have seen, maintains that there is but one substantial form in man which constitutes his humanity, the rational soul. Duns, on the other hand, maintains that beside the soul there are other substantial forms coexisting in man, namely, corporality, animality, rationality and so forth. The reply was to be : you are multiplying entities without necessity. Duns, however, above all delighted in distinctions. He invented a distinction he called " formal and real," as that as we have seen between animality and rationality in man or between wisdom and goodness in God. Of this he says : " It is a distinction in every way antecedent to our thought ; wisdom is in the thing from the nature of the thing ; and goodness is in the thing from the nature of the thing, but wisdom in the thing is not goodness in the thing."

Nor was Duns less opposed to St. Thomas in his system of Theology. St. Thomas is an Intellectualist, or more truly perhaps he maintains everywhere the perfect harmony of the intellect and the will in God. Duns comes near to asserting that the essence of God consists in His will. He tends to reduce the rôle of the intelligence to the profit of that of the will.

According to to him, God's love for Himself is not founded in a necessary instinct, as it were, but in free will. Every will being free, God's will is free also, but is so perfect that His will is at once free and necessary. Thus St. Thomas places Beatitude with Aristotle in vision, the act of understanding : Scotus places it in an act of the will. And to the will of God he ascribes not merely the existence but the very natures and essences of all creatures. He believes that God could have given to real beings different essences, and accordingly that He could change not only the laws of the universe, but the moral law and, in consequence, certain of the commandments. It is from this position that his disciple Ockham proceeds to that Nominalism which is but a symptom of the decay of Scholasticism.

That decay, however, might seem to be evident enough in Duns himself. He is less sure of the power of reason than is St. Thomas ; both are agreed, of course, that it is the business of the reason to bow to revelation, but Duns is far more doubtful of the extent of religious truth which reason can maintain. He is more than sceptical of the philosophical arguments for the immortality of the soul, the resurrection of the body, even the omnipotence of God. Yet it is, after all, in an appeal to the reason that the Subtle Doctor laid the foundation of the dogma of the Immaculate Conception. *Decuit, potuit, ergo fecit,* he repeats, how dangerously, after Eadmer, and refutes the objections of St. Thomas by maintaining that, far from being excluded from Redemption, the Virgin obtained from her Son the greatest of all Redemptions that she alone of all creation was born without sin. Characteristically enough, it is his passionate support of this mystical doctrine that will go furthest, it seems, to win him beatification ; for if his distinctions, his division upon division, till all is reduced to a sort of impalpable dust, won him pre-eminence in the schools of his day, it was the defence of this mystery which founded his cultus, as we may see in more than one altarpiece from more than one Franciscan sanctuary.[1]

[1] See CARMICHAEL : *Francia's Masterpiece* (Kegan Paul).

XI

WILLIAM OF OCKHAM

WILLIAM of Ockham in more ways than one might seem to gather up in himself the so various influences that had appeared in the Franciscan Order since its foundation; his life is symbolical, as it were, not only of what the Order had experienced, but also perhaps of its future, a future in England certainly disastrous for the friars and full of unexpected tragedy. As a Schoolman he passes on into the full decadence of Scholasticism prepared by Duns Scotus; as a friar he is excommunicated as Elias was, and for disobedience and heresy, but a disobedience and heresy into which he is led by a cause the very opposite of that which led Elias astray. He defends certainly with too much passion and self-will that Evangelical Poverty which Elias would not suffer, and in his championship of this cause he too flees to the Emperor and repudiates completely the Temporal Power of the Pope. Thus we find in him much of the past, much of the future, and indeed he seems to stand there facing both ways, like one of those hermæ which the ancients sometimes used as terminal marks or even as milestones upon their highways.

Born, as is generally thought—for indeed we know as little of his early life as we do of that of Duns Scotus—in the Surrey village whose name he bears, probably about 1280, he was almost certainly after

1290 a member of the Franciscan house at Oxford;
for though Sir Henry Savile speaks of an entry in a
manuscript at Merton proving him to have been a
fellow of that college, there would seem to have been
as little foundation for the statement as for Leland's
similar assertion about Duns Scotus. Duns Scotus,
however, if, as we believe, he was at Oxford till 1304,
was probably, as tradition maintains, Ockham's master.
It is strange that of none of the three famous English
Franciscans—Bacon, John Duns and Ockham—is it
possible to give the date or the place of their entering
the Order. There at Oxford in the first years of the
fourteenth century he received the degree of B.D. and
later passed to the University of Paris, where he in-
cepted D.D. and where he became acquainted with
and greatly influenced Marsiglio of Padua, Rector of
the University 1312–13. Already known as the author
of a commentary upon the Sentences composed at
Oxford, and now immersed in study and teaching,
Ockham found time for political theory, and it was his
political views which, Clement VI asserts, influenced
Marsiglio. All his knowledge and his energy seem to
have been placed at the service of his Order when in
1321 the question of Evangelical Poverty arose.

Always there had been debate in the Order as to the
vow of absolute poverty enjoined by St. Francis.
Clement V had tried in vain to settle these quarrels,
but the " Spirituals," who clung to the most severe
interpretation of the Rule, refused to submit, and in
Southern France and Italy especially not only rebelled,
but definitely declared that the Pope had no power to
dispense them from their Rule since it was that of the
Gospel. In 1317, in the time of the new Minister-
General Michael of Cesena, John XVII not only

ordered the " Spirituals " to obey their superiors, but caused their opinions to be examined, and in the following year many of these were condemned in the Bull *Gloriosam ecclesiam*, and many of the rebellious were burned at the stake. Meanwhile a new quarrel had broken out among the opponents of the " Spirituals " in the Order. This was concerned with a question of historical fact that struck at the very foundation of the Franciscan Order. It was maintained that Christ and His disciples possessed property. If this were so, the reason for the Franciscan vow was gone.[1] A general chapter of the Order was held at Perugia in 1322, and after much debate the chapter accepted the doctrine of Evangelical Poverty, that is to say that Christ and His Apostles had no possessions either individually or in common, and this decision was signed by the Minister-General Michael of Cesena, the English Minister-Provincial William of Nottingham, and others, and it is possible that William of Ockham took part in the debate. But this decision was most displeasing to Pope John, as might have been expected, and in December of the same year he revoked the Bull *Exiit* of Nicholas III which had declared Franciscan poverty to be equivalent to that of the Apostles, and in the following year, 1323, in the Bull *Cum inter nonnullos* declared it heresy to assert that Christ and His Apostles possessed no property either separately or in common.

The controversy, already bitter enough, was complicated by the political situation. Lewis IV of Bavaria

[1] In the Bull *Exiit qui seminat* Nicholas III had defined the poverty of the Franciscans both individually and collectively as equivalent to that of the Apostles, and had therefore transferred to the Roman Church all the Franciscan holdings in land and houses as Innocent IV had already (1245) declared should be done.

had defeated his rival Frederick, Duke of Austria, in 1322. Now the Franciscans were his partisans. In October, 1323, the Pope began the examination of the question of right to the German throne. Lewis replied by calling the Pope heretic and antipope, and charged him, among other crimes, with doing away with the poverty of Christ, doubtless prompted by the Franciscans. Lewis was excommunicated in the following year.

That Ockham was an eager opponent of the Pope we know, if only from this, that on December 1, 1323, John XXII ordered the Bishops of Bologna and Ferrara to inquire about a public sermon delivered by Ockham in Bologna wherein he had charged the Pope with heresy on account of his definition of Evangelical Poverty. If Ockham could be found he was to be sent to Avignon. Apparently he could not be found ; but later he repeated his offence at Paris, and in 1327 we find him at Avignon with Michael da Cesena and Bonagrazia of Bergamo. Upon April 9, 1328, the Pope reproved them publicly for the decision of the Perugia Chapter in 1322. A few days later they drew up a secret protest and resolved, in spite of the prohibition of the Pope, to flee from Avignon. They escaped down the Rhone in a boat, and though pursued reached Aigues-Mortes safely on May 28. Here they found a galley awaiting them sent by the Emperor, and on June 8th they came to Ghibelline Pisa, where they were welcome. On coming into the Emperor's presence tradition has it that Ockham greeted him with the words : *O imperator defende me gladio, et ego te defendam verbo*. Upon the 6th of June the Pope published his Bull of excommunication against the fugitives, and there we learn that Ockham was guilty not only of heresy in his sermons, but in his writings. From this time forward Ockham attached himself to the Emperor and his party, remaining at his court during his sojourn in Italy and returning with him to Bavaria in 1330, living at Munich in the Franciscan convent there in safety, and forming a refuge and a rallying point for that strong minority of the Order which the Pope could not reduce to submission. There, after Michael da Cesena's death in 1342, Ockham alone led the rebellion, writing furiously during some twenty years.

The first of his works, a work of great erudition, was the *Opus nonaginta dierum*, written in ninety days in which he answered the Pope's condemnation of the Franciscan doctrine regarding poverty. This was composed in 1330, immediately after his arrival at Munich. It was quickly followed by the *De Dogmatibus Papæ Johannes XVII* and the *Epistola ad Fratres Minores in Capitulo apud Assisium*. But to attack Pope John was one thing, to attack the Papacy and the whole idea of the Papal government of the Church another. This, however, was what Ockham proceeded to do after Pope John's death in 1334, and it is perhaps not surprising that when Lewis was seeking in 1336 to make peace with Benedict, he was ready not only to abandon, but to destroy, Ockham and his *fraticelli*. In this unhappy progress Ockham, having composed a *Compendium errorum papæ* wherein he charges Pope John with no less than seven heresies, proceeds in his *Defensorium* addressed in the Franciscan name to all Christians to indict Papal authority. And this was followed by other works not less anarchic and violent. Moreover, political events both gave him his opportunity for attack and confirmed him in it. The protection of Lewis, upon which he relied for his life, was at one time at least, as we have seen, precarious. Ockham was determined to maintain it. In 1338 his opportunity came. The electors of Reuse declared that their elected needed no confirmation by the Pope. Lewis followed this up and appealed from the Pope to a General Council, and Ockham seized the occasion to write a defence of the Imperial authority : the *Tractatus de Potestate Imperiali*. A violent discussion followed concerning the whole nature of the Imperial and Papal authority, and in this, too, Ockham took part in writing his *Octo Quæstines* and more profoundly and thoroughly in his great *Dialogus*. He appears as a thorough Protestant in that he is an advocate of secular absolutism. He denies the Pope any temporal power or the right to interfere in any way in the affairs of the Empire. We find him, surely three hundred years too soon, even advocating the validity of an adulterous " marriage," that of Lewis's son on grounds of political expediency, and the absolute power of the State in such affairs !

But William of Ockham did not persevere to the end. He grew weary of his isolation and his heresy, and after Lewis was dead he sent the seal of office he had received from Michael da Cesena (he claimed to be the Vicar of the Order), to the true Minister-General, William Farinerius, and recanting his heresies, was reconciled to the Church in 1349. He received absolution it might seem only to die, at any rate, his death, which found him still in the convent at Munich, was not long delayed ; and there he was buried.

In William of Ockham we find, in all his philosophy, not only a too eager appetite for something over simple—it is to him must be attributed the " Law of

Parsimony," Ockham's razor as the schoolmen called it;
Entia non sunt multiplicas sine necessitate—but an
increasing skepticism, a growing distrust of the power
of the human reason. He it is who definitely asserts
that the reason cannot prove the immortality of the
soul or the existence or the infinity of God. He comes
thus, perhaps, to forego the Realism of his predecessors
for a sort of conceptualism very welcome to the modern
mind, and as sure of welcome in comparison with the
Thomist or Scotist ideas, as is his theory of Papal
authority. *Doctor Invincibilis*, they called him; he
might certainly, as Rashdall says, seem to be " the
perfection of common sense," at any rate, to the
modern world.

With Ockham we find ourselves well into the fourteenth century. He is indeed the last of the great
schoolmen, and he stands up like some prophetic
figure almost on the threshold of that greatest of
catastrophies, the Black Death, which was to change
the very spirit of the world. He is the last, also, of a
great English company, Franciscan, too, in which
we reckon some of the greatest minds, and certainly
the most original, of that day; Alexander of Hales,
Adam de Marisco, Roger Bacon, Duns Scotus, William
of Ockham. Is it not significant that among these
there should appear already two such rebellious spirits
as Roger Bacon and William of Ockham?

XII

THE GREY FRIARS CHURCH IN LONDON

THE fourteenth century which was to hold so much disaster for Christendom and not least for the Friars Minor, opened very gloriously for the Franciscans in England, and not only at Oxford as I have tried to show.

We have seen the foundation of the Friars church and house in London, we have seen the establishment of the friars in the great city, within the wall by Newgate, and their popularity with the citizens. That popularity, only dimmed for a moment in 1256 when they intervened on behalf of the Jews condemned for the murder of Hugh of Lincoln, was probably increased by the support given by the friars to Simon de Montfort, especially in 1264, nor did this support on the other hand deprive them of royal favour. In 1290 in their church a service was held for Eleanor of Castile, the beloved wife of Edward I, and in the next year the heart of Eleanor of Provence, the queen-mother, at the time of her death a nun at Amesbury, was there buried. To the next queen, Margaret of France, second wife of Edward I, the Friars Minor of London were to owe everything; she was to be nothing less than the second founder of the London convent.

As early as 1302 the Queen had acquired land and houses in St. Nicholas parish of the value of sixty marks for the friars,[1] and further extensions were received for the friars in 1302, 1303 and 1305–6. In 1306 Sir William Walden laid the foundation-stone of a magnificent new church in the name of the Queen.

The account given in the *Prima Fundatio*, under the heading, " Founders of the New Church," is as follows :—

" To the perpetual memory of the founders and coadjutors of the Church and to remove the wonder of certain ignorant persons who are amazed at the work and whence its cost was drawn ; in the first place be it known that in the year of Our Lord 1306 the most illustrious Lady, Lady Margaret the queen and wife of Edward I. began to build the choir and the church, to the building of which she brought together in her life-time 2000 marks and bequeathed 100 marks in her testament to the same work. Her sepulchre is before the great altar in the same choir.

" Be it remembered that William Walden, Knight, placed the first stone on Monday in the foundation of the new church in the name of the aforesaid Queen in the year of Our Lord 1306.

" Item. Other friends built the nave of the church giving each according to his devotion, viz., Lord John of Brittany, Earl of Richmond,[2] the especial father and friend of the friars minor gave in support of the church of the said friars about 300 pounds sterling, a precious chalice of gold, various precious vestments, tapestries and many other gifts too numerous to set forth for the provision and necessities of the brethren.

---

[1] See *Prima Fundatio* in *Monumenta Franciscana*, I, 503, and for what follows cf. E. B. S. SHEPHERD : *The Church of the Friars Minors in London* in *Arch. Journal*, LIX (1902), p. 238 *et seq*., and C. L. KINGSFORD : *The Grey Friars of London* (Aberdeen University Press, 1915).

[2] Died 1305.

"The Lady Mary Countess of Pembroke[1] granddaughter of the Lord John of Brittany aforesaid gave also in support of the aforesaid church 70 pounds sterling and many other gifts and did much honour to the brethren.

"The Lord Gilbert de Clare, Earl of Gloucester,[2] gave for the aforesaid church 20 great beams (trabes) from his forest of Tonbridge of the price of 20 pounds and as much or more in money by means of Friar Geoffrey of Aylesham his confessor.

"The Lady Margaret Countess of Gloucester[3] sister of the said Gilbert gave for the construction of a certain altar in the said church 26 pounds thirteen shillings and four pence.

"The Lady Eleanor le Spencer[4] sister of the said Gilbert gave for the construction of a certain altar 15 pounds.

"The Lady Elizabeth de Burgh[5] another sister of the same Gilbert gave ten good pieces of wood (ligna) of the price of 10 pounds and five pounds sterling in support of the said Church.

"Arnaldus de Tredemar citizen of London bequeathed in support of the aforesaid church 100 pounds sterling. . . .

"Friar and Lord Robert Lyle, baron de Lyle,[6] who after the death of his wife assumed the religious habit, gave in support of the church 300 pounds sterling and did many other things for the friars in particular and general.

"Bartholomew de Alemaina merchant gave in support of the said church 40 pounds sterling and 10 pounds for the convent.

---

[1] Died 1377.   [2] Died 1314.   [3] Died 1342.
[4] Died 1337.   [5] Died 1360.   [6] Died 1342.

" After this came the most illustrious lady, Lady Isabella[1] the queen, mother of Edward III, and finding the church which her aunt Queen Margaret begun not yet finished but incomplete expended about 70 pounds or more upon it.

" Lady Philippa, by the grace of God Queen of England and wife of Edward III[2] gave in support of the aforesaid church 48 pounds 13 shillings and 4 pence ; and for the covering of the church 13 pounds and 6 shillings and 8 pence.

" Robert Lovelyn gave 5 pounds and John Enfeld 20 marks.

" And so by these and other devoted persons the aforesaid work was completed in 21 years ; for it was begun in 1327."

The last statement is curious. At first sight it might seem that " begun " should be " finished," for if the church was begun in 1306 as stated, and completed in twenty-one years, it would have been finished in 1327. But it is possible that the statement really refers only to the work of Queen Isabella, who came to England in 1327 ; and that her work which completed the church, then definitely stated to be incomplete, took twenty-one years to finish, bringing us to 1348. In any case, the church was wholly a building of the first half of the fourteenth century, and completed—this is the important thing—before the Black Death of 1348-9.

There follows in the *Prima Fundatio* a series of entries " concerning the glazing of the windows," which was begun " after the completion of the work and the covering of it." The first window on the north at the east end was the gift of Lady Isabella, mother of

[1] Died 1358.   [2] Died 1369.

Edward III. The middle window over the great altar was the gift of the cloth workers and drapers of the city of London. Of the windows at the west end the middle and principal one was " completely repaired anew by the illustrious King Edward III after a great wind (? the storm of January 15, 1362) by which it was blown down and he had it glazed at his own charges for the soul of the most illustrious Queen Isabella his mother who is buried in the Choir."

There were in all fifteen windows on the north, fifteen on the south, three at the east end and three at the west end, of which the two respectively in the midst were great windows. There seems to have been no clerestory.

Following these entries, is a description of the church as follows :—

" Firstly the church contains in length 300 feet of the feet of St. Paul. In breadth it contains 95 feet of the feet of St. Paul. In height from the ground to the roof 64 feet of the feet of St Paul. And as is patent, all the columns are of marble and all the pavement is of marble."

This marble was Purbeck. The whole seems to have been surmounted by a central tower.

Thus stood the church founded by Queen Margaret and so built by four queens, and certain noble lords and ladies. It stood almost due east and west, a little to the south of east and the north of west, its eastern end abutting upon Stinking Lane, its south side standing back from Newgate Street, but more at the east end than at the west where the south buttresses of the west front abutted into the street. Beyond it to the north, covering the whole nave, stood the Great Cloister surrounded by the Chapter House on the east, the Library, founded by Richard Whittington, thrice Lord Mayor of London, on the north, the Great Dorter and the Little Dorter on the west and south. To the west again was the Guardian's Lodging and beyond this again to the west the Little Cloister with the Infirmary to the north. The gate-house stood to the south of the Little Cloister, well to the west of the church in Newgate Street, not more than 200 feet within Newgate.[1]

The church itself in its eastern part occupied the site now filled by Christ Church, Newgate, built by Sir Christopher Wren, 1687–1704, which occupies the first six bays of the church of the Grey Friars. This eastern part of the old church consisted of the choir and sanctuary surrounded by four chapels ; the chapels of All Hallows and of the Apostles to the north and south of the sanctuary respectively, the chapel of St. Mary and St. Francis to the north and south of the choir. The choir was closed on the west by a great screen. Beyond this was an ambulatory or transept 25 feet wide enclosed on the west by another screen. Beyond this was a space of 20 feet closed again on the west by a screen and divided into two parts from east to west by a passage way. Here were four chapels, two to the north of the passage and two to the south. Beyond the third screen to the west lay the nave and two aisles.

The whole church was crammed with tombs, for Franciscan churches were favourite places of burial, partly perhaps because of the universal popularity of the "Third Order," the *Tertius Ordo de penitentia* instituted in 1221, whereby men and women living

---

[1] Cf. E. B. S. Shepherd, *op. cit.*, and the full translation in Dugdale, *op. cit.*, VI, pp. 1514 *et seq.*

in the world an ordinary Christian life were, as it were, affiliated to the Franciscan Order and had the right to be buried in the Franciscan habit which it was commonly believed gave those dying in it a special claim upon St. Francis' intercession ; and secondly, because of the promise of which Brother Masseo speaks, made by Our Lord to St. Francis, " All they that shall love my Order with their whole heart and the brothers that shall persevere shall by the grace of God make a good end."

The tombs of the Grey Friars church must have been as famous as those of Westminster Abbey. Behind the high altar the heart of Friar Peckham, Archbishop of Canterbury, was buried. Before the high altar was the tomb of Queen Margaret the founder of the great church, and there in the choir was the heart of Queen Eleanor, wife of Henry III, the tomb of Isabella, Queen of Edward II, and the heart of that king, the tomb of Joan de la Tour, Queen of Scotland, daughter of Edward II, the tomb of Isabella, Countess of Bedford, daughter of Edward III, and of many other noble lords and ladies ; but the tombs filled the whole church and the cloister was also full of them.[1]

The magnificence of the whole building, the greatness of its founders, must have given to the church an unique reputation. It rose there in those curiously feverish and proud years of the first half of the fourteenth century, a great, a royal, almost a national monument. While it was building the disasters of the reign of Edward II passed into the immense glory of Edward III and his victories; the avenging of Bannock-burn at Hallidon Hill, the invasion of France, the victory of Creçy, the fall of Calais. Little did the

[1] For a full list of tombs see KINGSFORD, *op. cit.*, pp. 134 *et seq.*

builders dream that they were on the eve of an universal
disaster without precedent, and perhaps without a
successor. They built the great church for the beloved
Order to the glory of God, in honour of St. Francis,
in that loveliest decorated style, the style of the fourteenth century before the Black Death, which for joy
and happiness surpasses every other in the world.
They covered their shafts and capitals and mouldings
with foliage and life, and could not curb their invention
nor prevent their hands from beauty and joy. They
forgot everything in their delight, and when they
lifted up their eyes behold Death was upon them ;
and suddenly, in scarcely more than twelve months,
the face of England, of Europe was changed, the
Middle Age was at an end.

Of that noble building nothing remains ; perhaps
a few marble fragments from the pavement, which
was all of marble, in Wren's church of Christ Church.
Nor of the glory of these years has any Franciscan
building come down to us, and assuredly they were
full of building, for it was the golden moment of the
friars' glory, save only what is left to us of the friars
church at Reading which I have already described.
The Black Death perhaps destroyed the friars, their
buildings it could not destroy, yet time and rage
and fire have consumed these also, things too beautiful for the world which emerged from the catastrophe
to await the revolution we know as the Reformation.

XIII

THE BLACK DEATH

THE cloud that was rising in the East and that was to threaten with extinction not the friars alone, but the whole of medieval civilisation, which in fact it destroyed, was the Black Death. This enormous pestilence, perhaps the most universal disaster which history records, in less than two years swept away two-thirds of the population of Italy, half of that of France, half of that of England.[1] The friars suffered far more severely. It is generally admitted that everywhere the poor suffered far more than the rich ; it is certain that the mortality of the secular clergy was much higher than that of the lay people ; the friars combined the qualities of the poor and the clergy, which caused them to suffer so terribly ; they inhabited the worst quarters of the towns and dwelt amid hovels, and their chief business was the service of the sick and the wretched. Wadding himself ascribes the decay of the friars to this pestilence, and it is certain that the Franciscans in England never recovered from it.

The disease which, without exaggeration, may be said to have destroyed the Middle Age came to Europe from the East, in the caravans along the trade routes between Asia and Europe. In Europe we first hear of it in the Crimea, in a small fort the Genoese had built there on the Straits of Kertch. Tradition has it

[1] See GASQUET : *The Black Death* (1908), p. 225.

that the pestilence arose from the decay of innumerable unburied corpses in China where famine, drought, flood and earthquake had during the first years of the fourteenth century, brought appalling calamity in their train. We know that in 1346 the pestilence was raging in the country through which the northern trade route ran, and we have the accounts of Gabriele de' Mussi, a notary of Piacenza and a witness of the Black Death in Lombardy, as to its advent.

" In the year 1346," he tells us,[1] " a great number of Tartars and Saracens in the East were the victims of a death both mysterious and sudden. Whole districts and many provinces, great kingdoms, cities, castles and villages crowded with population, were suddenly attacked by the death and in a short time were dispeopled. There was in the East a place called Tana, north of Constantinople, under the rule of the Tartars and there the Italian merchants who much resorted thither were besieged by a host of Tartars and ere long the city fell. These Christian merchants were then received with their property within the walls of Caffa which the Genoese had built in that country. The Tartars followed the fugitives and besieged Caffa, threatening it with starvation. Suddenly the death appeared in the Tartar host, and they, terrified, for vengeance, with their engines of war, hurled the bodies of their dead over the wall into the city and soon the air becoming tainted and all wells poisoned, the disease spread through the city. Now when the Italian ships left Caffa bound for Genoa, Venice and elsewhere some of the sailors were already infected with the

[1] See *Giornale Legustico* (Genoa, 1883), Vol. X, p. 139 *et seq.* My quotation is a paraphrase rather than a translation.

disease. Thus the death was brought to Italy, and first to Genoa in the early days of 1348."

Of its appalling career in Italy we have many records, of which the account of Boccaccio, which serves as an Introduction to the *Decameron* and tells us of what befell in Florence, was the most famous. What he there sets down, horrible though it be, is fully borne out by other writers, for instance, the historian Matteo Villani, whose brother Giovanni was carried off by the disease. So far as I know it was in Italy that it got the name by which it is known.[1] Old Agnolo di Tura, who tells us that in Siena he " carried with my own hands my five little sons to the pit and what I did many others did too," calls it the *mortalità oscura* and asserts that " in Siena and in the suburbs there died at this time (namely between May and August) eighty thousand persons." In the Chronicle of Tommaso Fecini we read that of every ten Sienese nine died ; while an anonymous writer declares that out of every four three perished. The grass grew in the streets. Nor was it much less fatal in the other cities of the peninsula. In Italy alone 30,000 Franciscans perished.[2] From Genoa it spread also into Southern France, to Marseilles and Avignon. In Marseilles we read that " the Bishop with the whole Chapter of the Cathedral nearly all the friars, Preachers and Minors together with two-thirds of the inhabitants perished." In a month some 57,000 persons died. The pestilence spread all through the country leaving desolation behind it. In Avignon, in three months, 62,000 bodies were buried ; in Paris and St. Denis, 80,000, among them two queens, Joan

---

[1] Dr. Gasquet is under the impression that the name of the Black Death was coined in the seventeenth century to differentiate it from the Great Plague, *op. cit.*, pp. 7–8.   [2] GASQUET, *op. cit.*, p. 52.

of Navarre, daughter of Louis X, and Joan of Burgundy, wife of Philip of Valois. From Paris it spread into Normandy and so into England, where it appeared in the autumn of 1348.

It was expected. In August the Bishop of Bath and Wells had sent letters through all his diocese ordering " processions and stations every Friday in each collegiate, regular and parish church to pray God to protect the people from the pestilence which had come from the East into the neighbouring kingdom." By then it would seem the Black Death was already in England. " In the year of our Lord 1348," we read in the *Eulogium Historiarum,* written by a contemporary monk of Malmesbury Abbey, " the cruel pestilence terrible to all future ages came from parts over sea to the south coast of England unto a port called Melcombe (Weymouth) in Dorsetshire. Sweeping through the southern districts it destroyed countless people in Dorset, Devon and Somerset."[1]

Now the summer and autumn of 1348 were very wet in England, and more than one Chronicler records that from Midsummer Day to Christmas it rained every day. Such a condition of things perhaps helped the disease, which we read, " passed most rapidly from place to place killing before midday many who in the morning had been well and without respect of persons (some few rich people excepted) not allowing those destined to die to live more than three or at the most four days." Bristol, the great port of the west,

[1] Dr. Gasquet points out that at this time Weymouth was a considerable port, that in 1347–48 it furnished Edward III for his siege of Calais with 20 ships and 264 seamen, which compares wonderfully with Bristol's 22 ships and 608 seamen and London's 25 ships and 662 men. He considers it not improbable that it was by the return of these boats from Calais to Weymouth that the plague was brought into England.

suffered no less than other cities. " There," we read, " died suddenly almost the whole strength of the town for few were sick more than three days or two days or even half a day." At Bodmin, according to the Friars Minor, 1500 persons perished while the Augustinian Friars there were practically exterminated. And this is typical of what was happening to the mendicant Orders all over the West.

The Death went on through the country to Gloucester, Oxford and London ; and the whole country was gradually involved in the immense catastrophe. " There was," we read, " no city, nor town, nor hamlet, nor, save in rare instances, any house, in which this plague did not carry off the whole, or the greater portion of the inhabitants." Knyghton a contemporary gives a very striking account of the pestilence at Leicester. " There were scarcely any who took heed of riches or cared for anything . . . and sheep and oxen wandered through the fields and among the crops ; there was no one to go after and collect them ; but there perished an untold number in out of the way ditches and under hedges."

London was attacked between St. Michael's day and All Saints, 1348. " For want of room in churchyards to bury the dead of the city and of the suburbs one John Garey, procured of Nicholas, prior of the Holy Trinity within Aldgate, a toft of ground near unto East Smithfield for the burial of them that died." Here, when the plague was stayed, the King founded the Cistercian monastery of Our Lady of Graces. But this was not enough. Other cemeteries were established, and in one of them the Charterhouse of London was subsequently founded. North, south, east and west the pestilence raged, and when in 1349 it was stayed fully a half of the inhabitants of England had perished.

In all this we hear little or nothing of the friars, who, however, must have suffered very severely, at least as severely as the clergy. In Italy it is said not less than 30,000 died of this pestilence; in England we are without the means to measure their suffering, but we may arrive at some idea of what it was—scarcely less than complete destruction—if we piece together the few facts within our knowledge.

In London we have proof that a hundred friars died of the disease, in the recent excavation of the pit made at the time of the epidemic, in which not less than a hundred bodies were found, upon them the lead crosses used by the Franciscans, but not inscribed as was usual with the formula of absolution.[1] In Winchester their suffering does not seem to have been less. For the two Franciscan houses of Winchester and Southampton three priests were ordained in 1347-8, but not one was presented thereafter till 1359. In Norwich the whole community seems to have perished. In Bristol and in Gloucester few can have remained; and, indeed, so universal were their sufferings, that Wadding, the Franciscan annalist, attributes to the Black Death the decay of the Order. "This evil wrought great destruction to the holy houses of religion carrying off the masters of regular discipline and the seniors of experience. From this time the monastic Orders and in particular the mendicants, began to grow tepid and negligent both in that piety and that learning in which they had up to this time flourished. Then, our illustrious members being carried off, the rigours of discipline relaxed by

[1] *Antiquary*, LII, 72, and V.C.H., *London*, I, p. 504.

these calamities could not be renewed by the youths received without the necessary training rather to fill the empty houses than to restore the lost discipline.[1]

The Black Death was stayed in September, 1349. Those fourteen months of its passing had however layed the whole country desolate ; as has been said, about half the population was swept away, and England was not so populous as it had been in 1348, before the pestilence, until the time of Elizabeth. The result as might be expected amounted to a revolution. In the Black Death we see the real barrier between the medieval and the modern world.

If we are in any way to seize the effect of this disaster we must generally understand the condition of affairs in England after the visitation. " Through this pestilence," say the Commons in Parliament, "cities, boroughs and other towns and hamlets throughout the land have decayed and from day to day are decaying and several are entirely depopulated."[2] The ordinary relation between the peasant, and, indeed, the working classes generally, and the rich was suddenly in a few months completely overturned and revolutionised. There was no longer any connection between the value of wages and the necessities of life. The country was face to face with revolt and starvation. The Commons passed hard laws to maintain the state of affairs *ante pestam*, but such action was futile. The peasants replied by moving from their own village to another county, the class of free labourers was wonderfully increased, some became mere vagabonds without house or home. The ranks of such men must often have been swelled by fugitive friars whom a desolate

---

[1] *Annales Minorum*, VIII, 22.
[2] 25 Edw. III (1350–51), *Rolls of Parliament*, II, p. 227.

convent no longer disciplined or maintained. Their duties, and perhaps their vows forgotten, stupid with fear or desperate, they wandered about the ruined country, from broken town to broken town, through cities half silenced by death, where all the innocence and joy of life, so characteristic of the world before the pestilence, were extinguished. Nor was it only that men and towns were ruined ; their hearts were changed. Consider then the architecture *ante pestam*, the Decorated style with its joy as of flowers, its happiness as of spring, shaft and moulding and capital covered with foliage as though men could not curb their invention or prevent their hands from beauty and joy. It is broken ; the song ceases in the midst of the melody, and thus prevented in its flight you may see it still very well in that marvellous fragment at Winchelsea, the church of St. Thomas of Canterbury, which was never finished ; and instead of the fullness of joy which is the Decorated style, men turned when they began to build again to the sombre and insular gravity of the Perpendicular, in which lies hid all the scepticism of the Renaissance and the modern world.

The effect of the Black Death upon the friars was, as Wadding assures us, fundamental, and that both materially and spiritually. Materially they suffered a loss of perhaps two-thirds of their number, but as it happens their Order and their convents were almost certainly enriched. That the Franciscan houses in England increased we know. In 1340 they numbered 52 ; in 1385 they were not less than 60.[1] But this was in all likelihood not all. Fear and misery, fear above all and hope of some relief here or hereafter, doubtless drove the dying to bequeath or give their goods to the

---

[1] See *Archivum Franciscanum Historicum*, Vol. I (1908), pp. 21-22.

friars and their convents, in England as in Italy, during the catastrophe, and this was by no means necessarily the fault of the friars, rather is it a proof of their devotion. Nevertheless it brought evil in its train; for, largely, those friars who survived the Death were the scum and refuse of the Order, those who had refused the service of the sick, those who had fled, the selfish and the fearful. It was they who not only continued and represented the Order when the plague was stayed, but entered as heirs into the gifts of the dead. The strength and splendour of the Order, the flower of the friars died in the by-ways in that appalling catastrophe, the wasters remained to carry on the convents now enriched almost alone in a stricken world and wholly forgetful of the poverty of St. Francis. In the licence that followed the Death, in the anarchy of the revolution, in the long work of the rebuilding of England, they bear their part; but it is scarcely a noble or a glorious one. We hear of no Agnellus, no Roger Bacon, no Duns Scotus. The friar of *Piers the Plowman* and of *The Canterbury Tales* is very different from these, and when the new spirit expresses itself it is by the mouth not of a friar but of a secular priest, John Wyclif, who, though he cannot claim anything of the spirit of St. Francis, is the heir after all of the most characteristic English Franciscans, the Scholastics, Duns Scotus and William of Ockham.

XIV

LANGLAND, CHAUCER, WYCLIF AND THE FRIARS

WE have so few documents which give us any direct information with regard to the sufferings of the mendicant Orders, and especially of the Friars Minor in the awful catastrophe of the Black Death, and of the condition of the Franciscan Order in England, when at last in 1349 it was stayed, that but for the evidence of two poets, who wonderfully mirror the time for us in their works, we should be largely unable to affirm what, after all, innumerable hints and isolated facts have led us to suppose, namely, that in that pestilence the Friars Minor suffered nothing less than a revolution. As it happens, in the pages of Langland and of Chaucer we find ample confirmation of this disaster.

Langland, the earlier of the two, the supposed author of *Piers the Plowman*, was born it would seem about 1332, probably at Cleobury Mortimer in Shropshire, some eight miles from those Malvern Hills he loved so well. Though he seems to have had the ear of England, to have had an immense success with his great work, no contemporary has spoken of him, and there has lately been put forward a theory that in his famous poem we have the work not of one but of several hands. Such a theory contested most strongly by Jusserand scarcely concerns us here, and I shall deal with the work on the old hypothesis, namely, that it is the work of William Langland.

Of the facts of his life, unfortunately we know very little. That he was poor and of low degree seems certain, but he was free born and born in wedlock and possessed of intelligence of a high order. That he went to school, perhaps at the monastery of Great Malvern, he himself tells us, " when I was young many years ago my father, and my friends found me at school till I knew truly what Holy Writ meant and what is best for the body, as that Book tells us, and safest for the soul if only I live accordingly. And yet assuredly found I never since my friends died a life that pleased me except in these long clothes," that is, in the habit of an ecclesiastic. This he repeats when in his poem Reason demands of him what work he can do, or what craft he knows, useful to the community, and he answers that the only life he ever cared for is that of the priest. In fact, he seems to have been in Minor Orders and to have been licensed as an acolyte, exorcist, reader and ostiarius. Why he never took Holy Orders we do not know. Perhaps he married, indeed he speaks of " Kytte my wyf and Kalotte my daughter," perhaps he neglected his opportunities, he speaks of having learned " too little Latin in youth." For a time he seems to have earned a living as a canonical singer, for in London where he lived in poverty and disregarded " even among lollards of London and lewede heremytes; " he earned his living as he says with such tools as " *Paternoster* and my primer, *Placebo* and *Dirige* and my *Psalter* sometimes and my *Seven Psalms*. Thus I sing for the souls of such as help me : and those that find me any food guarantee I trow that I shall be welcome when I come occasionally in a month, now at some gentleman's house and now at some lady's . . ." He tells us, too, that he " roamed about robed in russet like a mendicant in utter poverty." He certainly knew England well and above all London, and as his poem proves he had probed the life of his times to its depths. At last we seem to find him back amid his beloved Malvern Hills, but what his end was and where it found him, if not there, we do not know.

Now in the supposed work of this wanderer and dreamer we have one of the most remarkable poems of the fourteenth century. The " Vision of William concerning Piers the Plowman " may stand as a vision though not as poetry or a work of art beside the *Divine Comedy*. " Place Langland," says Jusserand, " at whatever distance you will from Dante, he is the only poet of the century whose mystic visions deserve to be mentioned after the epic of the illustrious Florentine." " He is," says Professor Hales, " as exact and realistic as Dante however inferior in the greatness of his conception or in nobleness of poetic form." In truth his work has little of the art of a poem, it is full of the chaos of life, the life of fourteenth century England after the Black Death ; it is full of pictures, and passionate with a terrible and righteous anger on behalf of the poor. In many ways Langland is the true ancestor of Bunyan, for if the form of his work and his subject-matter are very different, the atmosphere and the mood of it are the same, English alike in their *naiveté*, their puritanism, their sincerity and love of allegory.

All the England of the fourteenth century lies hid in this book ; and it is thus not only a grand, strange and beautiful work, but a document as valuable as

Chaucer's *Canterbury Tales*, which indeed it supple-
ments, for the life of the time. As in that work
we see the England of the time pass before our eyes,
monks, friars, pardoners, clerks, knights, shopkeepers,
labourers, tavern haunters, women of all sorts; and,
indeed, as Jusserand says, " it is impossible to form an
idea of English society at this important period, when
it received its definitive characteristics, without com-
paring these two series of paintings equally interesting
from the manner in which they are alike and unlike."

But what is this wonderful vision?

> In a somer seson · whan soft was the sonne,
> I shope me in shroudes · as I a shepe were,
> In habite as an heremite · unholy of workes,
> Went wyde in this world · wondres to here.
> Ac on a May mornynge · on Malverne hulles
> Me byfel a ferly · of fairy me thoughte;
> I was wery forwandred · and went me to reste
> Under a brode banke · bi a bornes side,
> And as I lay and lened · and loked in the wateres,
> I slombred in a slepyng · it sweyned so merye.[1]

The poet fell asleep, and as he slept he dreamed a
dream. A marvellous vision came moving before him.

---

[1] Or as Prof. Skeat modernises it :—

> In a summer season when soft was the sun
> I enshrouded me well in a shepherd's garb
> And robed as a hermit, unholy of works,
> Went wide through the world, all wonders to hear.
> And on a May morning on Malvern hills
> Strange fancies befel me and fairy-like dreams.
> I was weary of wandering and went to repose
> On a broad green bank by a burn side;
> As I lay there and leaned and looked on the waters
> I slumbered and slept, they sounded so merry.

Lost in a wild waste, but where he could not tell, he beheld in the east on high near the sun a tower on a hilltop, and beneath a valley and therein a dungeon dark and dreadful ; and between a fair field full of folk, of all manner of men, the mean and the rich, all working or wandering. Some were ploughing and their play was seldom, some sowing, some earning in the sweat of their brow the gain for great ones to waste. Some passed in glorious apparel, others in prayer and penance. Hermits and anchorites and beggars and bedesmen and pilgrims and palmers and friars of all the four orders, pardoners and priests and bishops, a king and his knights, the clergy and the commons, rich and poor, bond and free, in short, all England and the world. That fair field set as we see between heaven and hell, between the "Toure of Treuthe" and the "Dongeon of Wronge," is indeed the world, and the "loveli lady in lynnen yclothed," who explains all things to the sleeper is Holy Church. It is thus the England of the fourteenth century passes before us judged by one who says, "when all treasures are tried, truth is the best."

Now in this vision or picture of England on the morrow of the Black Death, how do the friars fare? All sorts and conditions of men, friars, priests, merchants, lawyers, are shown to be corrupted by love of Meed, corrupt gain, save only the monks who escape censure altogether ; but the friars, far from being subject to a special attack, are not so bitterly assailed as the lawyers. Nevertheless, they are assailed, and the picture we get of them is very different from that we have seen in the thirteenth century ; indeed, Langland himself very definitely states the difference when he speaks of Charity :

> And in a freres frocke · he was yfounde ones,
> Ac it is fer and fele yeres · in Frauncey's tyme ;
> In that secte sitthe · to selde he hath be founde.
> Riche men he comendeth · and of here robes taketh,
> Of tho that leelliche lyuen · and louen and by-leyuen.
> *Beatus est diues sine macula.*[1]

There we have as Langland sees it the great difference between the friars of St. Francis's time and those
of the thirteenth century ; the true friars and the
false. This difference he continually emphasises. He
speaks of Walsingham, of the great shrine of Our Lady
there, and the road thither on which he found a crowd
of hermits with hooked staves followed by their
wenches.

> I font there freres · all the foure ordres,
> Prechinge the peple · for profyt of heore wombes,
> Glosynge the gospel · as hem good liketh,
> For couetyse of copes · construeth hit ille ;
> For monye of this maistres · mowen clothen hem at
> lyking,
> For moneye and heore marchaundie · meeten ofte
> to-gedere.
> Seththe charite hath be chapmon · and cheef to
> schriuen lordes,
> Mony ferlyes han bi-falle · in a fewe yere.[2]

[1] Ed. Skeat : *Passus*, C. xvii, 352.

[2] Skeat modernises as follows :— (Prologue A.55 *et seq.*
  I found there some friars of all the four orders
  Who preached to the people for personal profit ;
  As it seemed to them good, put a gloss on the gospe
  And explained it at pleasure ; they coveted copes.
  Many of these masters may wear what they will;
  Their money and merchandise meet well together ;
  Since Charity was chapman and chief to shrive lords
  What sights we have seen in a few short years !

"What wonders have befallen in a few years!"
The Black Death and its appalling consequences, the
depopulating of England and the decay of the
friars.

That decay might seem for the most part to consist
in just this :

> . . . that freres folweden · folk that was ryche,
> And peuple that was poure · at lytel prys setten. . . .[1]

This passionate champion of the poor, whose hatred
is poured only upon Antichrist and Meed and Falseness and Wrong, who will have nothing to do with
Lollards and such as attack the Church as it is, or the
established order of things, finds, and continually
asserts, that the friars are corrupted by love of money,
are like the rest of the society of that catastrophic
time, followers of Lady Meed.

I have said that Langland treats the friars less
severely than is generally supposed ; far less severely
than, for instance, the lawyers ; nevertheless he rates
them sore enough. "Falseness for fere," he says,
"fled to the friars."

And Wrath declares that he was "sumtyme a
frere," and adds that "folk would far rather be
shriven by the friars than by priests." This was a
general complaint of the priests and prelates of the
time,[2] and Wyclif roundly asserts "if there be any
cursed juror, extorcioner or adulterer he will not be
shriven at his own curate but goes to a flattering friar
that will asoil him falsely for a llitte money by year,
though he be not in wille to make restitution and leave
his cursed sin."[3] This quarrel, however, was nothing

---

[1] Ed. SKEAT : *Passus*, C. xvi, 9.   [2] Cf. *Passus*, B. V, 145.
[3] WYCLIF : *Works* (ed. Arnold), III, 394.

new, it had existed ever since the entry of the Mendicants into England.[1]

Langland also generally blames the friars' preaching,
and though this touches the Dominicans most nearly
it would apply also to the Franciscans.

> Freres fele sithes · to the folk that thei prechen
> Meuen motifs meny tymes · insolibles and fallaces,
> That bothe lered and lewed · of here by-leyue douten ;
> To teche the ten commandmens · were ten sithe
>   bettere.[2]

But when all is said his attack upon the friars consists mainly in an exposure of their venality and greed,
their love of money. . . . In this charge he can be
bitterly ironical :—

> Who perfourneth this prophecye · of the peple that
>   now lybbeth
> *Dispersit, dedit pauperibus.* . . .
>
> If any peple perfourme that texte · it ar this pore
>   freres !
> For that thei beggen abouten · in buildynge thei
>   spene,
> And on hem-self sum · and such as ben her laboreres,
> And of hem that habbeth thei taken · an gyve hem
>   that ne habbeth.[3]

And what he would have them be and do is set forth
as clearly in his work as what they are. " Do," he says
to them,

> " as Antony did · Dominik and Fraunceys,
> Benet and Bernarde · the which hem first taughte
> To lyue bi litel and in lowe houses · by lele mennes
>   almesse." [4]

[1] See LITTLE *Studies*, pp. 105–8, 114–22.
[2] SKEAT : *Passus*, C. xvii, 230.   [3] *Ibid.*, B. XV, 320.
[4] *Ibid.*, B. XV, 413.

Above all, he tells them, be as one, remain in unity one with another and with the Church, and put away your logic for love—for love to be holy.

> ". . . Ac o thing ich yow preye,
> Holdeth yow in Unite · and haueth non enuye
> To lerede ne to lewide · bote lyueth after youre reule.
> And ich wol beo youre borw · ye shulleth haue brede and clothes,
> And other necessaries ynowh · you shall no thyng lakke,
> With that ye leue logyk · and lerneth for to louye.
> For love lefte thei lordshupes · bothe londe and scole,
> Frere Fraunceis and Domynyk · for loue to be holy.[1]

Such is the verdict of the poet who knew the people as perhaps no other English poet ever has known them. He has this at least in common with St. Francis, that he was the apostle of the poor and loved them. Yet prejudiced in his favour as everyone must be who has read and re-read his marvellous *Vision*, we must not take his verdict on the friars as wholly just ; it was much too passionate for that, and Langland was too narrow a mind to be wholly fair. He is one of the first of the puritans, he abhors the arts, minstrels, for instance, he treats as scurvily as lawyers, theologians, physicians and wastrels. He gives us the fullest picture of fourteenth-century England, of England that is on the morrow of the plague, but we cannot wholly accept it, or at least without question, for more reasons than one, the greatest being Chaucer.

Chaucer, born in 1340, some eight years later than

[1] SKEAT : *Passus*, C. xxiii, 245.

Langland, died in the year 1400 ; they are thus full contemporaries.

It is possible that Langland read the Prologue to *The Canterbury Tales*, it is impossible that he appreciated it. The two writers might stand as types of English character, both fully expressed in our literature. Chaucer, the virile artist, the man of the world, cultured, travelled, exquisitely a poet, looks on the world, and especially upon fourteenth-century England, with an eye not less keen than Langland's, but with a complete and joyful sanity, full of humour, eager and ironical. It is a relief to turn to his joyful pages from the self-accusation and gloom of the *Vision*. Yet his verdict upon the friars is certainly not less severe than Langland's ; it is less sorrowful, less bitter, more full of irony. No individual friar, no type as it were summing up the mendicants, disengages itself from Langland's sombre pages ; Chaucer gives us one of those immortal figures, which he and Shakespeare alone seem to have known how to create. He is, of course, one of the nine and twenty who assemble at the Tabard to go on pilgrimage to Canterbury.

> A Frere there was, a wantown and a merye,
> A limitour, a ful solempne man.
> In all the ordres foure is noon that can
> So muche of daliaunce and fair langage.
> He hadde maad ful many a mariage.
> Of yonge wommen, at his owne cost.
> Un-to his ordre he was a noble post.
> Ful wel biloved and famulier was he
> With frankeleyns over-al in his contree,
> And eek with worthy wommen of the toun ;
> For he had power of confessioun,
> As seyde him-self, more than a curat,

For of his ordre he was licentiat.
Ful swetely herde he confessioun,
And plesaunt was his absolucioun ;
He was an esy man to yeve penaunce
Ther as he wiste to han a good pitaunce ;
For unto a povre ordre for to yive
Is signe that a man is wel y-shrive.
For if he yaf, he dorste make avaunt,
He wiste that a man was repetitaunt.
For many a man so hard is of his herte,
He may nat wepe al-thogh him sore smerte.
Therfore, in stede of weping and preyeres,
Men moot yeve silver to the povre freres.
His tipet was ay farsed ful of knyves
And pinnes, for to yeven faire wyves.
And certeinly he hadde a mery note ;
Wel coude he singe and pleyen on a rote.
Of yeddinges he bar utterly the prys ;
His nekke whyt was as the flour-de-lys ;
Ther-to he strong was as a champioun.
He knew the tavernes wel in every toun,
And everich hostiler and tappestere
Bet than a lazar or a beggestere ;
For un-to swich a worthy man as he
Acorded nat, as by his facultee,
To have with seke lazars aqueyntaunce.
It is nat honest, it may nay avaunce
For to delen with no swich poraille,
But al with riche and sellers of victaille.
And over-al, ther as profit sholde aryse,
Curteys he was, and lowly of servyse.
Ther nas no man no-wher so vertuous.
He was the beste beggere in his hous ;
And yaf a certeyn ferme for the graunt ;
Noon of his bretheren cam ther in his haunt ;
For thogh a widwe hadde noght a sho,
So plesaunt was his " *In principio* "

Yet wolde he have a ferthing, er he wente.
His purchas was wel bettre than his rente.
And rage he coude, as it were right a whelpe.
In love-dayes ther coude he muchel helpe.
For there he was nat lyk a cloisterer,
With a thredbar cope, as is a povre scoler,
But he was lyk a maister or a pope.
Of double worsted was his semi-cope,
That rounded as a belle out of the presse.
Somwhat he lipsed, for his wantownesse,
To make his English swete up-on his tonge ;
And in his harping, when that he had songe,
His eyen twinkled in his heed aright
As doon the sterres in the frosty night.
This worthy limitour was cleped Huberd.

Such was the friar, not necessarily a Franciscan, as
Chaucer himself saw him. It is a wonderfully human
picture and seems to assure us that Langland the
churchman was right to be angry and sorrowful.
Chaucer, unlike Langland, is able however to see and
to show us the essential humanity of Huberd and his
like. We may not approve them, but we cannot altogether refuse them our sympathy. But when we
remember Blessed Agnellus and the brethren of the
thirteenth century we must confess that the falling
off is astonishing. Huberd is a sheer adventurer, a
vagrant man, a cheap jack and a rogue. His story
against Summoners, told to humiliate and to spite the
Summoner of the pilgrimage, is only not disgraceful
because it is so human. The Summoner replies in kind
and with interest.

This Somnour in his stiropes hye stood ;
Up-on this Frere his herte was so wood,
That lyk an aspen leef he quook for yre. . . .

His story is a sheer attack upon the friars full of
bitter hate, and therefore cannot be received as
evidence or at least must be received with caution.
There are a few passages which outside evidence
supports as by no means overstating the truth. And
at least we get a picture which those who heard it could
accept as realistic. The tale deals with a Yorkshire
friar of Holdernesse ; we see him first preaching :—

> And specially, aboven every thing
> Excited he the peple in his preching,
> To trentals, and to yeve, for goddes sake
> Wher-with men mighten holy houses make . . .
>
> . . . . . .
>
> "Trentals," seyde he, "deliveren fro penaunce
> Hir freendes soules, as wel olde as yonge,
> Ye, whan that they been hastily y-songe. . . . "

Then we see him begging :—

> And whan this frere had seyd al his entente,
> With *qui cum patre* forth his wey he wente.
> When folk in chirche had yeve him what hem leste,
> He wente his wey, no lenger wolde he reste,
> With scrippe and tipped staf, y-tukked hye ;
> In every hous he gan to poure and prye,
> And beggeth mele, and chese, or elles corn.
> His felawe hadde a staf tipped with horn,
> A peyre of tables al of yvory,
> And a poyntel polished fetisly,
> And wroot the names alwey, as he stood,
> Of alle folk that yaf him any good,
> Ascaunces that he wolde, for hem preye.
> "Yeve as a busshel whete, malt or reye,
> A goddes kechil, or a trip of chese,
> Or elles what yow list, we may nat chese ;
> A goddes halfpeny or a masse-peny,
> Or yeve us of your brawn, if ye have eny ;

A dagon of your blanket, leve dame,
Our suster dere, lo ! here I write your name ;
Bacon or beef, or swich thing as ye finde."

There is, too, a wonderful picture of the greeting of
one Thomas and his wife by this friar.

So longe he wente hous by hous, til he
Cam til an hous ther he was wont to be
Refresshed more than in an hundred placis.
Sik lay the gode man, whos that the place is ;
Bedrede up-on a couche lowe he lay.
" *Deus hic*," quod he, " O Thomas, friend, good day,"
Seyde this frere curteisly and softe.
" Thomas," quod he, " god yelde yow ! ful ofte
Have I up-on this bench faren ful weel.
Here have I eten many a mery meel ; "
And fro the bench he droof awey the cat,
And leyde adoun his potente and his hat,
And eek his scrippe, and sette him softe adoun.
His felawe was go walked in-to toun.
Forth with his knave, in-to that hostelrye
Where-as he shoop him thilke night to lye.
" O, dere maister," quod this syke man,
" How har ye fare sith that caparch bigan ?
I saugh yow noght this fourtenight or more."
" God woot," quod he, " laboured have i ful sore ;
And specially, for thy savacioun
Have I seyd many a precious orison,
And for our othere frendes, god hem blesse !
I have to-day been at your chirche at messe
And seyd a sermon after my simple wit,
Nat al after the text of holy writ ;
For it is hard to yow, as I suppose,
And therefore wol I teche yow al the glose.
Glosinge is a glorious thing, certeyn,
For lettre sleeth, so as we clerkes seyn.

[194]

Ther have I taught hem to be charitable,
And spende hir good ther it is resonable,
And ther I saugh our dame ; a ! wher is she ? "
" Yond in the yerd I trowe that she be,"
Seyde this man," " and she wol come anon."
" Ey, maister ! wel-come be ye, by seint John ! "
Seyde this wyf, " How fare ye hertely ? "

The frere aryseth up ful curteisly
And hir embraceth in his armes narwe.
And kiste hir swete and chirketh as a sparwe
With his lippes ; " dame," quoth he, " right weel,
As he that is your servant every deel.
Thanked be god, that yow yaf soule and lyf,
Yet saugh I nat this day so fair a wyf
In al the chirche, god so save me ! "
" Ye, god amende defautes, sir," quod she.
" Algates wel-come be ye, by my fey ! "
" Graunt mercy, dame, this have I founde alwey.
But of your grete goodnesse, by your leve,
I wolde prey yow that ye nat yow greve,
I wol with Thomas speke a litel throwe.
Thise curats been ful necligent and slowe
To grope tenderly a conscience.
In shrift, in preching is my diligence,
And studie in Petres wordes and in Poules.
I walke, and fisshe Cristen mennes soules,
To yelden Jesu Crist his propre rente,
To sprede his word is set al myn entente. . . ."

In that unequalled picture we seem actually to hear
and see the friar of the later fourteenth century. The
humour and above all the irony of the creation is
completed by the friar's account of himself.

" Therefor we mendinants, we sely freres,
Been wedded to poverte and continence,
To charitee, humbleesse and abstinence,

[195]

> To persecucion for rightwisnesse,
> To wepinge, misericorde and clennesse.
> And therfor may ye see that our preyeres—
> I speke of us, we mendinants, we freres—
> Ben to the hye god more acceptable
> Than youres, with your festes at the table.
> Fro Paradys first, if I shal nat lye,
> Was man out-chaced for his glotonye ;
> And chaast was man in Paradys, certeyn.
>   But herkne now, Thomas, what I shal seyn.
> I ne have no text of it, as I suppose,
> But I shall finde it in a maner glose,
> That specially our swete lord Jesus
> Spak this by freres, whan he seyde thus ;
> ' Blessed be they that povre in spirit been.' '

We must not be tempted to take Chaucer too
seriously. After all he wrote to amuse and we may
defend ourselves for thinking that this picture is
full of malice by the fact that it is the Summoner,
the enemy of the friar, who tells it for revenge.
Yet, in fact, the story is not altogether original ; it
has sources[1] and there is too much of the like, only
less artistic, in the writings of the time. Take this
curious song for instance[2] :—

> Of thes frer mynours me thenkes moch wonder,
> That waxen are thus hauteyn, that som tyme weren
>   under ;
> Among men of holy chirch thai maken mochel
>   blonder ;
> Nou he that sytes us above make ham sone to
>   sonder !
>   With an O and an I, thai praysen not seynt Poule,
>   Thai lyen on seynt Fraunceys, by my fader soule.

[1] See *Ch. Soc Orig. and Anal.*, p. 135, and Skeat, III, 452.
[2] Wright's *Political Poems*, I, 268.

[196]

First thai gabben on God, that alle men may se,
When thai hangen him on high on a green tre,
With leves with blossemes that bright are of ble ;
That was never Goddes son, by my leute.
    With an O and an I, men wenen that thai wede,
    To carpe so of clergy, thai can not thair crede.

Thai have done him on a croys fer up in the skye,
And festned on hym wyenges, as he should flie[1]
This fals feyned byleve shal thai soure bye,
On that lovelych Lord so for to lye.
    With an O and an I, one sayd ful stile
    Armachan distroy ham, if it is Goddes wille.

Ther comes one out of the skye in a grey goun,
As it were an hog-hyerd hyand to toun ;
Thai have mo goddes than we, I say by Mahoun,
Alle men under ham, that ever beres croun.
    With an O and an I, why shuld thai not be shent ?
    There wantes noght bot a fyre that thai nere alle
      brent.

Went I forther on my way on that sme tyde ;
Ther I saw a frere blede in myddes of his syde ;
Both in hondes and in fete had he woudes wyde.
To serve to that same frer, the Pope mot abyde.
    With an O and an I, wonder of thes dedes,
    To se a Pope holde a dische whyl the frer bledes.

A cart was made al of fyre, as it shuld be ;
A gray frer I sawe therinne, that best lyked me.
Wele I wote thai shal be brent, by my leaute ;
God graunt me that grace that I may it see.
    With an O and an I, brent be thai alle !
    And alle that helpes therto faire mot byfalle.

[1] A reference to the Seraph seen by St. Francis when he received the Stigmata on Monte La Verna.

Thai preche alle of povert, bot that love thai noght;
For gode mete to thair mouthe the toun is thurgh
soght.
Wyde are thair wonnynges, and wonderfully wroght;
Murder and horedome ful dere has it boght.
 With an O and an I, for sixe pens er thai fayle,
 Sle thi fadre and jape thi modre, and thai wyl the
 vassoile.

This strange poem makes one think. In attacking as
it does not merely the failings of the friars but their
whole history and even the vision of St. Francis, it
throws suspicion upon all the evidence against the
mendicants. It is the work of an enemy, and strongly
urges upon us the question whether we can admit
against the friars the attacks of their foes. Among
these foes must certainly be reckoned even Langland
and Chaucer. Langland was a narrow-minded
puritan, passionately defending his own views of
things, eagerly on the side of the poor it is true, but
only on his own terms. He attacks the friars because
their way of life does not agree with his. Chaucer, as
a man of the world, naturally hates the friars and
uses the weapon of the cultured against them, irony.
Both these witnesses are full of prejudice ; we
shall be unjust if we accept their evidence without
question.

But have we on the other hand any evidence in
favour of the friars ?

It might seem that the best evidence in their
favour is common sense. It is certain, to begin
with, that the Black Death of 1348, its recurrence in
1361 and return again in 1369 and 1375, had brought
upon England a misery without precedent, unless,
indeed, one may compare with it the Saxon or Danish

invasions. But that was not all, the fourteenth century had been crammed with disaster. Opening with the treason of the Templars, in England the miserable reign of Edward II, ending in the murder of the King, was scarcely relieved by the victories of his great successor, when the pestilence fell upon the country. In 1318 the greatest earthquake ever experienced in England occurred, in 1348 came the Black Death, in 1362 the great storm, of which Langland speaks, devastated the country, in 1376 the Black Prince, the hope of England, died. The most terrible and the most universal disaster, the Black Death, emptying the land of labour, was the cause of the great Peasants Revolt in 1381, and, whoever may have been behind that amazing movement, it is unanswerable evidence of the misery of the country at large. In these circumstances it would have been a miracle had the friars not also been in a state of decay. The exile of the Papacy in Avignon, the miserable schism which followed the return of the Popes to Rome in 1370, are signs of the times, evidence above all of the restlessness within the Church and the weakening of authority. Nothing we know would lead us to believe that the friars of the fourteenth century were as worthy of our love and respect as the friars of the thirteenth. Doubtless the complaints and stories, of which the literature of the time is full, are exaggerated ; but it is impossible to deny that they had a large basis of truth. Nor is it any answer to these charges to urge that in the previous century St. Bonaventura, for instance, had been as outspoken in his attack upon the abuses of the Church as Wyclif was in this. Popular opinion was, in the thirteenth century, wholly or almost wholly on the side of the mendicants ; it is now as universally opposed to them. I do not see how such an impression is to be got rid of; it seems to me overwhelming.

As for an explanation of the decadence of the friars, apart from the natural tendency of any movement to lose impetus the further it travels, the human weakness which finds it more and more difficult to refuse the fulness of life and wealth and the possession of material things; an enormous responsibility must be ascribed to the Black Death. If it destroyed half the population of England it is certain that the proportion of deaths among the friars was much higher; in places, we know all perished. Those who died were almost certainly the best: those who eagerly sacrificed themselves to save their fellow men. It is probable that by inheritance in this great catastrophe the friars acquired a very large amount of wealth, and it was the wastrels of the Orders, or at least the more selfish, who had the administration of it. Such a course of events would be enough to explain the decadence of which every writer of the time complains.

Nor were these writers confined by any means to the puritan dreamers such as Langland, or to cultured and travelled men of the world of whom Chaucer, who happened also to be a supreme poet, is of course the most splendid example. The most serious religious movement of the time, that led by Wyclif, came at last to be among the friars' enemies.

I say it came at last to be among the most eager opponents of the friars; that it was not so at first is both obvious and certain. It was only in the last few years of Wyclif's life that he conceived an enmity towards the friars. No Englishman not a friar had more in common with the Franciscans than Wyclif.

Langland, Chaucer, Wyclif

To begin with, one must seize the fact that Wyclif was a great Schoolman, the successor, in a sense, at Oxford of the Franciscans Duns Scotus and William of Ockham. The importance of his reform movement was largely due to the fact that it was put forward, not by an obscure idealist such as Langland, but by the most famous scholastic thinker of the day. Nor was this all. His poor priests closely resemble the friars of St. Francis, they are from the same mould. That they were opposed by the friars goes for nothing ; the friars had ceased to live in accordance with the Rule of their founder. It is here we find the best excuse for Wyclif's later enmity to them, or at least that most flattering to Wyclif himself. He had always opposed the *religiosi possessionati ;* and at one time he eagerly compared the poverty and mendicancy of St. Francis with the manual labour of SS. Peter and Paul, and contrasted both with the riches and honours of the ecclesiastics of the time. It was fundamentally the growing wealth and seclusion of the friars which turned Wyclif from a friend to an enemy. Mr. Little cites a passage from Matthew Paris in which the Benedictine speaking of the friars says, " they wandered through cities and villages . . . and had the ocean for their cloister."[1] Well, Wyclif begins by attacking them for living " closed in a cloister."

Wyclif, then, had much in common with the friars, and especially with their profession of poverty which he saw was gradually becoming a profession only. There was this, too, and it is of very great importance ; the friars, like Wyclif, were opposed to the monks and bishops on the questions of papal tribute and the power of the crown to deprive the Church of its

LITTLE : *Grey Friars in Oxford*, p. 82, n. 3.

possessions. In 1374 the Friars Minor had taken part against the Archbishop on the question of papal tribute; the Archbishop asserting in the council held at Westminster: "The Pope is lord of all, we cannot refuse him." And it was certainly a friar, probably a Friar Minor, one Frater Joannes, who long before Wyclif declared that the King had the right to deprive ecclesiastics of their temporalities, which after all Marsiglio of Padua if not William of Ockham had always maintained. The Franciscans, with the exception of the Observants as we shall see, continued to hold this opinion at the Reformation.

Wyclif's quarrel with the friars, in so far as it was not a quarrel with the Catholic Church, was a question of possessions, of property, in holding which, and that more and more largely, the Friars Minor certainly had forsaken the Rule of St. Francis. But there was much more than this, especially in the last years of Wyclif's life. The friars were orthodox in matters of dogma, and when Wyclif began to question the doctrine of the Eucharist they opposed him; and this formidable opposition is the real reason for his late attack upon them.

Among a host of accusations he brought against them: covetousness, simony and foul merchandise— the first definite and fundamental charge he brings is that they upheld the "idolatrous" doctrine of the Eucharist. Then he returns to the old question of Evangelical Poverty and accuses them of maintaining the theory of the mendicancy of Christ; and, thirdly, he asserts that they taught the people to rely for salvation on prayers and masses instead of on a good life. This last accusation is the only one that we can take seriously; but even here it is certain there is no case against the friars, whose indulgences[1] did not differ from others of that day or, indeed, from those of the Middle Age as a whole.

Wyclif, then, as a witness against the friars, is far less formidable then we are wont to believe, and, indeed, but for the popular voice of England which joins in his accusations of growing wealth and forgetfulness of the Rules and ideals of their founders, his attack upon the friars would in the circumstances be negligible. As it is we must be careful to distinguish his general attack upon the Catholic Church and Faith from his particular accusations against the friars as mendicants and religious. It seems the more tragic, in so tragic a time, that the one man who might have renewed the Friars Minor, with whom he had so much in common, should have come to find in them only enemies, and this chiefly because they maintained the fundamental dogmas of the Faith he would have had them betray and deny. His charges against them are indeed perhaps as good evidence as we could have that the core of Franciscanism was still sound in spite of the disasters in which so much had become little more than a dream of the Golden Age.

[1] The Catechism tells us that an Indulgence is " a remission of the temporal punishment which often remains due to sin after its guilt has been forgiven."

XV

THE DECAY OF THE FRIARS

THE years of the fourteenth century which had
seen the friars at the highest point of their
fortunes in England, in the Oxford of Duns Scotus and
William of Ockham, in the London which saw their
great church founded and built for them by four
queens, witnessed also, as I have tried to show, in
part at least as a result of the Black Death, their full
decadence, a decadence which was never really stayed
till the Reformation swept them, as an Order, out of
England altogether. That decadence, exposed as it
was by Langland and the author of *Jacke Upland*, by
Chaucer and Wyclif, was, as we have seen, largely the
result of a sudden acquisition of wealth directly produced by the enormous mortality of the pestilence,
when pious and despairing men commonly left all
their possessions to the friars, while others endowed
masses to be said in perpetuity for the departed.
The friars thus enriched began to forget the traditions
and rule of their Order. Instead of going about
among the poor they began to build large and noble
convents in which they lived like monks enclosed, as
Wyclif tells us, and their place in the service of the
people began to be filled by secular priests, the admirable figure of one such being perhaps the noblest
portrait in all *The Canterbury Tales*. But to forget
their service to the poor, to the people generally, was

to forget the very reason of their being. It was the excellent fulfilment of this service in the thirteenth century that had first won them so great a welcome in the towns of England, and had during many years secured them the affection of the people and the respect of all men. The fundamental cause of this neglect was the growing wealth of the Order. The dispute as to the Rule of Poverty was as old as the Order, but it did not come to have a really practical significance till the last quarter of the thirteenth century.

It was in 1279 that Bonagratia, then just elected General of the Order, asked, amid the disputes as to Evangelical Poverty then rife among the friars, for a definition of the Rule of Poverty from Pope Nicholas IV. In the Bull *Exiit qui seminat* of August in that same year, the absolute renouncement of property *in commune* by the Order was confirmed, all property coming to the Order being vested in the Holy See, which appointed *Nuntii* or trustees to hold all such property for the friars. Four years later, in 1283, this was however changed. In the Bull *Exultantes* of January, 1283, Martin IV established the *Syndici Apostolici*, that is to say, he permitted the Ministers Provincial and the Custodians of Custodies to appoint men who should receive in the name of the Holy See all inheritances or alms given to the Friars Minor. These *Syndici* were, however, less independent than the *Nuntii*; they were not only appointed by the Franciscan officers, but were compelled at their orders to disburse what they had received. It is obvious that it was becoming, and that not slowly, more and more difficult for the Order now enormously expanding, immersed in learning and the schools and fast accumulating property, to keep the Rule. The rebellion, for it was nothing less, of the Spirituals is evidence enough. We see Pietro Giovanni Olivi, first in the Province of Ancona and then as General of the Order (1294), forbid the accumulation of property and the investment of money. In 1310 Gonzalvez of Valleboa, Olivi's successor, did the same. But these commands were bound to be disputed, and in fact gave rise to the *Magna Disputatio* at Avignon (1310–12), where both parties argued before the Pope Clement V. The Spirituals, indeed, were set upon obtaining permission to separate from the Order. They asserted that " there will never be peace in the Order till leave is given to those who do desire it to observe the Rule literally. "Clement V in his Bull *Exivi de Paradiso* compromised : and in this way : The Pope divided the precepts of the Rule into two categories, namely, those which bound under pain of mortal sin and those which bound under pain of venial sin. At the same time the Rule of Poverty was maintained. The whole decision was, as I have said, a compromise. Clement persuaded certain French Spirituals who had withdrawn from the community to return to their convents, at the same time deposing certain Ministers who had attacked them. They returned, but the way things were going was obvious. In 1313 Gonzalvez was succeeded by Alexander of Alessandria, who soon died, and in the following year the deposed Ministers were restored. The Spirituals rebelled, even seized the convents in question, and were excommunicated. Finally they appealed to the General Chapter of Naples in 1316. This General Chapter of Naples elected Michael of Cesena, an opponent of the Spirituals, who nevertheless insisted upon Franciscan Poverty. The Spirituals who had acquired along with their zeal for Evangelical Poverty a host of strange notions, several of which were clearly heretical, were now dealt with by John XXII who completely suppressed them, and in 1317 restored a sort of unity to the Order.

There followed the long discussion, put forward first from outside the Order, as to Evangelical Poverty, that is to say, as to whether Christ and his Apostles did or did not possess property either in common or individually. This quarrel flamed up into a furious scholastic strife between the Franciscans and Dominicans, and though this helped the unity of the Franciscan Order, as the Pope sided with the Dominicans, an extraordinary situation full of danger presently declared itself. In 1322 John XXII, ever an enemy of poverty, renounced the trusteeship of the Holy See to the Franciscan possessions and insisted upon the ownership of the Order (*Ad Conditorem*).

By this amazing act the Pope may be said to have deprived the Franciscan Order of its individuality; it was after all the Rule of Poverty which had distinguished it from every other Order in the Church. It was a cruel blow; but, said Pope John, " great is Poverty; but greater is Obedience."

Much may doubtless be said for the papal decision. The quarrel had become an anarchy; the rule of poverty was obviously inconvenient, and day by day became more difficult of observance; and then even in St. Francis' day the Papacy had ever been suspicious of Poverty.[1] But the immediate result of Pope John's act was to unite the Order against his regulations, and certain zealots under the fugitive Angelo da Cingoli in the March of Ancona founded an independent Franciscan Order, the Fraticelli, denying that

[1] *Leg. Trium Soc.*, 49.

John XXII was really Pope, as he had repealed the Rule of St. Francis, and, as they considered, the Gospel of Christ. To these rebels now adhered the more zealously Franciscan among the friars proper, with Michael of Cesena, the deposed General, whom Pope John had succeeded in supplanting at Paris in 1329 by Gerardus Odonis. The Michaelites went out, but in spite of everything the Order as a whole remained faithful to the Holy See, the controversy being simply dropped. Indeed, Benedict XII, John's successor, in his Bull of November, 1336, the regulations of which were imposed on the Order by the Chapter of Cahors, does not so much as mention the rule of poverty.

But the battle was lost and won; the rule of poverty was gone, to be honoured thereafter rather in the breach than in the observance, and its disappearance was confirmed by the Black Death. It is true that the Chapter of Marseilles attempted to revive the old statutes, and that the General Chapter of Assisi in 1354 confirmed this attempt and produced a code based on the Narbonne Constitutions of 1260; but the Papal edicts remained in force and the vast majority of the Order were now ready and willing to submit to them and to undertake the ownership of their property and wealth, of late so largely increased. "Conventualism," [1] that is to say, the community of property and wealth, was founded and established in the Order. But with the recognition and establishment of Conventualism by John XXII the Order was really and finally divided. The movement still strong within the Order, which had

---

[1] The term Conventual as defining a distinct section of the Franciscan Order was not, however, used in an official document till 1431.

in spite of many excesses always proclaimed the rule of poverty as fundamental of Franciscanism, remained, and little by little increased. These " Observants " held to the strict observance of the Rule which forbade the friars to hold property in common or individually, it forbade the investment of monies or the accumulation of goods or wealth. I shall speak of them and of how they gradually increased till they formed a separate congregation and presently appeared in every country in Europe, in the next chapter. They were formally acknowledged by the Council of Constance in 1415.

We see, then, how the movement, both within the Order and without, led to the large abandonment of the rule of poverty by the official body of the Friars Minor. This was, as I have said, confirmed by the Black Death, and, with that calamity, may be said to have been among the more potent causes of the decadence of the Order.

That decadence was by no means stayed at the end of the fourteenth century ; it went on, and the records of the friars in the fifteenth century, such records as we have, show them as very different from those predecessors of theirs to whom England, and indeed the world, opened their arms in the earlier days of the Order. In England certainly there is little to record that might lighten that impression of decline. The Franciscans had certainly been with Simon de Montfort in his rebellion against the Crown. Now, whether we consider them in this, in any large view of the history of England, mistaken or no, at least they were on the side to which, on the whole, the future belonged. In their obstinate loyalty to King Richard II, a loyalty which refused to believe

o   [209]

him dead, they were certainly blind to the trend of events.

King Richard II was deposed and murdered in Pomfret Castle on St. Valentine's day, 1399. But when later a report was spread that he was still alive, the people, who were at least uneasy, under the usurper, Henry IV, believed it. Whether or no the Grey Friars had any hand in inventing that report, they certainly spread it, and were suspected of hatching a conspiracy against the life of the new King. Several of them were arrested, amongst others Friar Richard Friseby of the convent of Leicester, an old man and a Master of Theology, who being asked what he would do if King Richard were living and present, answered, that he would fight for him till death against any man whomsoever. He was executed, his head exposed on London Bridge, and brought to Oxford on the Vigil of the feast of St. John Baptist, the very day on which the rebels were to meet in " the plain of Oxford." In the presence of the procession of the University we read " the herald proclaimed : ' This Master Friar Minor of the Convent of Leicester, in hypocrisy, adulation and false life, preached often, saying that King Richard is alive, and roused the people to seek him in Scotland ' ; and his head was set on a stake there in Oxford."[1]

Eight other friars from the convent of Leicester were arrested and convicted on their own confession of having been concerned in organising an armed rebellion to restore the deposed King. All were hanged and beheaded at Tyburn without ecclesiastical

---

[1] Cf. *Eulog. Hist.*, 391 *et seq.* LITTLE : *Grey Friars*, p. 87, and PARKINSON : *Collectanea Anglo-Minoritica* (1726), p. 185. Other Leicester friars also perished and a friar of Aylesbury.

protest and before an enormous crowd of spectators.
There can be no doubt that the Friars Minor were
whole-heartedly against the new dynasty and spread
disaffection by every means in their power, especially
the confessional and the pulpit. They thus made
enemies of the House of Lancaster, whose short-
lived glory shed no reflection upon them. They more
and more withdrew into their convents, and this
literal conventualism was, of course, confirmed by
the Wars of the Roses. It is curious, if not significant,
that when Richard III was slain at Bosworth fight, his
body, " all naked across the back of a horse," was
taken to Leicester and laid dishonourably in the
church of the Grey Friars there.

Well might Jacke Upland make his " mone to
God."[1]

> Freer, how many orders bee in earth ?
> And which is the perfectest order ?
> Of what order art thou ?
> Who made thine order ?
> What is thy rule ?
> Is there a perfecter rule
> Than Christ himself made ?
> If Christ's rule be most perfect,
> Why rulest thou thee not thereafter ?
> Without more, why shal a freer
> Be more punished
> If he break the rule
> That his patron made,
> Than if he break the hests
> That God Himself made ?

. . . . . .

---

[1] See WRIGHT's *Political Poems and Songs* (Rolls Series), Vol. II, p. 18
et seq. Skeat denies that *Jacke Upland* was ever intended as verse.
He is probably right.

Why be ye wedded faster to your habits
Than a man is to his wife?
For a man may leave his wife for a year or two,
As many men done;
And if you leave your habite a quarter of yeare
Ye sholde be holden apostataes. . . .
Maketh your habit you
Men of religion or no?
If it doe, then ever as it weareth,
Your religion weareth;
And after that your habit is better,
Your religion is better;
And when yee have liggen it beside,
Then lig ye your religion beside you? . . .
What betokeneth your great hood,
Your scaplerie,
Your knotted girdle,
And your wide cope?

.   .   .   .

Why use you all one colour
More than other Christian men doe?
What betokeneth that ye been clothed
All in one manner clothing?
If yee say it betokeneth
Love and charitie,
Certes then ye be oft hypocrites. . . .
Why may not a freer weare clothing
Of another sect of freers,
Sith holinesse stondeth not
In the cloths?

.   .   .   .

Why make yee so costly houses
To dwell in, sith Christ did not so,
And dede men should have but graves,
As falleth it to dede men?
And yet ye have more courts
Than many lords of England;

For ye now wenden throgh the realme,
And ech night will lig
In your own courts,
And so mow but right few lords doe.

. . . . .

Why make ye men believe
That he that is buried
In your habit
Shal never come in hel,
And ye weet not of your selfe
Whether yee shall to hell or no?[1]
And if this were sooth,
Ye should sell your high houses
To make many habites
For to save many mens soules.

. . . . .

What manner men
Needeth for to beg?
For whom oweth
Such men to beg?
Why beggest thou
So for thy bretheren? . . .

. . . . .

Whose ben all your rich courts that yee han,
And all your rich jewels,
Sith ye seyen that ye han nought
Ne in proper ne in common?
If ye saine they ben the Popes
Why gather yee then of poore men and lords
So much out of the King's hand
To make your Pope rich? . . .

. . . . .

[1] Here as so often throughout this popular attack one feels one is
face to face with the malice of the populace, so ignorant that one is at
a loss where to begin one's answer. Whether such ignorance is genuine
or not is of course questionable.

The Franciscans in England

Why hold ye not Saint Francis
Rule and his testament,
Sith Francis saith that God shewed him
This living and this rule?
And certes, if it were Gods will,
The Pope might not fordo it,
Or els Francis was a lier
That saied in this wise.
And but this testament that he made
Accord with Gods will,
Or els erred, he is a lier
That were out of charitie;
And as the law saith, he is accursed
That letteth the rightful last wil of a dead man.
And this testament is the last will
Of Francis that is a dead man;
It seemeth therefore
That all his freers been cursed.

.   .   .   .   .

Freer, what charity is this,
To the people to lie
And say that ye follow Christ in povertie
More than other men done?
And yet in curious and costly housing
And fine and precious clothing,
And delicious and liking feeding,
And in treasure and jewels,
And rich ornaments,
Freers passen lords
And other rich worldly men. . . .

.   .   .   .   .

Freer what charity is this,
To prease upon a rich man,
And to intice him to be buried among you
From his parish church,
And to such rich men give letters of fraternitie,
Confirmed by your generale seale

[214]

And thereby to bear him in hand,
That he shal have part of all your masses,
Mattens, preachings,
Fastings, wakings,
And all other good deeds
Done by your brethren of your order,
Both whilest he liveth,
And after that he is dead ;
And yet ye witten never whether your deeds
Be acceptable to God ? . . .

. . . . .

This popular and very formidable indictment—formidable chiefly on account of its revelation of malice and an abyss of ignorance which may, or may not, be genuine—was answered by Reginald Pecock (1395 ? – 1460 ?), a Welshman, who became successively bishop of St. Asaph and Chichester. In his work the *Repressor of Over Much Blaming of the Clergy*,[1] he defends the friars with more subtlety than success. His book, a monument of fifteenth-century English and logical argument, is futile in that it altogether misses the vulgar intelligence represented in " Jacke Upland." Its subtlety and casuistry merely annoyed the ignorant, whose would-be " clever " points he takes seriously, failing altogether to appreciate that there was not a tittle of sincerity in them. He seems always to be pleading a hopeless cause, and valuable as his work is as a record of the theological opinions of his day, it is still more, and in spite of itself, an explanation of the more human causes of the revolution that was coming.

[1] *The Repressor* (Rolls Series), Vol. II, p. 537 *et seq.* The real and most skilful answer to *Jacke Upland* and in the same manner was *The Reply of Friar Daw Thopias.* See WRIGHT : *Political Poems and Songs*, II, 39 *et seq.* It is too long to give here.

In that part of this famous work where the friars and especially the Franciscans are defended, it might almost be the rude verses of Jacke Upland that Pecock has set himself to answer. Certain folk, says he, object to the habits worn by the religious orders, and also these same folk are angered because certain monasteries contain stately mansions for the reception of lords and ladies, and spacious churches resembling cathedrals. Moreover, the same people object that the Franciscans who may not touch money nor bear it, may keep it in their coffers and count it with a stick's end and may handle jewels and costly plate. He sets himself the task of answering these objectors with an extraordinary elaboration of argument.

He begins with three arguments in favour of the habit worn by religious. Firstly, he says it is reasonable that persons belonging to these orders should be distinguished by some sign from others, and no sign is so appropriate as the whole clothing for this purpose. Are not the different sexes and the different crafts distinguished by their different clothing? Are not the servants of one lord always known apart from those of another by their livery? And since this is so, is it not requisite that the brethren of the various religious orders should be recognised by their various habits? Secondly, he says the habits of the religious orders serve to remind the brethren of the vows and charges which they have undertaken to perform and are also profitable signs to secular persons. Thirdly, he argues that a sober and somewhat unsightly habit imposed by Rule restrains the religious from that vainglorious love of dress into which they might otherwise fall.

The " Repressor " then turns to the stately mansions and churches complained of and justifies them in four arguments. Firstly, he says it is expedient that lords and ladies when they come into cities be lodged in places where they may be removed from the world and may associate with religious persons and attend divine service. Secondly, the hospitality afforded to persons of rank within these mansions moves them to defend the rights of the religious houses. Thirdly, the presence of such persons has a good effect on the conduct of the brethren themselves. And fourthly, these great folks will be more ready to give alms to the mendicant orders if they are lodged within their monasteries, and so the poor will be relieved instead of more alms being solicited from them by the friars.

With regard to the great churches of the religious orders, and more especially of the mendicants, he points out that they admit larger congregations and hold them more conveniently, and offer to more persons opportunities to repair thither at other times for the settling of disputes and the like than smaller churches could do. And he adds that if it be said that evil comes from these stately buildings, greater evil does not arise than is suppressed, and no evil at all arises which may not easily be remedied.

This purely utilitarian argument with regard to that which the Middle Age had regarded as the House of God shows us at once that we are in a new era, indeed on the threshold of the modern world. Not so had the men of the thirteenth century thought of these things. Consider, then, the Abbey of Westminster for instance. It was built for a congregation of some eighty monks at the most ; the people were admitted only to the last bays of the nave. Yet how great a church it is ! The men of the thirteenth century believed they did not build their churches for men, but as sanctuaries for God where seven times every day the Divine Office should be said in His praise, and where, morning by morning, there should be renewed the mystery of His Sacrifice upon the Cross. For these services, for the performance of that Sacrifice, offered for the dead as well as for the living, no congregation was necessary. The church was not built for the people but for God. It is only in the fifteenth century we find great buildings explained and defended precisely as we should explain and defend them to-day, when we erect a new church " to accommodate " a congregation of 300 or 600 or any number of persons ; in other words, we build not for God but for men.

Having thus explained, in the best modern manner, the reasons for the stately churches of the mendicants, Pecock turns more especially to the Franciscans, and particularly to the accusation against them of counting money with a stick. In their defence he offers two arguments. Firstly, he says that whenever anything is to be avoided it is praiseworthy to avoid all familiar approaches to that thing. Love of money is such a thing, and therefore to abstain from handling money is praiseworthy. Secondly, he says the Franciscans, being bound by their religion to renounce the excessive love of money, are reminded of their vows by this abstinence from the bare touch of money. It may be said that they should with equal reasonableness abstain from counting it with a stick, or from handling precious jewels and plate ; but to count money with a stick is a less familiarity than to handle it ; and there is not so much danger in familiarity with jewels, as familiarity with money. Moreover, even if this were not so, it does not follow that if a man for the sake of devotion abstain from one thing he should therefore abstain from another, when he is not obliged to abstain from either. And, again, this will be found true, that it is, more or less, self-denial to abstain from the touch of money, and this self-denial, undertaken for love of God, will receive its reward, as will all other acts of self-denial.

Just there this sophistry comes to an end. It scarcely seems necessary to refer to the Second Rule of the Friars Minor still preserved at the Sacro Convento in Assisi and still the Rule of the first Franciscan Order, to expose the hollowness of the argument. In that Rule we read : " I strictly enjoin on all the Brothers that in no wise they receive coins or money either themselves or through any interposed persons. Nevertheless, for the necessities of the sick and for clothing the other brothers, let the Ministers and Custodes alone take watchful care through spiritual friends according to places and times and cold climates as they shall see expedient in the necessity, saving always that as has been said they shall not receive coins or money." To receive coins and count them not with the hands but with a stick was not to keep the Rule but to attempt to get round it without brutally breaking the letter of it.

The defence is disappointing and inadequate, and forces us to the conclusion that no defence was possible. Nor was this only the case with regard to money, though it is there the fundamental cause of the decay of the friars is to be found. Those stately churches and noble convents that had spread over the land since the Black Death were very different from anything St. Francis had dreamed of for his children. How great and how noble they were, their few ruins, all that is left to us of them, still testify. Consider, then, the Grey Friars steeple of King's Lynn, the tower of Richmond in Yorkshire, the work at Shrewsbury, the Jesse window in St. Mary's church there, the work at Bridgenorth and at Lichfield, the ruins at Walsingham and Gloucester : all works in the perpendicular style that obtained in England after the Black Death and through the fifteenth century.

No, it is not the defence of Reginald Pecock that will save or extenuate the memory of the Friars Minor in their decay ; not by words but by deeds did St. Francis found his Order and set out to convert the world. And for deeds we must go not to the official Franciscans at all, but to those rebels who had now for more than two hundred years raised their voices against the repudiation of the rule of poverty, and though from time to time involved in absurdities and heresy, had yet persisted, at least, in their loyalty to the Rule as St. Francis gave it and to the genius and the memory of their great and holy founder. In the tremendous revolution that was coming it is they, and not the brethren of the main part of the Order, as we see it in England, who will stand firm for the whole Faith of the Catholic Church.

XVI

THE OBSERVANTS

THE rule of poverty, as we have seen, had from the earliest days of the Order divided the Friars Minor. The mystic spouse of St. Francis had been the cause of a certain disunion even in St. Francis' lifetime, the Pope himself had hesitated to sanction this indissoluble marriage, and immediately St. Francis was dead Frate Elias, his successor, tried to put her out of the Order. But there were always many who passionately desired to remain loyal to her, who were ready to sacrifice everything else for this, and though in their enthusiasm they involved themselves, as I have said, in many absurdities, and at last in many heresies, which shut them altogether out of the Order, even among those who remained there were always a few who desired above all things to follow and observe the rule of poverty as St. Francis had established it. It was the decision of Pope John XXII in 1322, the Bull *Ad conditorem canonum*, which finally made the full observance of that rule impossible. In these circumstances that befell which might have been expected. In the various countries where the Franciscans were established, in Italy, in France, in Spain, in Portugal, and in Germany, but especially in the first two, independent movements within the Order appeared, each varying from other, and at first certainly without any uniformity, for the strict observance of the Rule of St. Francis, and especially with regard to poverty; for it was rightly perceived by the best friars everywhere that the life and continual regeneration of the Order must and would depend upon just that poverty, not only of each friar individually but of the Order itself as a community which it had been their Founder's hardest task to maintain.

How hard that task was we may gather from those strange little chapters in Thomas of Celano's *Second Life of St. Francis*.[1] There we read: "Once when St. Francis was returning from Verona and was intending to go through Bologna, he was told ' that a house of the brethren had just been built there.' No sooner did he hear the words ' a house of the brethren' than he turned aside and passed onward another way without going to Bologna. Furthermore, he ordered all the brethren to leave the house with haste, in consequence of which when the house was quitted even the sick were not left behind but turned out with the rest. Nor were they allowed to go back until the Lord Ugo (then Bishop of Ostia and Legate in Lombardy) had made it publicly known that the house belonged to him. He who was then turned out of the house sick bears witness to these things and writes them down. St. Francis would not let the brethren live in any dwelling, even a small one, unless it were certain that there was some owner to whom the property belonged; for he always aimed at his sons' observing the laws of pilgrims—namely, to be gathered under another's roof, to pass onward peaceably, and to thirst after their native land. So even in the hermitage of Sartiano, when one brother asked another where he was coming from, and the answer came, ' From

[1] Cap. XXVIII–XXIX.

[222]

Brother Francis's cell,' the Saint, on hearing it,
replied : ' Since thou hast put Francis's name to the
cell, appropriating it to me, look out for another in-
habitant for it, for I will not stay in it any more. Our
Lord (he said) when He was in the wilderness, where
he prayed and fasted 40 days, did not have a cell made
there, nor any house, but abode beneath a rock of the
mountain. We may follow Him in the manner enjoined by having nothing in the way of property ;
though we cannot live without having the use of
houses.' "

It was just this which John XXII finally overthrew
in 1322. Till then the Holy See held the title to all
the possessions of the Friars Minor, the Bull of 1322,
Ad conditorem canonum, restored the ownership to the
Order. Within twelve years of that Constitution the
revolution within the Order had begun, and first, as
we might expect in Italy.

In the year 1334 a certain Giovanni della Valle was
living at San Bartolommeo di Burgliano, a high place
between Foligno and Camerino, in exact accordance
with the Rule while still within the Order. A year
after the Black Death, in 1350, a companion of
Giovanni's, a lay brother of the Order, Gentile da
Spoleto, was granted an exemption from the Order,
in order to live in accordance with the strict Rule of
St. Francis. But here, as elsewhere, absurdities and
abuses crept in and Gentile was soon surrounded by a
rabble, among whom were certain *fraticelli*, so that
in 1354 his exemption was withdrawn, and in the
following year he was expelled from the Order, and
imprisoned. Now among his companions was a
follower of Giovanni della Valle, one Paoluccio de'
Trinci, born in Foligno in 1309, the son of Vagnozio

de' Trinci, of the noble house of Foligno. His mother was an Orsini. This man, the real founder of the Observants, was allowed to return to Burgliano in 1368. Burgliano, as I have said, was a solitary place high up in the hills between Foligno and Camerino. Snakes abounded there and as a protection against them the friars, who by rule and custom went barefoot wore wooden sandals (*zoccoli*), and it was from these sandals that the Observants came to be named in Italy as *Zoccolanti*.

Fra Paoluccio's reform succeeded. Within five years his followers were in possession of not less than ten small houses in Umbria and the Marches, and to these was presently added the capital and sacred house of San Damiano in Assisi. The cause of this success in Central Italy is, perhaps, not far to seek. The Fraticelli enjoyed complete liberty in Perugia, they lived as they pleased, chiefly in the great country villas of the nobles. They despised and insulted the Franciscans, that is the Conventuals, as we must now call the official Order; they elected their own Generals, and, as one might suppose, were themselves split into various factions. Nevertheless, they were not without power, and that a growing power. It was then, in fact, to combat them that the Conventuals used the Observants. They called in Fra Paoluccio and his friars, and in 1374 ceded to them the small convent of Monte Ripido, near Perugia. Thence Fra Paoluccio began his work of exposing the Fraticelli, and when he had shown them to be heretics the people drove them out. Thus, and for this cause, the superiors of the Order, and Pope Gregory XI, supported and regularised the Observants in Italy. In 1388 Frate Enrico Alfieri, the General of the Order, appointed

Fra Paoluccio Commissary General of his followers who upheld the Observance, the *Regularis Observantia*, and permitted them to penetrate into all parts of Italy, really to preserve the Order. Fra Paoluccio died in 1390, and was succeeded as Commissary-General by Giovanni da Stroncone. In 1414 the Observance held no less than thirty-four houses in the peninsula.

Successful though the Observance had been in the circumstances of the time, it might easily have perished but for the work of two men, S. Bernardino of Siena, 1380–1444, and S. Giovanni da Capistrano, 1386–1456, of whom the first has been called, erroneously, the founder of the Observants : he was rather their St. Bernard ; what St. Bernard had been to the Cistercians S. Bernardino was to the Observants.

This is not the place to examine the lives and struggles of these two great men. It will be enough to say that together they gave a definite character to a movement that, as I have said, was appearing independently throughout the Continent. Now if S. Bernardino represented the spiritual energy and enthusiasm of the movement, S. Giovanni was, as it were, its intellectual force. Their work had been so successful, and the strength of the movement in France, in Germany, in Spain and Portugal was so great that in 1430 Pope Martin V summoned the whole Franciscan Order, both Conventuals and Observants, to a general Chapter at Assisi to inaugurate a general reform of the Order. In that General Chapter Guglielmo of Casale was elected General, but the man who dominated it was S. Giovanni da Capistrano. The Italian Observants had continually

P

refused to avail themselves of any exemption from their ordinaries, or in any way to separate from the Order, and now all at the General Chapter of Assisi swore to abide by its decisions. Nevertheless, not much more than a month later Guglielmo da Casale, the Minster-General was released from the oath and obtained from the Pope in the Bull *Ad Statum* of Aug. 23, 1430, permission for the Conventuals to hold property precisely as other Orders did. The rule of poverty was definitely thrown overboard, and from that time to our own day the Conventuals and the Observants have practically been separate congregations. The cleavage indeed was at last so obvious, definite and apparently irremediable that even S. Giovanni proposed to divide the Order, in spite of the fact that S. Bernardino still opposed this. It is now we see convents till then in the hands of the main Order, the Conventuals, withdrawn from them and handed over for the use of the Observants. And at last, in 1438, even S. Bernardino is compelled to recognise the real state of affairs and to allow himself to be appointed, though after all by the Minister-General, Vicar-General of the Italian Observants, in which office, in 1441, he was succeeded by S. Giovanni. Two years later, in 1443, the then Minister-General, Antonio di Rusconibus, appointed two Vicars-General of the Observants, one for the Cismontane communities, Italy that is, and the Orient, and this office was filled by S. Giovanni ; and another for the Ultramontone communities, and this office was filled by the Frenchman, Jean Perioche of Maubert. In 1446, by the Bull *Ut sacra ordinis minorum*, the office of Vicar-General was secured to the Observants and made permanent and virtually independent of the

Minister-General. In spite of various attempts at reconciliation and a reunion of the whole Order, this state of affairs was confirmed, enlarged and regularised by Leo X in 1517. In the Capitulum Generalissimum summoned by him to meet in Rome at Pentecost, 1517, the Observants were declared to be an independent Order; all other Franciscan reforms were suppressed and annexed to the Observance which was then erected as the true Order of St. Francis, the Observant-General being given the title of *Minister-Generalis totius ordinis Fratrum Minorum,* and to him was given the ancient seal of the Order.

Such, most briefly told, is the story of the rise and triumph of the Observance. But as I have said that movement appeared independently in every country in Europe, and at any rate till 1430 pursued in each country an independent career. The movements that most concern us in this book are those which appeared in France and Germany.

The movement for the strict observance of the Rule of St. Francis first appeared in France as early as 1358, but it was not really till 1388 that in Touraine, in the convent of Mirabeau, it obtained a firm footing. Thence it passed all through that Province, and through Burgundy and Franconia. In 1407 Benedict XIII exempted these reformers from the jurisdiction of the Provincials of the Order, and, as early as 1408, thirty years before the Italian Observants would accept such a governour, gave them a Vicar-General, Thomas de Curte. From the Council of Constance the French Observants obtained a Provincial Vicar for each Province, and a Vicar-General to be supreme over all.

In Germany, where later S. Giovanni greatly

extended the reform, the Observance first appeared about 1420, in the Province of Cologne.

Now it was, as it happens from that Province of Cologne, that at the request of James I of Scotland the Observants first came to Great Britain in 1447, under the leadership of Cornelius Von Ziriksee. Scotland had first been a part of the English Province; but in the time of Elias (1232–39) it had been separated from England and itself raised to the dignity of a Province, only, on the disappearance of Elias, again to be annexed to the English Province. This endured till 1329, when Scotland was once more separated from England, its six cloisters receiving the title of *Vicaria*. It appears to have received the Observants before the English Province, but it is doubtful if this is really so. We cannot definitely assert that the Observants had a convent in England until Greenwich was founded in 1480, but we know that as early as 1454, King Henry VI used every sort of argument to persuade S. Giovanni da Capistrano to come over to England, promising to welcome his arrival with the building of some convent in his kingdom for the Observants. Parkinson argues[1] that " there were at that time many Observants in the nation, otherwise *the building of convents for the Observants* would have been building houses for nobody." It is possible that there were Observants in England, and that as in Italy, at any rate till 1430, they refused the exemption, and were not, as in France, formed into a separate body under proper superiors. At the same time, we must remember that when in 1454 the King, Henry VI, besought S. Giovanni to come to England, and promised to build him convents, he was sick, indeed in the same letter he asks for some

[1] *Collectanea*, p. 202.

relics of S. Bernardino, and that he probably hoped by introducing the Observance into England to win the intercession of the Saint and his own recovery from God. This is more or less borne out by S. Giovanni's letter : [1] ". . . Moreover, concerning the building of new monasteries to the honour of God and the memory of S. Bernardino, I add no more to your pious disposition, but that, as I have said, Faith without good works is not available ; wherefore if you are pleased to build the said monasteries I would have you to know that you build not for me nor for others but for yourself so many everlasting palaces in heaven. For our days are short, and in a little space of time death cuts us off from all that is here below and we, poor wretches ! carry nothing away with us but the virtues and vices, the good or evil which we have acted in this life. If therefore your Majesty intends to provide for your soul by building the said places or monasteries for the Observants I will write to the Most Revd. Father Vicar of France and to some guardian in the neighbourhood whom I do most earnestly recommend to your Majesty to consult with in this affair. Moreover . . . I here send you some of the relics of S. Bernardino which I had by me. For if you desire them with very great fervour of devotion and faith they may through the divine mercy conduce to your recovery. . . . Oh, how earnestly do I wish that I could have waited upon you in England ; but the defence of the Faith which obliges me to go into Hungary will easily excuse me to your Highness. . . ."

Such is the reply of S. Giovanni. It lends little colour to Parkinson's contention. However, Francesco

[1] PARKINSON : *Collectanea*, p. 203.

a Sta. Clara declares, in his *History of the Minors*,[1] upon which Parkinson founded his work, that in 1471 Edward IV wrote to Pope Sixtus IV that " he would withdraw himself from his obedience to his Holiness and arm against him in case he subjected the Observants to the Conventuals." Sixtus IV had been a Conventual, and it certainly might seem that Edward IV must have been acquainted with the Observance to defend it so warmly. However that may be, the same writer declares that in 1480, nine years later that is, " King Edward IV being much affected and edified with the great fame of the exemplary lives of the Observants, sent for Br. William Bertholdi, their Vicar-General on this side the Mountains, and treated with him about the bringing of that sort of religious men into England and gave them their first place of abode in the House of Greenwich which Pope Sixtus IV this year gave them leave to accept." [2] In 1481, according to the same author, three Observant convents were founded in England, and in 1484 " the English Franciscan Province was incorporated amongst the Observants in the General Chapter held at Burgos in Spain. . . ."

But it was King Henry VII who in 1499 really erected the Observants in England. He seems to have been specially devoted to them, and in 1499, by a special grant from the Pope took three convents from the Conventuals, namely, Canterbury, the first English Franciscan house ; Newcastle, the head of the northern custody, and Southampton, and gave them

[1] FRANC. A STA CLARA, *Hist. Min.*, p. 35.

[2] This letter is in the library of Corpus Christi College, Cambridge. MS. CLXX, No. 43, p. 72. Printed in *Archæological Journal*, XXIII (1866), p. 55.

to the Observants. Two houses, also, he newly established, namely, that at Richmond, close to the Royal
Palace, and that at Newark, which, however, some
claim as having been originally a Conventual establishment. Thus with Greenwich, which he is said
to have rebuilt, and certainly confirmed and patronised, there were in 1499 six Observant houses in
England, concerning which I find the following
particulars :—

Greenwich.

This was the first Observant house in England.
King Henry VII, in his Charter dated 1485,[1] tells us
that his predecessor, Edward IV, had by the Pope's
licence (in 1480), given to certain Minorities or
Observant Friars of the Order of St. Francis a piece
of ground adjoining his palace where certain ancient
buildings stood. These friars built on this site several
small buildings in honour of the Blessed Virgin,
St. Francis and All Saints. Henry VII confirmed by
his Charter the use of the site and buildings to the
friars, and founded a convent of these friars, to consist
of a warden and twelve brethren at least. Some say
he rebuilt the convent later ; but this probably refers
to his rebuilding of the works erected in the time of
Edward IV. As we shall see, Queen Katharine,
Henry VIII's first queen, greatly favoured this convent
and the Observants generally, who in return valiantly
espoused her cause. One of the Observant friars of
Greenwich, Friar John Forrest, was her Confessor.

---

[1] Rot. Cart., I Hen. VII, No. 24 (1485), now in the Record Office.
This document grants to the Observant Friars a certain parcel of land
with buildings thereon adjacent to the Royal Manor and Palace. The
document is printed in the *Archæological Journal*, XXIII (1866), p. 55.

Here as at Newcastle, it is said[1] that the Observants were suppressed in 1534, and their house given to the Austin friars. The convent was near the Royal Palace.

Richmond.

This house was founded near the Royal Palace by Henry VII in 1499. [2]

Newark.

This house was a new Observant foundation by King Henry VII in 1499. In 1509 he left 200 pounds to the convent " that by his succour and aid was newly begun in the town of Newark."

Canterbury.

The house, the first Franciscan house in England,

[1] KILBURNE : *Survey of Kent*, p. 115.

[2] In enlarging the Red Cross Hospital, Richmond Green, in August, 1915, by making a doorway into the adjoining house, Abingdon Lodge, the workmen came across a fresco of floral design, which was removed to the Public Library for expert examination as to whether it is part of the Convent of Observant Friars formed there in 1499 by Henry VII and suppressed in 1534.

The fresco was on a plaster partition of Abingdon House, and shows, what was not known before, that part of this building was demolished when the present Red Cross Hospital, known as the Old Friars, was erected in the eighteenth century. The fresco was in a room of which only the partition on one side now remains. On the other side—the interior of Abingdon Lodge—there is some fine old oak panelling.

The priory is known to have been in close proximity to the Palace and to this spot, if not actually on it, and possessed a fine church and extensive cloisters. In the survey of 1649 the building adjoining the Palace, called the Friars, is referred to as containing " 3 rooms below styrs and 4 handsome rooms above styrs," and was at that time used as a chandler's shop. The Old Friars was formerly the property of the Marquis of Hertford, and is believed to be the building to which Horace Walpole refers as having been known as the London Coffee House and having been a branch of White's Club, at which the nobility met for week-end cardplaying.

founded, as has already been noted (see *supra*, p. 19 *et seq*.), in September, 1224, was one of those Franciscan houses which were given for the use of the Observants. This would seem to have befallen in 1499.

Newcastle.

This house, the foundation of which has already been noted as dating from before 1239 (see *supra*, p. 91 *et seq*.), which was the head of one of the seven Franciscan custodies of the English Province, was handed over for the use of the Observants by Henry VII in 1499.

Southampton.

This house, the foundation of which has already been noted as dating from before 1235 (see *supra*, p. 62), was one of those Franciscan houses which were given to the Observants. This befell in July, 1499, when Henry VII handed it over for the use of the new congregation.

The year 1499 was indeed a notable one for the whole Order in England. According to Parkinson, it was in this year, at the General Chapter held at Mechlin that the English Observants " were solemnly formed into a Province with the consent of all its parts; so that the whole Franciscan Province of England, made up of a coalition of the Conventuals and Observants, was now incorporated in the Observance, and hereafter had two votes in all General Chapters, as appears in the Acts of the said Chapters; and thus the Province continued till the decree of Leo X, intituled *Bulla Concordiæ et Liberæ Unionis*, 1517, when the whole Order of Observants prevailed, and got the superiority over the Conventuals. However, the English Franciscans were always one single body or Province of friars. For neither the Chronology of General Chapters nor the histories of our nation say that the Observants ever withdrew themselves from the obedience of the Order though they lived in separate houses; but on the contrary, the Conventuals in England united themselves with the Observants; so that the Vicar-Provincial of the Observants was at first subject to the Provincial of the Conventuals, and at last the Conventuals were made subjects of the Provincial of the Observants without any disunion of the Order, having all and always one Minister-Provincial upon whom all had a dependance." [1]

This state of affairs was peculiar to England and doubtless, partly due to the conservatism of the people, but chiefly the result of the King's patronage; King Henry III had originally established the Order in England, and it was King Henry VII who re-established it, and placed the Observants in supreme authority. In the year 1502 we read that the Observants of Greenwich " compelled the Conventuals to change their religious habits, not so much as to colour, though now somewhat more dusky, being spun with white and black wool as it came off the sheep without any dye; but in regard to the price and fineness of the cloth wherein lay the main difficulty. For whereas the Conventuals used cloth of four or five or six shillings an ell, they were now brought to coarse rough cloth of two shillings an ell, which was much more suitable to their state."

Thus, when Henry VII died in 1509 and his son

[1] *Collectanea of the Antiquities of the English Franciscans* (1726), p. 212.

ascended the throne as Henry VIII, the state of the Franciscan Order in England would seem to have been better than it had been since the Black Death; the future seemed bright. In fact, it had but rearisen to fight a last fight, and to bear witness, even unto death to the fundamentals of the Catholic Faith and the essential prerogatives of the Holy See.

XVII

THE ROYAL SUPREMACY

Remember not, Lord, our offences, nor the offences of our fore-fathers; neither take thou vengeance of our sinnes: spare us, good Lord, spare thy people, whom thou hast redeemed with thy most precious blood, and be not angry with us for ever. (*English Library*, 1544.)

WHEN Henry VIII came to the throne of England in 1509 he was no less an admirer of the Observants than his father had been. Two of the convents of these devoted friars, each built and established by a king, stood cheek by jowl with the Royal Palaces of Greenwich and Richmond. The former of these was especially patronised by Queen Katharine of Aragon who had appointed one of the friars there, John Forrest, to be her confessor, and used, whilst resident at Greenwich, to rise at midnight and join the friars in their devotions. Nor was the King himself at all behind her in his devotion to the Order. In 1513 we have a letter from him to Pope Leo X in which he greatly praises the Observants, and speaks of his peculiar and fervent devotion to the holy family of the Friars Minor of the Observance and eagerly supports and defends them.[1] This is more surprising than it otherwise would be, because the Franciscans, as a whole, were undoubtedly opposed to the new

[1] Letter printed in Ellis's original Letters, Ser. III, Vol. I, p. 165, from Vatican Transcripts, Vol. XXXVII, fol. 17.

learning which Henry delighted in. The Friars Minor were certainly included by Tyndale among " the old barking curs, Duns' disciples and like raff called Scotists the children of darkness, who raged in every pulpit against Greek, Latin and Hebrew." It was Friar Henry Standish, Franciscan Minister-Provincial of England, who attacked Erasmus at Paul's Cross and even at Court, and though there were certainly individual Friars such as Friar Richard Brynkley of Cambridge, also sometime Minister-Provincial in England, who were devoted to the study of Greek, and Friar Nicholas de Burgo, an Italian humanist, a protégé of Wolsey's, who later became an eager champion of the King's claims, the Order as a whole and the Observants, the more living part of it, in particular, were opposed to the new learning ; but it by no means necessarily follows that the Franciscans were equally opposed to the Reformation.

The movement we call the Reformation in England appears in three different phases, namely, a political and financial question, a spiritual question and a moral question. It was the two latter which decided the attitude of the Order and more particularly of the Observants. To the movement as a whole the friars were not necessarily opposed ; indeed, to its political and financial objects the Order was by tradition sympathetic. Thus, William of Ockham, as we have seen, defended secular absolutism, denied the Pope any temporal power or the right to interfere in any way in the affairs of the Empire, he acknowledged the right of the secular government to deprive the Church of properties held by her, and even defended the validity of an adulterous " marriage " on the grounds of

political expediency and the absolute power of the
State in such affairs. It might seem, therefore, that in
the quarrel that was now beginning the friars would
not necessarily have opposed the King in his sequestra-
tion of Church property or in his suppression of
religious houses or even in his assertion of the Royal
Supremacy. Indeed, the friars at Oxford, Mr. Little
tells us, " seem like most of the religious to have
accepted the supremacy [even] in its extended form
and to have taken the oath without demur " :[1] it was
the Observants who resisted and refused it.

If we ask why, of all the Franciscans, only the Observants seem to have refused this oath, we shall find the
answer in turning to the moral question involved in
the Reformation in England. The oath with regard
to the Royal Supremacy, administered to monks and
friars, involved an acknowledgment of the lawfulness
of Henry's divorce of Katharine and of his marriage
with Anne Boleyn, and a promise to preach and defend
these acts on every occasion. This moral question long
before any article of the Faith was in question, or
rather seemed to be in question, for the whole Faith
was as Blessed Thomas More (*ob.* 1535) saw, involved
in the Supremacy of the Pope, decided the Observants,
and, let us admit it, to their eternal honour.

It was in 1530 that Wolsey fell and died. It was in
1533 that Henry divorced Katharine. It was in 1534
that the King declared himself supreme head of the
Church in England and abolished in England the
authority of the Pope. It was in 1535 that Blessed
Thomas More was beheaded. Henry was excommunicated by the Pope. It was a progress from adultery
to apostacy.

[1] LITTLE : *Grey Friars in Oxford*, p. 114.

From the beginning the Observants, and especially the Observants of Greenwich, the first house of the Congregation in England, had defended and supported Katharine in her claim to be the lawful wife of Henry and in her protest against the divorce. In 1533, however, Cranmer, then Archbishop of Canterbury, pronounced the marriage null and void, and Henry, who had been living adulterously with Anne Boleyn, went through a ceremony of marriage with her. In 1534 Greenwich, the chief house of the Observants, the staunch allies of the Queen and the most formidable opponents of the divorce, was suppressed, and their house was given to the Austin friars.[1] The other five Observant convents suffered the same fate. And though all were thus extinguished, Richmond and Canterbury especially suffered, for they were involved in the affair of the holy Maid of Kent.

Elizabeth Barton the Nun or Maid of Kent was a young domestic servant in the service of a farmer of Aldington near Canterbury. In 1525, after a severe illness, she became subject to visions and ecstasies, and was gifted with prophecy. Archbishop Wareham had her examined by Dr. Bocking of Christchurch Priory with two of the monks there and two Observant friars and others. They reported favourably to the Maid, and the Archbishop placed her in the Benedictine nunnery of St. Sepulchre, Canterbury. There she fearlessly denounced the adultery of the King, and, her reputation spreading, became a danger to the project of the divorce. In 1533 Thomas Cromwell ordered

---

[1] The reason the Augustinian Friars were so favoured was that their prior in London at Easter, 1533, had proclaimed Anne Boleyn queen, and called on all to pray for her. His congregation rose and left the church in a body.

Cranmer, then Archbishop, to examine her, later she was sent to London where Cromwell dealt with her till her execution. Before this, however, in November, 1533, Dr. Bocking and John Dering, monks of Christchurch, Friar Risby, the warden of the Observant house of Canterbury, and Friar Rich, the warden of the Observant house of Richmond, with two secular priests and a layman were arrested and set up on a platform at Paul's Cross in London to do public penance. But this was not enough, the King and Cromwell had decided upon the death of all concerned, and on April 20, 1534, the holy Maid and her seven companions, including the Observant Friars, were done to death at Tyburn[1] after a trial in which they had never been heard in their defence or even examined by their judges. And to prevent comment upon this outrageous and illegal act, Cranmer prohibited all preaching in his diocese save under new and restricted licences; while in June, 1534, the clergy were required expressly to justify the King's adultery. Such were the foundations of the Reformation in England, such was the cradle of the Anglican Church.

The state of affairs was precisely this : Henry had defied the Pope and was living in open adultery with Anne Boleyn. The act of the Archbishop in prohibiting sermons save by licence of himself was, as Chapuys says, the act of an antipope ; it might stop the mouths of seculars and monks who had much to lose, it could not altogether prevent the friars, and especially the Observants, from denouncing the

---

[1] Friar Thomas Bourchier, who took the Franciscan habit at Greenwich in Queen Mary's time (1557), tells us that their lives were offered to Friars Rich and Risby if they would accept the King as Supreme head of the English Church. See *Hist. Eccl. de Martyrio FF. Ord. Min.*, and GASQUET : *Henry VIII and English Monasteries* (1888), Vol. I, 150.

iniquity, for the latter at any rate possessed nothing. The only way they could be dealt with was by total suppression. This is what happened :—

To begin with the chief house of the congregation, that of Greenwich : A spy was found within the convent, a lay brother, one Richard Lyst. He acted as Cromwell's agent and was later rewarded with a place at Cambridge. As early as February, 1533, he was at work complaining to his employer of the severity of the discipline of the convent, and especially of the attitude towards the King of Friars Forrest, Peto and Elstow. Of these three he especially considers Friar Forrest blameworthy, because the King had flattered him and had even " sent him some beef from his own table."[1] It is easy to see into this man's soul. After writing a threatening letter to Friar Forrest, he turns his attention to Friar Peto. This friar had not hesitated to speak his mind openly in a sermon preached before the King in the friars' church at Greenwich, which was close to the palace. Stow, in his *Annals*,[2] gives us the following account of the affair.

" The first that openly resisted or reprehended the King touching his marriage with Anne Boleyn was one friar Peto, a simple man, yet very devout, of the Order of the Observants ; this man preaching at Greenwich upon the two and twentieth chapter of the third Book of Kings, viz. the last part of the story of Ahab, saying, ' even where the dogs licked the blood of Naboth, even there shall the dogs lick thy blood also, O King,' and therewithall spoke of the lying prophets who

[1] *Letters and Papers H. VIII*, VI, No. 116.
[2] *Annals* (ed. 1615), p. 561.

abused the king, and 'I am' quoth he 'that Micheas whom thou wilt hate, because I must tell thee truly that this marriage is unlawful. I know I shall eat the bread of affliction and drink the water of sorrow, yet because our Lord hath put it into my mouth, I must speake it.' And when he had strongly inveighed against the king's second marriage to dissuade him from it he also said, 'There are many other preachers, yea, too many, which preach and persuade thee otherwise feeding folly and frail affections upon hope of their own worldly promotion and by that means they betray thy soul, thy honour and posterity to obtain fat benefices, to become rich abbots and get episcopal jurisdiction and other ecclesiastical dignities. These I say are the four hundred prophets who in the spirit of lying seek to deceive you; but take good heed, lest, being seduced, you find Ahab's punishment, which was to have his blood licked up by the dogs.' . . . The king being thus reproved endured it patiently and did no violence to Peto, but the next Sunday being the eighth of May, Dr Curwin preached in the same place, who sharply reprehended Peto and his preaching and called him dog, slanderer, base beggarly friar, closeman, rebel and traitor, saying that no subject should speak so audaciously to princes. . . . He, then, supposing to have utterly suppressed Peto and his partakers lifted up his voice and said: 'I speak to thee, Peto, who makest thyself Micheas that thou mayest speak evil of kings, but now thou art not to be found, being fled for fear and shame as being unable to answer my arguments.' And whilst he thus spoke there was one Elstow, a fellow friar to Peto, standing in the rood loft, who with a bold voice said to Dr Curwin : 'Good sir, you know that father Peto, as he was commanded, has now gone to a provincial council held at Canterbury, and not fled for fear of you, for to-morrow he will return again. In the meantime I am here as another Micheas and will lay down my life to prove all these things true which he hath taught out of the holy scripture. And to this combat I challenge you before God and all equal judges. Even unto thee, Curwin, I speak who art one of the four hundred prophets unto whom the spirit of lying is entered and seekest by adultery to establish succession, betraying the king unto endless perdition more for thy own vain glory and hope of promotion than for discharge of your clogged conscience and the king's salvation. . . .' This Elstow minced not and spake very earnestly, so that they could not make him cease his speech until the King himself bade him hold his peace.''

Next day the two Friars, Peto and Elstow, were brought before the council, and when the Earl of Essex threatened to throw them into the Thames, Friar Elstow answered : " Threaten these things to the rich and dainty folk who are clothed in purple, fare delicately, and have their chiefest hope in this world, for we esteem them not, but are joyful that for the discharge of our duties we are driven hence. With thanks to God we know the way to heaven to be as ready by water as by land and therefore we care not which way we go."

The two friars were exiled and Archbishop Cranmer solemnly declared that Henry's union with Anne Boleyn was true and valid.

Meanwhile, Katharine was strictly guarded at Bugden where it was found two Observants, Friars Payn and Cornelius, had secretly visited her. They were arrested, and, when nothing of importance could be discovered against them, Cromwell wished to examine them " by pains," in other words, to put them on the rack. He did not get his way. However, it would seem that Friar Forrest was now in prison.[1] He could however still write to Katharine and others whom he besought to pray for him, for he believed he had not three days to live. To the Queen he sent his rosary.

But the friars of Greenwich were not alone in withstanding to the utmost the wickedness of the King. Other Observants were equally bold. We hear of Friar Pecock of Southampton preaching on Passion Sunday, 1534, in the cathedral of Winchester, and relating the story of St. Maurice who refused to obey his king's command when it was contrary to God's law, preferring martyrdom, and vigorously and eloquently defending the primacy of Peter and the rights of the Holy See. When Cromwell sent to Southampton to find him he was still absent, and the mayor wrote strongly in his favour. What became of him does not appear.

It was now the King conceived the idea of suppressing all the Observant houses and giving them to the Austin friars who had sided with him in his quarrel with the Pope. Henry had by 1534 abolished the papal authority in England, and no obstacle to his will remained. John Hilsey, a Dominican, later Bishop of Rochester, and Dr. George Brown a prior of Austin hermits, were appointed grand visitors with commission to examine the various orders of friars, convent by

---

[1] See GASQUET : *Henry VIII and the English Monasteries* (1888), Vol. I, p. 189, and authorities there quoted. I am, of course, here much indebted to this work of Cardinal Gasquet's.

convent, concerning their acceptance of Henry as supreme head of the Church in England, and the oath of allegiance to Anne Boleyn, " the wet nurse of heresy," as the Imperial ambassador calls her, was to be administered to them, while each friar was to be solemnly sworn to preach and persuade the people to accept the royal supremacy and to repudiate the Pope. Each house, too, was to " show its gold and silver and other moveable goods and deliver an inventory of them." Well might the Imperial ambassador repeat that Henry was " very covetous of the goods of the Church which he already considers as his patrimony."

As we might expect, the rascaldom of the kingdom saw here an opportunity. False visitors appeared. One such, we learn, visited the convent of the Observants at Southampton where Friar Pecock was warden. Pecock wrote to Cromwell about it : " On the 15th July there came to us a father Black friar and without any authority took the keys from our porter and delivered them to one of his servants. Then by ringing the bell he assembled us in the chapter-house and said he was come as our visitor by the king's authority and read an instrument under seal, as he said, of my lord of Canterbury containing a transcript of the King's letters patent by which authority was given to Dr Brown, provincial of the Austin friars and Dr Hilsey provincial of the Black friars to be visitors. We took him to be Dr Hilsey ; for when I spoke with him in the town he did not deny it. We were willing to accept him as visitor, but we found by chance by one of his servants that he was not named in the commission and was not Hilsey. Not knowing what to do, we desired him to show us his authority and he showed us a letter to your mastership so ill-written that I could not read it plainly, under seal as he said of Dr Hilsey ; and knowing that he was a wise father and a good clerk we did not believe it, but begged him to show us the first writing again to see whether Dr Hilsey had any power to substitute. This he refused and so we would not let him proceed and he threatened us with the king's displeasure and yours."[1]

Hilsey at this time (July) was busy elsewhere. He was, in fact, in pursuit of two Observants, Friars Hugh Payn and Thomas Hayfield of the Newark Convent, in south-west England. He had followed them from Bristol through Somerset, Devon and Cornwall, and at last came up with them in Cardiff, as they were about to embark for Brittany disguised in secular dress. He sent them as prisoners to Cromwell with a letter saying : " In all places where they come they persuade the people to hold to the bishop of Rome calling him a Pope and saying that they will die in his cause and never forsake him while they live. They rail at the books set forth *cum privilegio* calling them heresies, and heretics that set them forth." He goes on to say that they have made people laugh at Anne's bastard, Elizabeth (who by the way was baptised in the church of the Observants at Greenwich), saying that it had been baptised in hot water which they declared was not hot enough for her.[2]

The persecution was now in full swing. The Friars Rich and Risby, who were involved in the affair of the holy Maid of Kent, had been executed in April and it was now proposed to deal with their convents of Canterbury and Richmond. In vain the Commissioners attempted to persuade the friars to take the oath :

[1] *Letters and Papers H. VIII*, VII, No. 982 (July 16).
[2] *Ibid.*, VII, No. 939.

they obtained nothing. Then they tried at Richmond to get the friars to appoint four of the elder members of the community to represent them and to act for them in the matter. This was done. The four appointed met the commissioners at the house of the Observants at Greenwich, but the friars there refused to leave the matter to be settled by deputies, saying " that as it concerned particularly everyone of their souls they would answer particularly every man for himself." The whole matter therefore was openly debated, and in the result each friar absolutely refused to admit that the Pope had no authority in England, for such a proposition was, they declared, " clearly against their profession and the Rule of St. Francis."[1] The Commissioners answered, firstly, that St. Francis made his Rule for Italy and that it did not apply in England ; secondly, that the clause referred to in the Rule was a forgery. But the friars were firm and the commissioners had to report to Cromwell that " all this reason could not sink into their obstinate heads and worn in custom of obedience to the Pope." Finally, they urged that the two archbishops, and most bishops, had admitted that the Pope had no authority in England, and suggested that they who set themselves up against them were presumptuous fools. But the friars answered that " they professed St Francis's religion and in the observance thereof they would live and die." " Sorry we be," wrote the commissioners,

---

[1] In the 12th article of the Rule we read : " I enjoin on the ministers by obedience that they ask of the Lord Pope, one of the Cardinals of the holy Roman Church to be Governor, protector and corrector of this brotherhood, so that being always subject and submissive at the feet of the same Holy Church, grounded in the Catholic Faith, we may observe poverty and humility and the holy Gospel of our Lord Jesus Christ which we have firmly promised.

" we cannot bring them to no better frame and order in this behalf, as our faithful minds was to do for the accomplishment of the King's pleasure."[1]

"A few days later," writes Mr. Gairdner, " two carts of friars were seen passing through the city to the Tower." Henry had determined to suppress the Observants in England. On August 11, 1534, the the Imperial Ambassador Chapuys wrote to the Emperor Charles V. " Of the seven houses of Observants, five have been already emptied of friars because they have refused to swear to the statutes made against the Pope. Those in the two others expect also to be expelled."[2] On August 29 Chapuys writes, " All the Observants of this kingdom have been driven out of their monasteries for refusing the oath against the Holy See, and have been distributed in several monasteries, where they are locked up in chains and worse treated than they could be in prison."[3] No less than fifty of them died in prison, a few escaped into France or Scotland by the assistance of " their secret friend and admirer Wriothesley ; " others from Greenwich seem to have got to Ireland, but a large number perished from cruelty and starvation, and we hear of no less than thirty-two chained two and two being sent to various prisons in England. Of one of them, Friar Francis Lybert, we know something in particular, for we have a letter written from the Grey Friars, Stamford, to " Master James Beckk dwelling at the sign of the Cross Keys the next house unto St Magnus Church in going down towards Belyngsgate."[4] This

---

[1] See WRIGHT : *Supp. to Monast.*, 41–44.
[2] *L. and P. H. VIII*, VII, 1057. I know of but six convents of Observants in England. See *supra*.   [3] *Ibid.*, VII, 1095.
[4] GASQUET, *op. cit.*, I, p. 190, and *L. and P. H. VIII*, VII, 49 and 50.

letter is as follows : " I recommend me unto you and your good bedfellow, thanking you for your great kindness in times past. If you wish to know of my poor fare, thanked be Almighty Jesu I am in meetly good case, as the world at this time requireth, being here at the Grey Friars at Stamford enclosed with my fellow father Abraham, in a poor lodging according to the king's command. Though we are treated as his prisoners, we shall always be his true bedemen and pray for his high and excellent estate and prosperous health. We desire to hear some tidings of our fathers in London and at Greenwich what they have done and what they intend to do. We hear that they are all sworn and have somewhat changed their government at which we marvel. Notwithstanding if they think that God is pleased with it, their conscience discharged, the world edified and any profit may come of it we desire to have a more perfect knowledge, and then we shall do as God shall inspire us—either suffer pain still and be enclosed or else go at liberty as they do.

" Father Abraham and I sent a letter to your wife at the feast of the Nativity of Our Lady, wherein he desired her to send him his gear which he left in the friar's chamber in the ' amerye ' at the bed's head, that is, a little mantle in which was wrapped a Romsey bottle of one pint and a half, a roll of wax, a new Psalter, a pair of new socks etc., I also sent a little bill with it desiring her to send a sure messenger to brother Feeld, in the Grey Friars London who should have delivered to the messenger certain things of mine bound in a handkerchief which I left with him when he was our porter and keeper of the infirmary, with my *Enchiridion Eckeii*, my penner and inkhorn, my

knives and such things as I left with brother Amna.[1]
I also begged her to send me my fire-box which I left
with a young man in your shop, and that all these
things should be sent to the father warden of this
house at Stamford. We have had ro answer to our
letter. Read this letter, read and burn it, for you
know what hurt hath chanced by letter writing, though
many never intended hurt thereby. Recommend me
to my brethren and especially to my poor sister in
Tower Street and my cousin at the Strand without
Temple Bar ; also to my poor father and mother if you
know of any going to them. Grey Friars, Stamford
25 Oct."[2]

We have seen the imprisonment and death for the
Faith of many of the Observant friars in the prisons of
London and of England, to which the violence of the
King condemned them when they refused to acknow-
ledge him, for the first time in history, as the Supreme
Head of the Church in England.[3] It remains to tell
of the barbarous death and martyrdom of perhaps the
chief among them, Friar Forrest, which occurred upon
May 22, 1538.

Friar Forrest, as we may believe, had been in prison,
perhaps in Newgate, since 1534 on a charge of heresy
and treason, the latter for denying the King's supremacy
and the former trumped up out of this ; the absurd
and insincere argument being that since heresy is to

[1] Amna was, I think, the " John Amney priest who in this year received
a licence to collect money within the King's east pale for the Grey Friars
of Canterbury who have no lands nor rents. See *Ibid.*, No. 1620.

[2] *L. and P. H. VIII*, VII, 1307.

[3] In 1537–38 Friars Anthony Brookby, Thomas Belchiam and Thomas
Cort all three proclaimed *venerabili* by Leo XIII, were thrown into
prison for preaching against the King's supremacy. Friar Brookby was
strangled with his own girdle ; the others died of ill-treatment.

be defined by the heretics as " that which is against Scripture," and since Scripture saith (Ecclesiasties v. 8) *Insuper universæ terræ rex imperat servienti*, to deny that the King is Supreme Head of the Church in England is heresy.

By such " monstrous reasoning " Friar Forrest was found guilty of heresy and treason, and so his enemies were able to award him the hideous death of agony they longed to see him suffer. Not the least among these enemies was Latimer, Latimer Bishop of Worcester, Latimer the idol of the Anglican thieves. This Latimer preached at the martyrdom, accepting the office in a letter to Cromwell, almost as barbarous as the death by which Forrest was to die. " Sir—If it be your pleasure as it is that I shall play the fool after my customable manner when Forrest shall suffer, I would wish that my stage stood near unto Forrest for I would endeavour myself so to content the people that therewith I might also convert Forrest, God so helping or rather altogether working. Wherefore I would that he shall hear what I shall say—*si forte*—if he would yet with his heart return to his abjuration I would wish his pardon. Such is my foolishness."[1]

Upon the 22 May a new gallows was set up at Smithfield over the faggots, from which Friar Forrest was suspended in a cradle of chains. Every sort of barbarism attended the scene. The chips of wood to light the fire were a broken and desecrated image venerated in North Wales. Stow gives us the scene. " Memorandum that on Wednesday the 22nd May in A° 1538 Friar Forrest of Greenwich a doctor of divinity was burnt at Smithfield. . . . In the wood when the Bishop asked him what state he would die in, the

---

[1] GASQUET, *op. cit.*, I, p. 199.

friar with a loud voice answered and said if an angel should come down from Heaven and teach him any other doctrine than he had received and believed from his youth he would not now believe him. And that if his body should be cut joint from joint or member after member burnt, hanged, or what pain soever might be done to his body, he would never turn from his old profession. Moreover he told the bishop that seven years before he [the bishop] dared not have made such a sermon for his life."

So died Friar Forrest for the Catholic Faith by fire, slung " by the middle and armholes all quick over the flames," clutching in his agony at the steps of the ladder to swing himself out of the fire. And they sneered at him, " for that so impatiently he took his death as never any man that put his trust in God." Blessed John Forrest was beatified by Pope Leo XIII on December 9, 1886. His relics would seem to be still buried at Smithfield near the corner of St. Bartholomew's hospital near the Priory Gate.

So perished the Observants in England, their convents having been, since 1534, in the hands of the Augustinians by gift of the King.

XVIII

THE SUPPRESSION, 1538-9

THE movement against the friars, the immediate cause of which had been the defiance of the Pope in the King's divorce of Katharine and the proclamation of Henry as Supreme Head of the "Church of England," resulted in 1534, as we have seen, in the suppression of the Observants and the handing over of their convents to the Augustinians, whose Minister, Dr. George Brown, had since that year been appointed as General in England over all the mendicants, in return for having married Anne Boleyn to the King. It culminated in 1538 with the absolute suppression and spoliation of all the friaries in England, and the martyrdom of Blessed John Forrest and in the following year of Friar Waire. Between these two dates, 1533-4 and 1538-9, lie all the greater incidents of the greatest revolution any European country has ever suffered. Within this brief period the traditions of more than a thousand years were utterly destroyed, the Faith that had been unquestioned in England for a millennium was uprooted, and the English people deprived of their religion. No similar catastrophe is to be found in the history of any other nation.

Henry had come to the throne in 1509; in 1521 he published his book against Luther, and received from Leo X in acknowledgment the title borne by his predecessor of Defender of the Faith. In 1525 he began the suppression of the smaller religious houses, and in 1530 Wolsey fell and died. To the office of this great man, that of Vicar-General, the King appointed a layman, Wolsey's secretary, Thomas Cromwell, and it is probably in the career and the corrupt soul of this adventurer, a soldier who had seen service in the Low Countries and had probably assisted at the horrors of the sack of Rome in 1529, that we owe the deciding impulse that encouraged the King in his lust and his rebellion. There follow in quick succession, the Divorce of Katharine in 1533, the proclamation of the King as Supreme Head of the Church of England in 1534, the abolition in the same year of the Pope's authority in England, the martyrdom in 1535 of Sir Thomas More, the revolt against these iniquities known as the Pilgrimage of Grace in 1536 and its unhappy failure, the general suppression and dissolution of the friaries, monasteries and convents in 1538-9, and the gradual erection upon this catastrophe of the aristocratic oligarchy which has ruled England ever since and which now, corrupted by alien blood and manners, is to-day degenerated into a sheer plutocracy. The edifice of Church and State erected upon the adultery of Henry in the sixteenth century and buttressed twice over in the seventeenth is a ruin tottering about our ears. A nation, like a man, bears its fate within itself, nor can it escape any more than the individual the result of its actions. So it is, and shall be, with our country, and we are witnesses of these things.

But in this book we are only concerned with the actions which now are come to full effect and with but one of those many crimes which to-day are demanding of us, who have almost forgotten them, payment.

The Observants with their six convents, Greenwich, Richmond, Canterbury, Southampton, Newark and Newcastle, perished in 1534; there remained more than fifty convents held by the Franciscan conventuals. In 1538 these also were destroyed. Perhaps they had been spared so long, when the religious houses of less than two hundred pounds a year had been suppressed, because, with the exception of London and York, which were undoubtedly almost as wealthy, as richly furnished, and as splendid as a Benedictine Abbey, they possessed very little property, offered little loot and were enormously popular; but the Pilgrimage of Grace, its brutal suppression and unhappy failure seem to have decided the King; it was probably rather from fear than from greed that he now proceeded against the friaries. " That thou doest do quickly " said our Lord when Satan entered into Judas, and it was as though he had heard the same command that the excommunicated King set about the destruction and murder of the Order of St. Francis in England. The whole was accomplished in a few months. Cromwell, of course, was the soul of the business, and his chief assistant was the renegade and perjured Dominician prior Richard Ingworth, who in 1537 had been appointed, as a reward for his apostacy, Suffragan bishop of Dover. To assist and succeed him the notorious Dr. London, now Warden of New College, Oxford, and rather a robber than a peacemaker, was appointed. This canon of Windsor had been put to open penance for adultery, and was to die in prison for perjury. Such were Cromwell's bravos. These, and other lesser instruments of the royal violence and fear, proceeded in their vile task, and what chiefly strikes us in the record of their work is the poverty of the friaries and the fewness of the friars. No doubt the disastrous years between 1534 and 1538 had ruined the friaries, while many of the friars, seeing what was coming and witnesses of the fate of the Observants, had fled away overseas or into Ireland. But as Ingworth reports to his master, " Divers friars are very loath to forsake their houses and yet they are not able to live." The whole business was, of course, accompanied by much brutality, and was not done without protest from the people. Thus, at Walsingham, we read of the " suppression of so many religious houses in which God was well served and many good deeds of charity done " as being condemned. " See," cried one, " how these abbeys go down and our living goeth away with them." But the ferocity with which the Pilgrimage of Grace had been suppressed had done its work of " frightfulness," men were perhaps afraid to protest against the barbarous acts of the King and of Cromwell, and the suppression and dissolution of the friaries were accomplished at last without a single hitch.

The best way, perhaps, in which we can follow this far-reaching act, which was yet not a tenth part of the suppression as a whole, is to follow as well as we are able the record of each individual house, to stand, as it were, by the death-bed of each. I shall therefore now proceed to record the fall of the Franciscan houses in order, custody by custody, and house by house, as I recorded their birth and establishment.

I. The London Custody

London (surrendered November 12, 1538).

In 1534 Friar Thomas Cudner, the Warden of this house, acknowledged the King as supreme head of the

Church in England.[1] He was succeeded in the
wardenship by a friend of Cromwell's, Friar Thomas
Chapman. This man writes to Cromwell in 1538,
" I remember the commandment you gave me to
make search of Forrest's friends, but you gave me too
short a time to answer—only a night and half a day."
He adds, " I will be true to my Prince and so will all
my brethren. I dare depose for them they were no
Observants. Your Lordship spoke to me of changing
my coat, we shall be ready to change when commanded."[2] It is obvious that this man was a traitor
to his Church and to his Order. He is even ready to
give up his habit. The whole convent, as appears in
another letter, was honeycombed with royalism,[3] and
delation was rife. It is not surprising, then, to find
that the house was willingly surrendered by Thomas
Chapman and twenty-six friars on November 12,
1538, " with all its possessions in London and elsewhere in England, Wales and the marches thereof."

I give two of Chapman's letters :—

Letter from Thomas Chapman, warden of the
London convent, to Thomas Cromwell. 1538. [Cott.
MS., Chap. E. IV., f. 115.] " Prudentissime mi
Domine. Dandumque tibi salutem.

" If it may be called to your lordship's remembrance
you commanded me to send the names of my brethren,
whereupon you might send a dispensation of our
papistical slanderers apparel, the which I think it
pleaseth God that we shall no more wear. For of
truth it hath not been rightly used many years, and

---

[1] *L. and P. Hen. VIII*, VII, 665 (14 May, 1534).
[2] *Ibid.*, XIII (1), 880, and XIII (2), 251.   [3] *Ibid.*, XIII (1), 658.

therefore I doubt not but God moves the hearts of princes to take it away and many other things more in the church of Christ, *sicut Ezechias* 4to Reg. 18, *confregit serpentem eneum quem fecerat Moyses : ex precepto dei.* Of the which act we may see that princes may change a thing that God did institute, when it is not used to God's intent. Also it is not unknown to them that be learned in God's law how God gave to the children of Israel and to clergy of Israel also, both cities and towns etc., but when they used them with idolatry and sin, then did the same God that gave the gifts move the Caldeans and Babylonians, yea as scripture saith that he called the Babylonians and the Caldeans to take away that he afore gave etc. And the apostle saith *prima*, Cor. x., *Hec autem omnia in figura nostri contingebant illis, Scripta autem sunt ad correctionem nostram.* No doubt but in those words the apostle spake of us and all that shall come after Christ. The which thing is now justly executed on us, we specially of the clergy, whom God as a loving father doth correct and calleth many to him by those that hath authority to change all customs, usages, and manners in living, and apparel, that hath been offensive to God's people ; the which authority we say is in the King's gracious hand and yours ; and therefore all my brethren desireth no other dispensation but your lordship's word, so known to be your word and commandment by the last letter, that your lordship can write. For as much as ye be our head (under the king's grace) we be exempt from all bishops till it shall please the king's grace to submit us to them ; I trust your lordship will take us as your subjects exempted from bishops ; and as for myself I am your bedesman and servant at all times to my life's end at your commandment and still remaining in such apparel as your lordship saw me in at Chichester and will till I shall know your pleasure to be therein and then shall obey with all readiness. I think long till your dispensation came for my brethren and so think they also. If your pleasure be to make your dispensation by every man's name, here I have sent them in this other letter. So fare ye well in God and all good prosperity for the which ye have and shall know the daily prayer of your orator the warden of the Grey-friars in London."

The following letter of submission accompanied the Deed of Surrender :—

" For as much as we the Warden and Friars of the house of Saint Francis in London commonly called the Grey Friars in London do profoundly consider that the perfection of Christian living doth not con-sist in dumb ceremonies, wearing a grey coat, disguis-ing oneself after strange fashions, ducking, noddings and bowing in girding ourselves with a girdle full of knots and other papistical ceremonies wherein we have been most principally practised and misled in times past : but the very true way to please God and to live a true Christian man without all hypocrisy and fained dissimulation is sincerely declared unto us by our Master Christ, his Evangelists and Apostles :— Being minded hereafter to follow the same, confining oneself unto the will and pleasure of our supreme head under God in earth the King's Majesty ; and not to follow henceforth the superstitious traditions of any forensical potentate or peer : with mutual assent and consent do submit ourselves unto the mercy of our

[259]

said Sovereign Lord. And with like mutual assent
and consent do surrender and yield up unto the hands
of the same or to our said house of Saint Francis
commonly called the Grey Friars in London, with all
lawns, tenements, gardens, meadows, waters, pond-
yards, feedings, pastures, commons, rents reversions
and all other our interest rights or titles, appertaining
unto the same : most humbly beseeching his most
noble grace to dispose of us, and of the same, as first
shall stand with his most gracious pleasure : and
further freely to grant unto every one of us his licence
under writing and seal to change our habits unto
secular fashion and to receive such manner of livings
as other secular priests commonly be preferred unto.
And we all faithfully shall pray unto Almighty God
long to preserve his most noble Grace, with increase of
much felicity and honour. And in witness of all and
singular the premises, and the said warden and Convent of the Grey Friars in London to these presents
have put our Convent Seal the XII day of November
in the thirty the year of the reign of our most Sovereign King Henry the Eight : or Anno 1538.

Chapman was, of course, granted a pension of
13 pounds 6 shillings and 8 pence, which he enjoyed
till 1544,[1] twenty of his friars received payments in
compensation.[2] The house was not rich, but the
church must have been worth more than Stow's
valuation of 32 pounds 19 shillings.[3] The plate alone
amounted to 1520 ounces gilt, 600 ounces parcel gilt,
770 ounces white plate. [4] In January, 1547, the King

[1] *L. and P. H.*, XIX (1), 368.   [2] *Ibid.*, XIV (2), 236.
[3] STOW : *Survey* (Strype), III, 130.
[4] *Monastic Treasures* (Abbotsford Club), 19.

granted to the City of London the church and the
buildings called " le Fratrye," " le Librarye," " le
Dorter " and " le Chapter House," and the ground
called " le Great Cloyster " and " le Little Cloyster."[1]
The church remained ; it was to be called Christ
Church and to be the parish church of a new parish
formed by the union of St. Nicholas and St. Ewen
with that part of St. Sepulchre's parish which was
within the wall. It was opened as a parish church
on January 30, 1547, and in September of that year
" was pulled up all the tombs, great stones, all the
altars with the stalls and walls of the choir and altars
in the church that was sometime the Grey Friars,
and sold, and the choir made smaller."[2] Stow says
" There were nine tombs of alabaster and marble
evironed with staikes of iron in the choir and one
tomb in the body of the church also coped with iron
all pulled down beside seven score grave stones of
marble all sold for fifty pounds or thereabouts by
Martin Bowes, goldsmith and alderman of London."

Thus spoiled, the church continued to be used till
the Great Fire of 1666 destroyed it altogether.

The Friary and conventual buildings were used by
the City of London as an Orphan school and known
as Christ's Hospital from 1552. With the exception
of the cloister they escaped the Great Fire, but, little
by little, were pulled to pieces, and then in 1825
modern buildings were erected by John Shaw. Christ's
Hospital itself was dissolved and the sale of its buildings ordered in December, 1889, and this was carried
out when, in 1902, the school was removed to the

[1] TROLLOPE : *History of Christ's Hospital*, App. XIII–XXIX. The
Letters Patent are here printed in full.
[2] *Chronicle of the Grey Friars of London* (Camden Soc.), p. 54.

country. The site of the convent is now covered with the buildings of the General Post Office; only the site of the church remains where Christ Church, built in 1704 by Sir Christopher Wren, stands.

Dugdale gives us the following:—

"The ornaments and goods being taken to the King's use the church was shut up for a time and used for a storehouse of goods taken prizes of the French; but in the year 1546, on the third of January, it was again set open; on which day preached at Paul's Cross the Bishop of Rochester, where he declared the King's gift thereof to the City for the relieving of the poor, which gift was by patents.

"St. Bartholomew's Spittle in Smithfield, valued at the Suppression at £305 6s. 7d., this Church of the Grey Friars and two parish churches, the one of St. Nicholas in the Shambles and the other St. Ewens in Newgate Market, were all to be made into one parish in the said Friars' church. In lands he gave for maintenance of the said church with Divine service, reparations, etc., 500 marks by the year for ever.

"The 13th of January, in the 38th of Henry VIII, an agreement was made betwixt the king and the mayor and commonalty of London by which the said gift of the Grey Friars' church with all its edifices and ground, the fratry, the library, the dorter, the chapter-house, the great cloister and the lesser tenements, gardens and vacant grounds, lead, stone, iron, etc., the hospital of St. Bartholomew in West Smithfield, the Church of the same, the lead, bells and ornaments of the same Hospital, with all messuages, tenements and appurtenances; the parishes of St. Nicholas and of St. Ewen, and so much of St. Pulcher's parish as was within Newgate were made one parish church in the Grey Friars' church and called Christ's Church, founded by King Henry VIII. A very odd foundation, to let two churches of four stand subverting the other two and a good hospital, to call himself a founder. ... He gave them the Hospital of Bethlehem with the laver of brass in the cloister by estimation 18 feet in length and two feet and a half in depth ; and the watercourse of lead to the said friar-house belonging, containing by estimation in length eighteen acres.

"In the year 1552 began the repairing of the Grey Friars' house for the poor fatherless children, and in the month of November the children were taken into the same to the number of almost four hundred. On Christmas day in the afternoon while the mayor and aldermen rode to St. Paul's, the children of Christ's Hospital stood from St. Laurence lane end in Cheapside toward Paul's all in one livery of russett cotton, 340 in number ; and the Easter after they were in blue at the Spittle and so have continued since. King Edward VI, or rather his governors took from the Hospital at the Savoy lands to the value of £600 per annum and gave the same to this new Hospital of Christ's Church ; as also license for the city to procure and take in mortmain to the value of 4000 marks a year for the use of the same. . . .

"Many persons of note were buried in this church, all of whose monuments were wholly defaced ; for there were nine tombs of alabaster and marble, railed in with iron in the choir, all pulled down, besides seven score grave stones of marble all sold for £50 or thereabouts by Sir Martin Bowes, Goldsmith and alderman of London. Thus was a beautiful church defaced by sacrilegious hands."

Leland : *Collectanea*, IV, 49–51, gives the following list of books " *in bibliotheca Franciscanorum Londini.*" The list is, of course, not exhaustive.

Vita S. Edwardi martyris, ignoto autore.

Historia Ivonis Carnotensis, *inc.* Assyriorum igitur rex.

Sigeberti monachi historia.

Chronica Martini.

Alexander de S. Albano (Necham) de naturis rerum.

Lincolniensis super Libros Dionysii de Hierarchia.

Floriloquium Fratris Joannis Walensis.

Nicolaus Trivet super libros Augustini de Civitate Dei.

Sermones festivales Holkoti, *inc.* Erunt signa in sole.

Collectiones Wallensis super Mattheum *inc.* Tria insinuantur.

Collectiones eiusdem super Leviticum, *inc.* Immolabit vitulum.

Sermones festivates fratris Thomas Winchelse *inc.* Omnis qui audit.

Alexander de S. Albano cog., Necham super Cantica Canticum sive in opus Epithalamicum, *inc.* Humilitas vera.

Holcot super librum sapientiæ.

Notingham super unum ex quatuor, *inc.* da mihi intellectum.

Lathbiri super Librum Trenorum.

Wallis super Psalterium *inc.* Beatus qui custodit.

Adam Wodham Franciscanus super Cantica Canticorum ; vir Scholasticus.

Costesey super Psalmos usque ad Psalmum Nonne Deo 168.

Pastoralia fratris Joannis Wallensis, doctoris Parisiensis.

Postillæ Alexandri de Hales super Job *inc*. Dicitur in Psalmos.

Expositio Wallensis super Valerium ad Rufinum de non ducen da uxore *inc*. Loqui prohibeor.

Opera Reverendi inceptovis Ockam Franciscani.

Expositio super Porphyrium.

Super Prædicamenta.

Super Libr. Periermenia.

Super libros Elenchorum.

Defensorium logices.

Tractatus eiusdem qui vocatur ; Dominus potest facere omne quod fieri vult non includit contradictionem.

Tractatus eiusdem de decem generibus.

Opinio Wiclivi de Universalibus.

Winchelsei super Logicum Stilo Scholastico.

Rhetorica Aristotelis, Latine.

Wiford de Sacramento altaris *inc*. Ratione solemnitatis.

Liber Rogeri Bacon Franciscani de Retardatione accidentium Senectutis et senii e conservatione quinque sensuum *inc*. Cogito et cogitavi.

Antidotarium eiusdem (Part II of above).

Hic liber erat excisus, cum alio eiusdem auctoris ex cujus erasi tituli vestigiis suspicor fuisse de universalibus.

Cowton super Sententias *inc*. Sic dicit beatus Ambrosius.

Bradwardein de Caussa Dei.

Quolibeta Joannis (? Gulielmi) (Okam inceptoris).

Idem de sacramento altaris.

Idem super Sententias.

Ware super libros Sententiarum.

Peccham super Sententias.

Questiones Peccham de vanitate mundalium.

Itinerarium eiusdem non insulsus liber *inc.* Confitebor tibi Domine.

Suttoni questio de unitate formæ.

Ockami quæstio de pluralitate formæ.

Quæstiones Pecchami de sacramento altaris.

Holcoti lectura super Sententias.

Fizaker super Libros Sententiarum.

Ricardus de Media villa super Sententias *inc*.

Abscondita produxit.

None of these books has actually been identified or is known to exist. A volume from the Grey Friars' Library in London, not included in Leland's list, is now in the British Museum (Roy. MSS., 4 D. IV). It is entitled, Postilla Bertrandi super Evangelista ; it contains three other works, viz. Johannes Wallensis De Viciis, the same author's Penitencia and Egidius Romanus : De Regimine Principium. On the first folio we read : *Iste Liber est de Conventu fratrum Minorum, London.*

CANTERBURY (Observant house since 1499, suppressed 1534).

This the earliest Franciscan house in England became an Observant convent in 1499, and was suppressed as such in 1534 (see *supra*) and given to the Augustinians. As an Augustinian convent it was

surrendered in 1538. On the 5th October in that
year we find Archbishop Cranmer, who had always
acted as Henry's pander with regard to Anne Boleyn,
writing to Cromwell from Lambeth : " I perceive
you have already suppressed certain friars' houses, and
I trust your proceedings will extend to Canterbury
that the irreligious religion there may be extincted.
As the Grey Friars, Canterbury, is very commodious
for my servant Thos. Cobham, brother to Lord
Cobham, I beg you will help him to the said house." [1]
But Cranmer did not get his way. The site was
granted to Thomas Spilman (31 Hen. VIII), and later
came to the Finch family, and in Elizabeth's time to
the Lovelaces, who lived here till 1629.

A charming fragment still remains to us from the
thirteenth-century house of the friars. See *supra*,
pp. 24–25.

WINCHESTER (surrendered 21 July, 1538).
This house was surrendered 21 July, 30 Hen. VIII,
with the house of Austin friars at Winchester to
Ingworth, Bishop of Dover. The friars were asked
by Ingworth whether they would reform certain
disorders, and conform to the injunctions, but all
said they were unable to continue for poverty and
desired to be assigned to other houses. Their stuff
valued by two men appointed by the mayor was
worth £9 os. 3d. The plate for the three houses of
Grey, Black and Austin friars was under four score
ounces.[2] Four days later Ingworth writes again to
Cromwell, saying, " The Grey Friars is a proper house
in building, no rents, small gardens and no lead but

---

[1] *L. and P. Hen. VIII*, XIII (2), 537.
[2] *L. and P. Hen. VIII*, XIII (1), 1432.

The Franciscans in England

two or three gutters. The city will make suit for it."

Inventory of the stuff of the Grey Friars at Winchester praised by Master Lurkyn (*sic*) alderman and Master Knyght. (*L. and P. Hen. VIII*, XIII (1), 1108):

	A pall and frontlet	12d.
	2 St. John's heads	2d.
	2 wooden paxes	4d. etc.
The Valans :	A pall and frontlet	2d.
	2 altar cloths	6d.
	2 candlesticks	6d.

Cloths, candelsticks and cruets for St. Clement's and St. Francis' altar.

In the Vestry : 18 corporasses, 3 sudories, a gold cushion 20d. 5 suits of vestments, 2 single vestments of requiem 33/– and other items.

6 bushels of wheat.
A pair of old organs, 4/–

kitchen utensils and bedding and other furniture in Master Denham's chamber.

Total   £9 0. 3d.

Added by Ingworth : Debts 16s. House and stuff in Knight's hands.

This site came into the hands of Winchester College, 35 Hen. VIII. Nothing remains. Leland, as I have already shown, points out the site (see *supra*, p. 62).

SOUTHAMPTON (Observant house since 1499 ; suppressed as such 1534).

This house was surrendered by the Austin friars 30 October, 1538.

Indenture of the stuff of the Austin friars (late

Grey friars) of Southampton delivered by the lord
Visitor under the lord Privy Seal to Nich. Dey, mayor
there and James Betts, customer, for the king (1538).
(*L. and P. Hen. VIII*, XIII (2), 545) :—

Choir : At the high altar a table of alabaster of the
Passion, above that a fair table painted and gilt with
a pageant of the Passion, curtains on bars of iron to
save the same. In the midst of the altar a proper
frame gilt for the sacrament ; at the altar's ends
2 small altars, a proper seat syleyd for priest, deacon,
subdeacon etc. Choir double stalled and well and sub-
stantially graven. A fair loft over the door with a good
clock and a bell to warn the clock. A bell in the steeple.

Church : 3 tables of alabaster at 3 altars, a sacring
bell ; a painted table, 12 closed seats and other seats,
2 branches for tapers, a lamp and basin.

Vestry : 6 suits of vestments honest but none better
than silk or chainlet, and many other vestments etc.
(18 items).

*Chapter House, Frayter, Fermery, Tailor's house,
Parlour and Kitchen :* Furniture detailed : the 3 first
have conduits for water and the last has leaden troughs.

The *Library* locked with 2 locks and many books in
it chained.

Besides this, certain stuff sold for £10 15s. to pay
debts to brewer, baker, barber etc., of £9 6s. The
visitor had 32s. and 4 chalices which were in pledge
52 oz.

The site was bought in 1545 by John Pollard and
William Byrt and in 1551 by Sir A. Darcy. Nothing
remains. All Leland can say is : "There was a
college of Grey Friars in the east south east part of
the town touching to the town wall betwixt the east
and south-east gates."

LEWES (surrendered 15 December, 1538).

On 15 December, 1538, Ingworth writes to Cromwell : " If the houses northward have made their releases to the king, knows of no house to release except Lewes."[1] And on the same day writes to say he has received " the house of Friars at Lewes to the King's use. All the implements, altars, bells, windows, gravestones, etc., except the roofs and the covering of them were not able to pay the debts. Most of the plate was abroad on pledge. All is appraised but none sold, and left in the hands of John Mylesent and Nich, Geney, Cromwell's servants. Has paid the debts £15 4s. The plate is 77 oz."[2]

Three days later, upon 18 Dec., Sir John Gage writes to Cromwell : " Hearing that Cromwell wishes to let to farm all his land at Lewes offers to take both the Ryes where the conies are, and the " brokes " lying to the said Ryes, the fields between the Place and the Friars ; and the Broadwater. . . .[3]

In 36 Hen. VIII the site was granted to William Heydon and Hugh Stukeley.

CHICHESTER (surrendered 8 October, 1538).

In the latter part of July, 1538, when Ingworth visited Chichester he found the Grey friars' house " in good order and so left them."[4] But on 8 October he received the surrender of the house. The debts were £7 and " to pay this and reward to poor friars " seven friars had signed the surrender—" he sold

[1] *L. and P. Hen. VIII*, XIII (2), 1059.
[2] *L. and P. Hen. VIII*, XIII (2), 1060.
[3] *L. and P. Hen. VIII*, XIII (2), 1091.
[4] *L. and P. Hen. VIII*, XIII (1), 1456.

£10.17 worth of stuff. The Visitor hath 8s. 8d towards his charges and 141 oz. of silver." [1]

Indenture of the stuff of the Grey Friars Chichester delivered by the Lord Visitor under the Lord Privy Seal to him. Bradbryge, mayor there, and Ellis Bradshaw for the King (*L. and P. Hen. VIII*, XIII (2), 562) :—

Choir : (6 items) a fair painted table etc., and 2 bells in the steeple.

Cloister : A fair laverys and a conduit coming to it.

Vestry : 4 suits, of red raw velvet, blue silk, silk payneyd, and silk with the ground green. Vestments altar cloths and suplices 3 each, and two great chests.

Ostre : 2 trestles, table and form, the ostre well syleyd. Parlour, well syleyd and benched. Brew house, 5 items.

Library : 4½ new stalls with divers old books and new press with almers for books.

Frayter : 7 tables and 7 forms.

The whole house new syleyd about the windows and all the windows well glazed.

Part of the church remains. See *supra*, p. 65.

The site of the house was granted to the Mayor and citizens.

SALISBURY (surrendered 2 October, 1538).

On 25 July, 1538, Ingworth writes to Cromwell that he found the Friars of Salisbury in good order. [2] He then, apparently, took an inventory, for on

---

[1] *L. and P. Hen. VIII* XIII (2), 562 .
[2] *L. and P. Hen. VIII*, XIII (1), 1456.

20 August, John, Lord Fitzwarren, writes to Cromwell, " Hearing that the visitor of the friars is coming to Sarum to dissolve and make sale of such things as he took an inventory of, I beg your Lordship's letters to him, that I may have the stuff of the Black Friars for my money before any other, and the place to dwell in for my rent ; and also for your servant Mr Goodale for the Grey Friars." On 21 September, however, Charles Bulkeley writes from " In the Grey Friars, Sarum," to Cromwell, " I beg your favour to get me the house of the Grey Friars in Salisbury which is like to be soon in the King's hands. I have had lodging in it this 20 years, at 26s. 8d a year, which is all the yearly profits they receive within the precinct of the house. I will give £100 for it and would use the timber and stone to build my own lodging, trusting there to keep twice as many persons as there now are friars who shall work for their living without begging. The jewels and goods come to about 100 marks ; I would gladly buy them too."

Indenture of the stuff of the Grey Friars, Salisbury, received by the lord Visitor under the lord Privy Seal and delivered to John Shaxton and John Goodale bailey of Salisbury for the King (*L. and P. Henry VIII*, XIII (2), 518) :—

Choir : The high altar, a table of imagery gilt, etc.
Church : Poor altars, one alabaster. Steeple, 2 bells—one a fair bell.
Vestry : 5 laten candlesticks, a golden cope with offeros imagery ; white, blue, green and black copes, altar cloths, etc.
Frayter, Parlour, Hall : a few articles of furniture.
Besides this there is sold to pay the debts, 3 suits of

vestments and 4 copes, all poor for £10; also a pair of organs broken, 2 candlesticks and the stuff of the chambers which was very poor for £4 2. The debts drew £19 great part being to brewers and others for necessaries and the rest to the warden; £11.12d satisfied all. The Visitor has for the King 59s. and 278 oz. of silver."

Then upon 2 October the house was surrendered by the warden and convent to the lord visitor. There were 278 oz. of silver. In 36 Hen. VIII, the site was granted to John Wroth.

Nothing remains.

WINCHELSEA (surrendered December, 1538) :—

On Aug. 25, 1538, Ingworth writes to Cromwell " At Winchelsea . . . the Grey Friars are very poor and not able to continue. Thinks the warden would have given it up if he had been at home. Has provided that there shall be no waste in the house. Mr. Lowes has sight of it."[1] On the 15 December he writes that he will go to Winchelsea; presumably to receive the surrender of this house.

The site was granted, 36 Hen. VIII, to William Clifford and Michael Wildbore.[2]

Almost nothing remains. (See *supra*, p. 65.)

WARE. (Surrendered December, 1538.)

This house, dating from 1347, was surrendered early in December, 1538,[3] and the site, 36 Hen. VIII, granted to Thomas Birch.

---

[1] *L. and P. Hen. VIII*, XIII (1), 1456.
[2] DUGDALE, Vol. VI (1830), 1533.
[3] *L. and P. Hen. VIII*, XIII (2), 1021.

II. Oxford Custody

OXFORD (suppressed July, 1538).

The friaries of Oxford, if we except the Observants, were attacked earlier than the other Franciscans because they suffered in the " reform " of the University which Cromwell sent the infamous Layton to accomplish in 1535. " We have set Dunce in Bocardo,"[1] he writes, " and have utterly banished him from Oxford for ever with all his blind glories. Is now made a common servant to every man, fast nailed up upon posts at all common houses of easement ; *id quod oculis meis vidi ;* and the second time we came to New College after we had declared your injunctions we found all the great quadrant court full of the leaves of Dunce, the wind blowing them into every corner. And there we found one Mr Greenfield a gentleman of Bucks, gathering up part of the said books' leaves (as he said) therwith to make him sewels or blansheres to keep the deer within the wood, thereby to have the better cry with his hounds."[2]

The study of the schoolmen thus abolished, the attack was directed upon the religious students, the object being especially to destroy the monastic life of the place : " We have further," Layton continues, " in visiting the religious students amongst all other injunctions adjoured that none of them for no manner of cause shall come within any tavern, inn, ale-house or any other house whatsoever it be, within the town and the suburbs of the same, upon pain once so taken by day or by night to be sent immediately home to his cloister whereas he was professed. Without doubt we

[1] The Old North Gate used as a prison. Dunce was Duns Scotus.
[2] WRIGHT : *Suppression* (Camd. Soc.), 71.

hear say this act to be greatly lamented of all the double honest women of the town and especially of their launders that now may not once enter within the gates and much less within their chambers whereunto they were right well accustomed. I doubt not but for this thing only the honest matrons will sue unto you for a redress."

There is no doubt that the measure taken in 1535 by Cromwell, and the threatening situation then obvious to all, here in Oxford perhaps more than elsewhere, caused the friars to depart for the most part overseas. On July 7, 1538, Dr. John London, Warden of New College, writes to Wriothesley that he has received the King's commission to Master Mayor, Mr. Pye, Mr. Fryer and himself "to look upon the friars in Oxford." He found all the houses in poverty and soon notes that the Grey Friars had made submission.[1] Writing to Cromwell on the following day, July 8, he says : " The Grey Friars have pretty wooded islands behind their house and the waters be theirs. They have an orchard, pretty gardens, and lodgings. It is a huge house much in ruins. They have impledged and sold most of the plate and jewels forced by necessity ; what remains is in the bill. Church ornaments old and worthless. Other stuff evil worth £10.

" They have taken up the pipes of their conduit lately and have cast them in sows to the number of 67 whereof 12 be sold for the costs of taking up as the warden saith. The residue we have put in safeguard. But we have not yet weighed them. And there is yet on the earth remaining much of the

[1] *L. and P. Hen. VIII*, XIII (1), 1335.

conduit not taken up. In their groves the wind hath blown down many trees, which so remain upon the ground. These friars do receive yearly out of the exchequer of the king's alms 50 marks. This house is all covered with slate and no lead."

On August 31 London writes to Cromwell to say that " he has caused all the four orders of Friars to change their coats. . . ." He adds that the warden of the Grey Friars, Edward Barkerfelde, S.T.P., desires a benefice with dispensation to reside in the University of Oxford, though above forty years ; and encloses a list of jewels and plate as follows : " A silver gilt cross. Four chalices. A pyx. A censer. A pair of small cruets. Five old masers with silver bands weighing with the trees 82 oz. A black horn with silver band and foot. Three dozen spoons. A knob of the cover of a maser."[1]

Later, London writes to Cromwell to urge that the site of the Grey Friars should be given to the City. This, however, was not done. On August 10, 1540, William Fryner and John Pye obtained a lease of the house and site with the grove of 5 acres for twenty-one years at 20s. a year. This grant did not include the churchyard, the garden called the Paradise, or the garden called Boteham ; moreover, all the trees and shrubs were reserved to the King and the buildings within the precincts were to be torn down.[2] Four years later, however, Richard Andrews of Hales in Gloucestershire, a land jobber of the period, bought for £1094 3s. 2d. a large number of monastic properties, among them the Grey Friars in Oxford.[3] He

[1] *L. and P. Hen. VIII*, XIII (2), 235 and 238.
[2] LITTLE : *Grey Friars*, p. 121–22.
[3] See LITTLE, *op. cit.*, p. 122. Pat. Roll, 36 Hen. VIII, Pt. 3, m. 37, and Orig. Rolls, 36 Hen. VIII, Pt. 4 ; V, m. 12.

bought woods and gardens and all, with the church-yard. The speculation was a good one, and in August of the same year Andrew and his partner sold to Richard Gunter, who had originally rented the Churchyard.

NORTHAMPTON (surrendered 28 October, 1538).

On 23 October, 1538, the Mayor and Corporation of Northampton write to Cromwell to say that " hearing that the four friar houses in the town are likely to be suppressed they ask him to speak to the King that the town may have part of them."[1] On the 28 October the surrender was made to Dr. John London of the house and all its possessions in England to the King's use. Ambrose Clerke and Roger Wall were appointed as attorneys to receive and deliver the premises to Dr. London. The surrender was signed by Friar John Wyndlowe the warden and 10 friars.[2] In 1539 a memorandum drawn up by Dr. London for Thomas Thacker notes that " At Northampton the Grey Friars church is covered with lead."[3] The site was granted 36 Hen. VIII to Richard Taverner.

Leland says : " The Gray Friars House was the best builded and largest house of all the places of the friars and stood a little beyond the chief market-place, almost by flat north. The site and ground it stood on longed to the city, whereupon the citizens were taken for founders thereof. There lay two of the Salisburys buried in this house of Gray Friars. And as I remember it was told me that one of the Salisburys

---

[1] *L. and P. Hen. VIII*, XIII (2), 678.
[2] *L. and P. Hen. VIII*, XIII (2), 705.
[3] *L. and P. Hen. VIII*, XIV (1), 3.

daughters was mother to Sir William Parr and his elder brother."[1]

READING (surrendered 13 September, 1538).

On 31 August, Dr. London, writing to Cromwell from Oxford, says he " has caused all the four orders of friars to change their coats," and he adds : " A friend of mine, the warden of the Grey Friars in Reading, also wishes license for them to change their garments. Most of them are very old men."[2]

The warden, Peter Schefford, being a friend of London's, there can have been no difficulty about the surrender which followed on September 13, and was signed by Friar Peter Schefford, Egidius Coventry, and nine others. In the preamble the friars state that they " are moved to do so by the consideration that the way to perfection does not consist in the wearing of a particular habit and that they are accused of hypocrisy and the people withdraw the support formerly given them. They beg license under the King's seal to change their habits."[3]

The fact that the people had withdrawn the support formerly given is understandable, for naturally if their suppression was generally expected people were loath to imperil their gifts as well as personally in fear.

Dr. London, on the day following the surrender, 14 September, writes to Cromwell, " I have taken a surrender of the friars in Reading and this day they shall change their coats. Of friars they be noted here honest men. In the house are three pretty lodgings ;

[1] LELAND : *Itin.* (1907), I, p. 9.
[2] *L. and P. Hen. VIII*, XIII (2), 235.
[3] *L. and P. Hen. VIII*, XIII (2), 340.

the warden keeps one, Mr. Ogle, the King's servant, another, and an old lady called my lady Seynt Jone the third. None is out by convent seal, but they say they promised one to Mr. Ogle. There is a goodly walk in their back side with trees, ponds, and an orchard, in all 20 acres. Household stuff, coarse. What little plate and jewels there is I will send up this week. There is a great trough of lead at their well and another in their kitchen and the bell turret is covered with lead. Church ornaments slender. The inside of the church, and windows decked with grey friars, I have defaced and yet made some money out of these things. On Monday I will pay their debts to victuallers and rid the house of them all." [1]

On the 17 September, London writes again, recommending that the church of the Grey Friars " be given to the town of Reading as their town hall is small and inconvenient." [2]

" I beset your good Lordship to admit me a poor suitor for these honest men of Reading. They have a fair toun and many good occupiers in it ; but they lack that house necessary of the which for the ministration of Justice they have the most need of. Their Toun Hall is a very small house and standeth upon the river where is the common washing place of the most part of the toun and in the session days and other court days there is such beating with battledores as no man can not hear another, nor the guest hear the charge giving. The body of the church of the Grey Friars which is selyd with laths and wins would be very commodious room for them. And now I have rid all the fashion of that church in pardons, images and

---

[1] *L. and P. Hen. VIII*, XIII (2), 346.
[2] *L. and P. Hen. VIII*, XIII (2), 367.

altars it would make a goodly Toun Hall. The Mayor of that toun, Mr. Richard Turner, a very honest gentle person, with many other honest men hath expressed unto me their grief in this behalf and have desired me to be an humble suitor unto your Lordship for the same if it should be sold. The walls, beside the corner stones be but chalk and flint and the covering but tile. And if it please the King's Grace to bestow that house upon any of his servants he may spare the body of the church which standeth next the street very well, and yet have room sufficient for a great man."[1]

On 18 September London again writes to Cromwell saying that he has sent up the surrender of the Grey Friars Reading with their plate such as it is. Has defaced inward the church and dorter leaving the rest till he knows Cromwell's pleasure, and despatched all the friars out of doors in secular apparel paying their debts and giving them each money in their purses. He adds a notable comment. "This is a toun of much poor people and they fell to stealing so fast in every corner of the house that I have been fain to tarry a whole week here to set everything in due order."[2]

He is indeed quite eloquent about this : "As soon as I had taken the Friar's surrender the multitude of the Poverty of the toun deserted thither and all things that might be had they stole away, insomuch that they had conveyed the very clappers of the bells. And saving that Mr Vachell which made me great cheer at his house and the mayor did assist me they would have made no little spoil.

[1] B.M. Cott. MS. Cleop., E. IV, fol. 225.
[2] *L. and P. Hen. VIII*, XIII (2), 377.

" In this I have done as much as I could to save everything to the King's Grace's use as shall appear to your Lordship at the beginning of the term, God willing who with increase of much honour long preserve your good Lordship." [1]

London was evidently accused of destroying more than was expected by his master in his inquisition. On October 29 he writes to protest, and notes, " I have not rased the houses so much as I perceive the King and your Lordship are informed. I had rased none save for the words of my Commission and did not extremely so but when the importunity of the people who would else have pitted all, compelled me." He then briefly rehearses what he has done. At Reading he says he " defaced the church, the windows being full of friars and left the roof and walls whole to the King's use ; sold their ornaments ' Selleys ' in the dortoir and certain utensils which else had been stolen."

In 1544 the King granted to the mayor and burgesses of Reading, for a new Town Hall, the church of the Grey Friars, the town paying a halfpenny rent annually. The house and site were granted to a groom of the King's chamber.

The church in some sort remains. See *supra*, pp. 67–68.

Leland merely says : " On the north side of Castle Street was a late a fair house of Gray Friars." [2]

BEDFORD (surrendered 30 October, 1538).

The surrender of this convent upon 30 October,

---

[1] B.M. Cott. MS. Cleop., E. IV, fol. 225.
[2] LELAND : *Itin.* (1907), I, 110.

1535, was signed by the warden, the vice warden and eleven other friars.[1] Upon that day London writes to Cromwell that " now I have taken the surrender of the Grey Friars in Bedford. I kept Mr Geffreys to help me till I got Mr Gostwik with whom according to your pleasure after I have dispatched them I will leave the house. Would God he had the perpetual custody for if sickness happen in his house he has I hear no other to resort to. This is a pretty house of plate, jewels and other necessaries, and they have long used husbandry. They intended to make away all and sold their cart and horses within these fourteen days. When I came I found six threshers in one end of the barn and two in another, and if more might have stood there more should have been there. With Mr Gostwik's help I trust to make them all secular priests for such friars I never met with. To declare what persons many of them be before time at the very warden's hands I chanced upon the bill enclosed. He had it in his sleeve and delivered it me instead of his inventory. It will move you to wrath. I trust to make a better inventory to the King's use than this bill and then repair to other places in this commission."[2]

On the same day, 3 October, John Gostwik wrote to Cromwell : " Dr London and I met 2 October at the Grey Friars in Bedford for the dissolution of the same. The warden had sold his house the Sunday before for £40 to Sir John Seynt John who I am assured has since surrendered it to the King. I desire a gift of it to me and my heirs (annual value 5 marks) and will give you £40. The King will have a great benefit

[1] *L. and P. Hen. VIII*, XIII (2), 525.
[2] *L. and P. Hen. VIII*, XIII (2), 526.

there in lead and other things. Mr Seynt John intends shortly to be at London about this."[1]

On the 29 October London reports to Cromwell that he has "sold the church ornaments at Bedford and certain utensils and saved all the lead with some utensils to leave with Mr Gostwik."[2]

The revenues of the monastery when suppressed were estimated only at 3 pounds 15 shillings 2 pence clear yearly value. The site to the north-west of the town in St. Paul's parish was granted by Henry VIII to Gostwik, who was master of the horse, and later came to the Earl of Ashburnham. A few remains are still extant, including certain vestiges of the cloister. A barn close by is said to have been the Refectory.

STAMFORD (surrendered 8 October, 1538).

The surrender of this house on 8 October, 1538, was signed by John Schewyn the warden and nine other friars.[3] On the 15th October London writes to Cromwell to say that he has received on the 14th, by Mr. Vincent, Cromwell's letters bidding him give to Vincent the custody of the Grey Friars in Stamford, and did so at once. " Within three hours after the Duke of Suffolk wrote that he trusted to have the house. When I had opened this to Mr Vincent he was contented, trusting you would help him to another house of the Friars. The town would be helped by the Duke living there. I have despatched the Friars all well contented and made the best I could of the moveables.

---

[1] *L. and P. Hen. VIII*, XIII (2), 527.

[2] *L. and P. Hen. VIII*, XIII (2), 719.

[3] *L. and P. Hen. VIII*, XIII (2), £64. The surrender is printed in DUGDALE, VI, 1514.

It would help this town if men expert in clothing were planted here. . . ."[1]

On the 29th October London writes to Cromwell that he has " left the Grey Friars their brewing vessels and could get but 8s. for all the kitchen stuff. Sold no glass at the Grey, White or Black Friars, but in the churches."[2]

The site was granted 32 Hen. VIII to Charles, Duke of Suffolk. It consisted of eleven acres beside the orchard, the whole was valued at but 41 shillings a year, for all the important buildings had been destroyed.[3]

NOTTINGHAM (surrendered 5 February, 1539).

The surrender of this house on 5 February, 1539, was signed by Thomas Basford, warden and seven other friars.[4]

Site granted 2 Edw. VI to Thomas Henneage.[5]

LEICESTER (surrendered 10 November, 1538).

The surrender of this house on 10 November, 1538, was signed by William Giles, warden, Simon Harmer, lector, and five other friars.

In 1513 the King's Letters Patent had been obtained by William Thomas and Roger Wigston for founding the hospital of St. Ursula, known as Wigston's Hospital, on ground within the precincts of the Grey Friars, and in 1520 William Fisher, the first master of the hospital, had obtained the addition of St. Francis garden.

[1] *L. and P. Hen. VIII*, XIII (2), 613.
[2] *L. and P. Hen. VIII*, XIII (2), 719.
[3] V.C.H., *Lancs.*, II, 229.
[4] *L. and P. Hen. VIII*, XIV (L), 229.
[5] DEERING : *Notts.*, 52.

The site was granted 37 Hen. VIII to John Belton and John Broxham.

Leland says : " The Grey Friars of Leicester stood at the end of the Hospital of Mr Wigeston. Simon de Montfort as I learned was founder there ; and there was buried King Richard III and a Knight called Mutton, sometime Mayor of Leicester."

GRANTHAM (surrendered February, 1539).

On 31 July, 1535, the Earl of Rutland writes to Cromwell that on July 29 the aldermen of Grantham and others have informed him that one of the Grey friars has impeached others of the house for using certain treasonable words. He tells Cromwell that he commanded to put the friars in prison till the King's pleasure were known, and has sent the aldermen with the depositions to Cromwell. There seems, however, to have been nothing in this. The accusing friar was but eighteen and his witness, who turned upon him, but thirteen.[1]

The convent was surrendered late in February, 1539. It was exceedingly poor.[2]

Site granted 25 Feb. 33 Hen. VIII to Robert Bocher and David Vincent one of the royal pages. The church was included in the Grant. They sold the site in 1542 to Austin Porter of Belton.[3]

AYLESBURY (surrendered 1 October, 1538).

The surrender of this house on 1 October, 1538, was signed by Henry Mertyn, warden, William Mey, vice warden, and five other friars. The deed has a preamble in which the friars are made to assert that

---

[1] *L. and P. Hen. VIII*, XIV (1), 348 and 413.
[2] *L. and P. Hen. VIII*, VIII, 1149.
[3] V.C.H., *Lincs.*, II, 218.

they " do profoundly consider that the perfection of Christian living doth not consist in dumb ceremonies, wearing of grey coat, disguising oneself after strange fashions, ducking and beating, in girding ourselves with a girdle full of knots and other like papistical ceremonies, wherein we have been most principally practised and misled in times passed." Henceforth they are made to assert they will follow Christ, conforming themselves to the will of the King their Supreme Head.

There was a close of six acres containing a pond called the Moote, fifteen other fields, gardens etc. " The site of the ' priory ' been worth 10s."[1]

On October 3rd London wrote to Cromwell that he has " committed the custody of the friars to Mr Geffrey the king's servant as he had been bidden. The house beside the plate and lead is worth little . . . so he need be charged only with the lead, the house, and the iron in the church windows."[2]

On 29 October he writes to say he has sold the glass windows, the ornaments and utensils at Aylesbury, and has left the house whole, but defaced the church which is well covered with lead and has a good new roof.

The site was granted 8 April 32 Hen. VIII to Sir John Baldwin, Lord Chief Justice of the Common Pleas, and became his county seat. Later it came to the Parkingtons, but in the Civil War it was so much damaged that it was deserted.

Leland says : " There was an house of Grey Friars in the town towards the south founded about the time of Richard II. The Lord Ormund was in time of mind counted chief lord of Aylesbury since Boleyn by

[1] *L. and P. Hen. VIII*, XIII (2), 501.
[2] *L. and P. Hen. VIII*, XIII (2), 526.

partition of land."[1]   The house had been founded in 1386 by James Butler, Earl of Ormund.[2]

III. CAMBRIDGE CUSTODY

CAMBRIDGE (surrendered 1538).

The surrender of this house before October 1st, 1538, was signed by William Whyte, warden, and Thomas Dysse, doctor, Robert Whight, doctor, John Fakun, vice warden, and twenty others.[3]   Upon October 23 the University applied for the house. The Vice-Chancellor wrote to Cromwell that " when they considered the king's ardent desire for the increase of virtue and good learning and Cromwell's continued and prosperous furtherance of the same, they cannot but have great hope that by turning the houses dedicated to vain religion into colleges of true and sincere doctrine, learning and virtue will be greatly augmented."   " They hear," he says, " that Master Hyde, sergeant at law, who has not been always friendly to the University is appointed keeper of the Grey Friars, the custody whereof was given by the visitors to the University.   They fear that this will be prejudical in their suit for obtaining the forfeited houses to be converted into places of learning which they hoped from Cromwell's comfortable words would be speedily brought to pass."[4]

It was certainly most ungrateful of the King to forget the University which had " got the right sow by the ear," as Henry phrased it, and had pronounced that Henry could put away Katharine and marry Ann

[1] LELAND : *Itin.* (1908), II, 112.
[2] Pat. 10, Rich. II, Pt. 2, m. 6.
[3] *L. and P. Hen. VIII*, XIII (2), 495.
[4] *L. and P. Hen. VIII*, XIII (2), 677.

Boleyn, and all this at the suggestion of Thomas Cranmer of Jesus College, Cambridge. So eager was the University for payment for its complaisance, its support of the King's adultery and encouragement of his lust, that on the 5th November, 1538, the Vice-Chancellor wrote again to Cromwell.

He points out that their complaint is now an old one, and he begs Cromwell, " as their Chancellor," to move the King that they may have the houses and sites of the friars for the erection of a new college. The advantage of this, he says—the church of the Franciscans is especially necessary to them—their pro-chancellor whom they have sent to the King and to Cromwell will explain.[1]

Something of their eagerness is explained by Ascham, who tells us that the buildings of the friary were so spacious that " they were not only an ornament and grace but had great convenience for holding the assemblies and doing all the business of the University." The site was at last granted by the King to the master and fellows of Trinity, of whom it was purchased by Frances Sidney, Countess of Sussex, for her foundation of Sidney Sussex College.

NORWICH (20 September, 1538).

Upon 17 September, 1538, we find the Duke of Norfolk writing to Cromwell, and, among other things, claiming his ancestors as the founders of the Grey Friars house in Norwich. He says he perceives from letters just received " how gracious the King is to me concerning the Grey Friars of Norwich and that your mind is, an the friars would give me the house, I should take it. The warden of the friars had already

[1] *L. and P. Hen. VIII*, XIII (2), 760.

come hither offering to give up the house to me, I intend within two or three days to ride to Norwich to take the surrender to the King's use, for I would not example to other founders to take surrender to their own use. . . ."[1]

On September 21 Norfolk again writes to Cromwell to say that he had intended yesterday to have ridden to Norwich to take the surrender of the Grey Friars, but he was ill, so he sent his son of Surrey, his treasurer and others of his Council who have taken his surrender, and left servants in charge. . . .[2]

On March 12, 1539, was granted to Norfolk " all the site of the late Friary and the Church, steeple, bells, churchyard, fisheries, orchards, yards and buildings both within and without the site to be held in free burgage by fealty only."[3] With the Norfolks it remained till 1544, when the King seized it and on November 6th granted most of it to Paul Gresham and Francis Baldero ; they soon sold most of what had been granted them, but what remained came back to the Norfolks when Queen Mary reversed their attainder. They held this till 1559, when the city bought it of the Duke, let it to Mr. Sotheran and bought it again in 1564 when most of the buildings were demolished.

Bury St. Edmunds (Babwell surrendered December, 1538).

On 27 September, 1538, Hilsey, Bishop of Rochester, writes to Cromwell to say that he has been at Babwell and spoken with the warden there to know whether he would surrender if the King sent to him.   He desired

---

[1] *L. and P. Hen. VIII*, XIII (2), 365.
[2] *L. and P. Hen. VIII*, XIII (2), 399.
[3] *L. and P. Hen. VIII*, XIV (1), 651.

Hilsey to receive his submission, and said he was ready to surrender if the King or Cromwell wished. Hilsey writes for permission to receive the surrender and notes that there is a bedridden friar there, and asks for orders concerning him.[1] Then, on December 10, Ingworth writes to Cromwell that, " since he was last with him he has received to the King's use among other friaries that of the Grey Friars in Babwell."[2]

From an estimate of the lead remaining on the church and other buildings of the friary, " as appeareth by the walls there yet remaining,"[3] we learn that the church was 167 feet in length, " and the sparre on the one side 25 feet which is in breadth 50 feet. The two aisles each 88 ft. and the sparre of either of them in one whole length 17 foot. . . . The cloister in length being four square 352 feet and the sparre in one length 12 feet. The cloister from the fratry to the kitchen 79 feet. . . ." There were, we learn, four bells weighing in all 30,000 lbs., the first bell being 13,000 lbs. These bells were exchanged with the town of Mildenhall. Anthony Dunryche had the brass pillars in the choir and the copper of the gravestones.

The site granted 33 Hen. VIII to Anthony Harvey at a rental of 10 shillings.[4]

KING'S LYNN (surrendered 1 October, 1538).

The surrender of this house upon 1 October, 1538, was signed by Edmund Brygat and nine others.

The site was granted 20 February, 1545, together with that of the White friars to John Eyre. Blom-

---

[1] *L. and P. Hen. VIII*, XIII (2), 437.
[2] *L. and P. Hen. VIII*, XIII (2), 1021.
[3] *L. and P. Hen. VIII*, XIII (2), 1213.
[4] TYMMS : *Bury Wills*, 5.

field, in his *History of Norfolk* (IV, pp. 564 and 568), states that Eyre sold to a priest who conveyed the site to the corporation of Lynn which still owns it.

The hexagonal steeple of the church remains. See *supra*, p. 000.

IPSWICH (surrendered 1538).

Upon 1 April, 1538, Lord Wentworth writes to Cromwell that " the house of Grey Friars at Ipswich and the warden and brethren there live in great necessity. As the inhabitants now extend their charity to the poor and impotent instead of such an idle nest of drones who devour the meat of the King's poor subjects, the friars have been compelled to sell their plate." Wentworth, who claims to have been " their founder in blood," sent for the warden and demanded why he sold the jewels of the house. He was told necessity compelled it, " for this twelve month they could not gather the worth of £5 and could not continue in the house three months longer." Wentworth therefore purchased the house for himself and heirs. There were no lands but " the bare site with a garden or two enclosed."[1]

The inventory of the house was taken upon 7th April by Ingworth. It was as follows :—

The Choir : 5 candlesticks, 2 hanging lamps, a holy water stoup and sprinkle, laten ; 20 books good and ill, a timber lectern, a small form.

The Vestry : A great chest and in it a great cloth to lay before the altar ; 4 silk pillows, 2 late my lady Curseyn's ; 16 cushions ; 18 hangings for the choir of small value ; a veil for the choir in Lent ; old Altar

[1] *L. and P. Hen. VIII*, XIII (1), 651.

cloths and vestments ; 2 old candlesticks and a broken pyx etc. In an old chest ; 2 rochets, 10 copes, a hearse cloth, 2 linen altar cloths, 17 albs, etc.

The poor contents of the kitchen, the buttery, the garner, the cheese house, the warden's upper and nether chamber, the chamber where the warden lies, the vicewarden's chamber, a house in the dorter are also given.

Plate : A cross with a crystal in it ; 2 gilt chalices, 12 spoons, etc. Total 259¾ oz. And other stuff.

COLCHESTER (surrendered December, 1538).

This house was surrendered in December, 1538.[1] Sir John Raynsforth besought Cromwell for the house.[2]

His prayer was not granted ; upon July 8, 1544, the site was granted to Francis Jobson and Elizabeth his wife, Andrew Dudely, Robert Heneage and Richard Duke for the sum of 430 pounds 10 shillings.[3] But in the year after the Dissolution, Jobson, who was a farmer, had paid 2 pounds 10 shillings 8 pence for the site of the house, the " olde halle," the " fermerye " and the chambers called " Syr Thomas Tyrrells lodgynge," the kitchen, bakehouse, brewhouse, two little gardens and 4 acres.[4]

YARMOUTH (surrendered December, 1538).

This house was surrendered in December, 1538,[5] and

[1] *L. and P. Hen. VIII*, XIII (2), 1021.
[2] *L. and P. Hen. VIII*, XIII (2), 1262.
[3] MORANT : *Hist. of Colchester*, p. 152. *L. and P. Hen. VIII*, XIX (1), 1035.
[4] V.C.H., *Essex*, II, 180.
[5] *L. and P. Hen. VIII*, XIII (2), 1021.

later it is noted that " the house was delivered to Mr. Millesent servant to the Lord Privy Seal, by the Visitor, of whom he bought most part of the things and his inventory was not there." The house was not " defasede ne rasede."[1] It was granted in the following year to Cromwell himself, and three years later to Sir Richard Williams *alias* Cromwell.[2] This is interesting. Thomas Cromwell was beheaded as we know in 1540. Sir Richard Williams *alias* Cromwell was his illegitimate son, the great grandfather of Oliver Cromwell, who by reason of the loot of the religious houses was one of the richest squires in England.

DUNWICH (surrendered December, 1538).

This house was surrendered in December, 1538,[3] and in 1545 came into the hands of that John Eyre of the Augmentation Office who obtained so much monastic property in East Anglia.[4]

WALSINGHAM (surrendered December, 1538).

This house was surrendered in December, 1538,[5] and, like Dulwich, came into the hands of John Eyre.

IV. THE YORK CUSTODY.

YORK (surrendered 27 November, 1538).

This capital house was surrendered upon 27 November, 1538, by William Vavasour, the warden and

---

[1] *L. and P. Hen. VIII*, XIII (2), 1212.
[2] DUGDALE : *Baronage*, tom. ii.
[3] *L. and P. Hen. VIII*, XIII (2), 1021.
[4] *Dep. Keeper's Rep.*, lx, App. II, 207. V.C.H., *Suffolk*, II, 126.
[5] *L. and P. Hen. VIII*, XIII (2), 1021.

twenty friars of whom five were novices. The warden received a pension of 5 pounds a year.[1]

The site was estimated at 7 shillings and 6 pence a year and the rents at 12 pounds 5 shillings and 5 pence. There were two bells and some lead. The jewels and plate consisted of three chalices, two cruets, ten spoons, two masers, one round salt parcel gilt, a wooden cross plated with silver, a standing maser with bands and foot silver gilt, a little standing cup, a——with cover gilt ; in all 109 ounces.[2]

The site was granted 34 Hen. VIII to Leonard Beckwith. Leland merely says, " The Grey Friars not far from the castle."[3]

LINCOLN (surrendered 23 February, 1539).

On 23 February, 1539, Ingworth writes to Cromwell that he is now in Lincoln where he has received four poor houses, nothing left but stones, and poor glass, but meetly leaded. In the Grey Friars is a goodly conduit, he says, which the Mayor wants for the city and he has promised to write in support of this.[4] As it happens we know that the conduit was then quite new for the Grey Friars had received licence to lay it on common ground on 8 April, 1535.[5]

The site of about 4 acres was let for 12 shillings a year to William Monson of Ingleby, who in January, 1540, obtained a twenty-one years' lease of it. In 1568 it was the property of Robert Monson, who in that year founded a free school here, and in 1574

[1] *L. and P. Hen. VIII*, XIII (2), 917.
[2] V.C.H., *Yorks.*, III, 291.
[3] LELAND : *Itin.* (1908), I, 55.
[4] *L. and P. Hen. VIII*, XIV (1), 348.
[5] *Hist. MSS. Com. Rep.*, XIV, App. VIII, 33.

conveyed the site of the Grey Friars with the Free Grammar School to the City of Lincoln.[1]

GRIMSBY (surrendered 9 October, 1538).

Upon 8 October, 1538, John Freman writes to Cromwell that he has dissolved the Grey Friars in Grimsby, " there was nine friars in the same." He adds that there remains to the King's use in bells and lead 80 pounds. He says he has deliyered possession to Mr. Atelyf.[2] The actual surrender is dated 9 October and was signed by Adam Howetun, warden, and five others.[3]

The site of 3 acres was let to Thomas Hatcliff and granted in October, 1543, to John Bellow and Robert Brokesby.[4]

SCARBOROUGH (surrendered 9 March, 1539).

The house was surrendered 9 March, 1539.[5] It was exceedingly poor, as Ingworth states to Cromwell on the following day.[6]

BEVERLEY (surrendered 25 February, 1539).

This convent was in the midst of the rising of 1536. The rebellion broke in Beverley on 8 October, just outside the Grey Friars on Westwood Green. The friars of the convent who had almost without demur taken the oath as to the King's supremacy in 1534[7]

[1] V.C.H., *Lincs.*, II, 223.
[2] *L. and P. Hen. VIII*, XIII (2), 567.
[3] *L. and P. Hen. VIII*, XIII (2), 572.
[4] V.C.H., *Lancs.*, II, 219.
[5] *L. and P. Hen. VIII*, XIV (1), 482.
[6] *L. and P. Hen. VIII*, XIV (1), 494.
[7] *L. and P. Hen. VIII*, VII, 953.

do not seem to have taken any part in it, but there was in their house an Observant called Friar Bonaventura who seems to have ruled the rising and even to have persuaded William Stapleton to lead it. He went with the rebels as far as Doncaster and then made for the Newcastle convent.[1]

The house was surrendered on 25 February, 1539. The site consisted of some 7 acres.[2] House granted 32 Hen. VIII to Thomas Culpeper.

Doncaster (surrendered 20 November, 1538).

The surrender of this house dated 20 November, 1538, was signed by Thomas Kyrkham, s.t.p., warden, and nine friars, three being novices.

The site was granted 36 Hen. VIII to William Giffard and Richard Welbore.

Leland says :—" There was a house of Grey Friars at the north end of the bridge commonly called the Friars Bridge, containing a three arches of stone. Here I marked that the north part of Doncaster town in the which is but little and that mean building standeth as an isle."[3]

Boston (surrendered February, 1539).

This poor house was surrendered in February, 1539.[4] Site granted 37 Hen. VIII to the Mayor and burgesses of Boston.

---

[1] *L. and P. Hen. VIII*, XII (1), 392. The Newcastle convent was now Augustinian, which may explain why Bonaventura is often said to have been an Austin Friar.

[2] *L. and P. Hen. VIII*, XIV (1), 348 and 413.

[3] Leland : *Itin.* (1908), L, 35.

[4] *L. and P. Hen. VIII*, XIV (1), 342, 348.

V. BRISTOL CUSTODY.

BRISTOL (surrendered 10 September, 1538).

Upon 27 August, 1538, Ingworth writes to Cromwell to say, among other things, that " of the three convents in Bristol, the Blackfriars are ready to resign ; but the other two are stiff, the Grey Friars because the warden is warden of Richmond and is in favour (though not worth 20 mks.)." [1] Nevertheless the house was surrendered on 10 September by Thomas Lewys and five others. The inventory of stuff was as follows :—

Vestry and Choir : 2 pair of great brazen candlesticks and 2 pair of small for the altar with a pair of timber candlesticks ; copes ; a vestment for deacon and subdeacon of red velvet broidered with half-moons. (Mr. Bowen has the vestment.) For the priest, deacon and subdeacon vestments of white roses, bors and beasts ; cloth, etc., in all 17 items.

Hall, harbour, buttery, chambers and kitchen ; the parlour seyleid with bowdley border and the kitchen where among other things named were 3 brass pots and 4 brass pans. The visitor has a cross doubting whether it be silver or no, a band with the foot of an horn and a chalice 51 ounces. There are many debts claimed but none paid, as the warden was not there. [2] The Mayor of Bristol, William Chester, writes to Cromwell on the same date, 10 September, to say that the " warden and convent of the Grey Friars in Bristol have surrendered their house to the king which is of the foundation and purchasing of the town,

[1] *L. and P. Hen. VIII*, XIII (2), 200.
[2] *L. and P. Hen. VIII*, XIII (2), 321.

built by ancient burgesses at their cost. . . . He begs therefore for a grant of the house of the Grey Friars and of the ground."[1] This suit was granted 33 Hen. VIII.

Leland says :—" The Grey Friars house was on the right ripe of Frome water not far from St. Bartholomew's Hospital."

HEREFORD (surrendered 25 August, 1538).

The surrender of this house upon 25 August, 1538, was signed by William Scryven, the warden, Friars John Trevelyan, John Elkins, Zakarias Carpenter, and 10 others. The inventory was as follows :—

Vestry : 6 suits of vestments, one of branched silk with lions, another with birds and trees and many single vestments, altar cloths etc.

Steeple : 2 bells and the third at the gate and a pair of organs.

Choir : 5 Mass books, 4 antiphoners, 2 choirs, 6 graduals, an epistle book, 4 legends and a martyrology, etc. Contents of the higher chamber, buttery, ostery and church very scanty. Also contents of kitchen. The visitor has a chalice, also maser and a borse price 6s. 8d. The debt was great.[2]

Ingworth seems to have had trouble here as elsewhere with the Grey Friars.[3]

The house was granted 36 Hen. VIII to James Boyle, the ancestor of the noble house of Boyle, Earls of Cork, Orrery etc.

Leland says :—" There be in the walls of Hereford

[1] *L. and P. Hen. VIII*, XIII (2), 322.
[2] *L. and P. Hen. VIII*, XIII (2), 184.
[3] *L. and P. Hen. VIII*, XIII (2), 200.

6 gates ; Wye Gate ; Friar gate standeth west, called of the Grey Friars house, standing without it. . . . There be few houses without Friar's Gate. . . ."[1]

BRIDGWATER (surrendered 13 September, 1538).

The surrender of this house upon 13 September, 1538, was signed by John Herys warden and seven others. The inventory of the stuff was as follows :—

Choir : A table of alabaster with 9 images ; 2 goodly candlesticks, a pair of organs, an iron gate about a tomb etc.

Church : 3 cloths before the altars, a chapel with a frame barred with iron.

Sextry : 21 copes of vevelt, silk, etc., also vestments etc.

Elsewhere a suit of damask with flowers of gold, a suit of blue silk with stars of gold and many other suits and vestments.

The visitor has in jewels and plate 358 ozs. The debt £18-£19.

The site was granted 35 Hen. VIII to Emmanuel Lukar.

Leland says :—" These things I marked in the west part of the town. One large parish church, a goodly house where sometime a college was of Grey Friars. William Briwere son of William Briwere the first, builded the house. One of the Lords Botreaux and his wife were especial benefactors to this house. Thereupon his heart and his wife's body were buried there. The accustomer of Bridgwater hath translated this place to a right goodly and pleasant dwelling house."[2]

---

[1] LELAND : *Itin.*, V, 67.   [2] LELAND : *Itin.*, I, 163.

EXETER (surrendered 15 September, 1538).

1. The surrender of this house on the 15 September was signed by Gregory Bassett and nine others. The inventory was as follows :—

Choir : An old table imagery of little worth ; a little tomb, laten, 6d. ; a pair of organs, 20s. 2 old timber lecterns £2 ; fair stalls 40s. ; a sacry bell and fair seats 6s. 8d. Two old altars in the church.

Sextry : 3 old copes of white damask, embroidered, 33s. 8d. ; a suit of crimson and velvet 33s. 4d. ; and other old vestments, 20 items in all ; a coffer bound with iron 13s. 4d. which is claimed as another man's but no friar knows who, for it was there before any can remember.

Steeple : 3 bells.

The visitor has 241 oz. silver. Debt £14 0s. 9d.[1]

The site was granted July 4, 31 Hen. VIII, to John Lord Russel. On March 16, 34 Hen. VIII, the reversion of site was granted to Humphrey Colles.

Leland says :—" There was an house of Grey Friars betwixt the north and west gate near the town wall, now a plain vacant ground called Frerenhay. Bytten Bishop of Exeter removed thence the Grey Friars and built them a house a little without the South Gate."[2]

GLOUCESTER (surrendered July, 1538).

Ingworth received the surrender of this house in July, 1538.

The inventory was as follows :—

[1] *L. and P. Hen. VIII*, XIII (2), 354.
[2] LELAND : *Itin.*, I, 228.

Choir: 3 altar cloths, very poor; books of the choir of little value.

Vestry: 6 copes of white damask with flowers, ray striped and green silk; 6 vestments, white damask, silk, yellow, chequer work, black worsted, black etc.; 17 chasubles one being blue taffeta with birds, lions; 3 albs and amices; 2 ragged altar cloths and other vestments.

Library: Many books of no value.
Master Payn has 147½ oz. of plate.[1]
The house was at this time " a goodly house much of it newly builded, especially the church choir and dorter, the rest small lodgings.[2]
The site was granted 35 Hen. VIII to John Jennings.
Leland says :—" The Grey Friars and Black Friars within the town."

DORCHESTER (surrendered 30 September, 1538).

The surrender of this house on September 30, 1531, was signed by William Jermen doctor and 7 friars.
The inventory was as follows :—

Choir: a table at the high altar of imagery after the old fashion; a small pair of organs; fair stalls well sileid, divers tombs etc.

Church: 4 tables and 3 great images of alabaster; a new tabernacle for the image of St. Francis; divers images stolen, tombs etc.

Steeple: 3 bells each more than other.

Vestry: priest, deacon and subdeacon of blue velvet embroidered and five other suits of damask,

---

[1] *L. and P. Hen. VIII,* XIII (1), 1109 and 1484.
[2] FOSBROOKE : *Hist. of Gloucester,* p. 296–97.

etc., with other vestments and copes, one with blue velvet embroidered. To pay Visitors charges there were sold : an iron gate about a tomb in church 40s. ; a white vestment with deacon and subdeacon 40s. ; old iron with a holy water stoup, etc. The Visitor had 126½ oz. of plate.[1]

Ingworth then writes to Cromwell from Salisbury that he has received all the houses in Dorchester. He says " the warden of Dorchester, a doctor, has been there many years, and is in high favour, so that he the writer had much trouble to come to a knowledge of the state of the house. There is a mill worth £10 a year which the warden has let, to Lord Stourton for £4 the repairs to be done by the King." He adds that he hears Lord Stourton has gone to London to sue to have the whole house on the plea that he has the mill and grounds. That Ingworth has seized the mill into the King's hands. . . .[2]

Lord Stourton failed to obtain his desire. In 1539 house and grounds were leased and in 1543 sold to Edmund Peckham cofferer to the King's household.[3] In 1548 Peckham sold to Thomas Wriothesley, Earl of Southampton and to Paul Dowel and later it came to Sir Francis Astley.[4]

BODMIN (surrendered 20 September, 1538).

The surrender of this house upon 20 September was signed by Walter Rodd the warden and eight other friars.

The inventory was as follows :—

[1] *L. and P. Hen. VIII*, XIII (2), 474.
[2] *L. and P. Hen. VIII*, XIII (2), 482.
[3] *L. and P. Hen. VIII*, XV, 555.
[4] HUTCHINS : *Hist. of Dorset*, II, 365–66.

Choir : On the high altar an alabaster table ; a frame of old organs without pipes etc.

Vestry : 7 suits of vestments of damask, bandkyn, silk and worsted with other vestments etc. The debt was £16 to discharge which the warden had a suit of white vestments not yet all paid for, a pair of organs, a little maser and two spoons. The visitor has 286 oz. of silver.

Leland says :—" There was a good place of Grey Friars on the South side of Bodmin town."

CARMARTHEN (surrendered 30 August, 1538).

Barlow, Bishop of St. David's, writing to Cromwell on 31 March, complains that on St. David's Day the people wilfully solemnised the feast and set forth relics in defiance of his admonition and the King's injunctions. He complains, too, of a sermon preached in the Cathedral to three hundred or four hundred persons on Innocents' Day, and desires that the See be transferred from St. David's to Carmarthen. For this purpose he wishes a grant of the Grey Friars' place in Carmarthen, where he says the King's grandfather is buried, for the accommodation of the canons and collegians of St. David's, which he calls a " desolate corner."[1] The wishes of this heretic and iconolast were not granted ; but on 30 August, 1538, the Grey Friars at Carmarthen was surrendered, the deed being signed by John Trahern and 13 other friars.[2]

CARDIFF (surrendered 6 September, 1538).

The surrender of this house was signed upon 6

[1] *L. and P. Hen. VIII*, XIII (1), 634.
[2] *L. and P. Hen. VIII*, XIII (2), 229, where also the inventory is given.

September by Thomas Guyn the warden and 8 other friars.[1]

VI. WORCESTER CUSTODY.

WORCESTER (surrendered 4 August, 1538).

This house was surrendered on 4 August, " considering that the friars were not able to live for very poverty, and no charity had come to them as of old, for in the space of six weeks they had run at least £3 in debt."[2]

The inventory is as follows :—

Ten suits, crosslets of gold, blue silk with fishes of gold, red silk with stars of gold, birds, harts and lions, Our Lady with burned gold, 13 single vestments with dragons, pelicans, ragged stuff, stars and Katherine wheels, green popinjays and silver heads etc., 3 poor chasubles, 12 poor altar cloths, 12 copes etc. . . . a pair of organs, a frame for the sepulchre etc., in the choir. Plate 86 oz.[3]

The house does not from this inventory seem so poor and Ingworth himself, writing to Cromwell on 7 August, states that " The Grey Friars is a fair house, well builded with not above 40s. a year in orchards and gardens, two aisles leaded, the rest tile and slate."[4]

The City applied for the house, and on October 5 the bailiffs, aldermen and Common Council write to Cromwell to thank him for his assistance in their suit, asking him to continue in the same and add that their walls and bridge are in need of repair, and that the

[1] *L. and P. Hen. VIII*, XIII (2), where also the inventory is given.
[2] *L. and P. Hen. VIII*, XIII (2), 32.
[3] *L. and P. Hen. VIII*, XIII (1), 1513.
[4] *L. and P. Hen. VIII*, XIII (2), 49.

stone of the Friars' houses is very meet for the purpose.[1] Latimer also writes a horrible and blasphemous
letter to Cromwell to the same end.[2]

The suit was granted in 1539.

COVENTRY (surrendered 5 October, 1536).

On September 20, 1538, the Mayor and aldermen of
Coventry write to Cromwell that it is reported that
the Grey and White Friars of this town are to be
suppressed. Their churches can be ill spared, for in
time of plague, sick people resort to them for divine
service. There are but two parish churches, and if in
time of plague people resorted to them they would
infect the whole City. "We beg you therefore to
intercede with the King that these two churches of
friars remain, the religious persons thereof to be reformed at the King's pleasure."[3]

This plea was of course disregarded. The Grey
Friars surrendered their house on October 5, 1538, the
deed being signed by John Stafford, warden, and ten
other friars.

The survey was as follows :—

Choir, 36 yds. by 10 yds. Rood Chapel, 3 yds. by
4½ yds. St. Nicholas Chapel, 11¾ yds. by 8 yds. The
North valence, 11 yds. by 7½ yds. The South valence,
9½ yds. by 7¼ yds. The body, 39½ yds. by 10 yds.
North aisle, 31 yds. by 5 yds. South aisle, 30¾ yds.
by 4¾ yds. The whole church newly covered with
lead within these twenty-four years. The house is
much in ruin. Adjoining is an old manor of the King's
called Chyldesmore where they say King Edward IV

---

[1] *L. and P. Hen. VIII*, XIII (2), 540.
[2] *L. and P. Hen. VIII*, XIII (2), 543.
[3] *L. and P. Hen. VIII*, XIII (2), 650.

kept a parliament. The hall is down but there is a proper park adjoining it and the lodgings might be repaired with tiles from the friary. The timber of the housing is stark, but the church roof is very good timber.[1]

On 20 October the Mayor and aldermen complain to Cromwell that in spite of their plea London, the King's commissioner, has defaced the church of the Grey Friars.[2] Two days later even London discovers that if he destroy the conduit of " the late Grey Friars," set almost a mile from Coventry, which is better than that of the town, and has a better head " much of the city shall lack water."[3] Nevertheless on October 29 he writes to Cromwell that he has partly rased the Grey Friars, " because the poor people lay so sore upon it."

In 34 Hen. VIII the site was granted to the town.

Leland says :—" There were two very fair houses of Friars in Coventry. The Grey Friars and the White Friars. . . ."

LICHFIELD (surrendered 7 August, 1538).

The surrender of this house on 7 August was signed by Richard Wetwod, who seems to have added the names of two others.[4] Ingworth writes to Cromwell that the warden is sore diseased in his face, has been little at home this half-year, and yet now is loath to give up his house though it is more in debt than all the stuff that belongs to it would pay, chalice, bells

---

[1] *L. and P. Hen. VIII*, XIII (2), 539.
[2] *L .and P. Hen. VIII*, XIII (2), 650.
[3] *L. and P. Hen. VIII*, XIII (2), 674.
[4] *L. and P. Hen. VIII*, XIII (2), 44.

and all, by twenty nobles.[1] On August 12 Thomas Legh writes to Cromwell that the visitor has dispatched the friars and put the house in the custody of Richard Wetwoode and the constables of the town. Of his own accord and also at instance of the bishop of Chester (to both of whom Wetwoode has formerly shown great pleasure) he desires Cromwell to favour the said Richard for the preferment of the house.[2] On August 23 Ingworth, writing to Latimer, notes that " the friars in these parts . . . have many favourers and great labour is made for their continuance. Divers trust to see them set up again and some have gone up to sue for them."[3] The sale of the Grey Friars stuff at Lichfield took place on October 4.[4]

In 36 Hen. VIII the site was granted to Richard Crumbilthorn.

Leland says :—" There was a house of Grey Friars in Lichfield in the south-west part of the town. . . . There cometh a conduit of water out of an hill brought in lead to the town and hath two castelets in the town, one in the east wall of this Friars Close on the street side. . . ."

SHREWSBURY (surrendered August, 1538).

The inventory was as follows :—

Two pairs of candlesticks, a branch with four sockets, and an old broken cross, all of latten. 3 altar cloths, 4 pillows, a table of alabaster for the high altar, a timber lectern, a brass lamp, a parclose of timber

[1] *L. and P. Hen. VIII*, XIII (2), 50.
[2] *L. and P. Hen. VIII*, XIII (2), 79.
[3] *L. and P. Hen. VIII*, XIII (2), 170.
[4] *L. and P. Hen. VIII*, XIII (2), 666.

In Lower vestry and high vestry : A fair chest and an almery. 18 corporas cases, 2 teneculles motley with good offeras with vestment and cope of the same suit. 17 chasubles, one white with swans, another yellow velvet with a red lion, 2 boxes with evidence etc. An old jug with a box, latten, a silver cross and chalice in the visitor's hands and other things. . . . Little lead, none rents, 3 or 4 acres of land.[1]

On 6 September Adam Mytten writes to Cromwell that " two naughty friars houses in Shrewesbury, one of Friars Minor, the other of Austin Friars, are suppressed by the lord visitor at their own request, and the custody given to him the writer. He asks Cromwell to help him to one of these houses for that they lie in the town he dwells in and he has served the king 16 years in Parliament being one of the " inseuysciant " of the Commons. Was northward (? Pilgrimage of Grace) with 100 men in the King's service."[2] Apparently this rogue got no answer, for on October 16 he writes again almost in the same terms.[3] But Mytten did not get his way. In 35 Hen. VIII the house and site was granted to Richard Andrews and Nicholas Temple.

A part remains, see *supra*, p. 90.

CHESTER (suppressed 15 August, 1538).

The surrender of this house upon 15 August, 1538, was signed by William Wall and six others.[4] It was delivered to Master Phoke Dutton, mayor there, and to Master Raffe Ragerson and Thomas Marten.

---

[1] *L. and P. Hen. VIII*, XIII (2), 88.
[2] *L. and P. Hen. VIII*, XIII (2), 293.
[3] *L. and P. Hen. VIII*, XIII (2), 626.
[4] *L. and P. Hen. VIII*, XIII (2), 96.

The inventory was as follows :—

The Choir : On the altar a fair table alabaster, two altar cloths with a frontlet and a stained cloth before the altar. Two candlesticks laten. An old table alabaster. Lamp basin, pair of organs, holy water stoup, a sort of books for the choir of friars use, sacring bells, two pillows on the altar etc.

The Vestry : 15 chesabulls for the priest, 16 tenacles, albs, amys, copes etc., and an old censer. . . . The visitor has a little chalice, maser and six spoons for the king. Debts £12. 8s. 11d. . . . No lead nor rents but yr gerdens.[1]

LLANVAIS (surrendered 19 August, 1538).

The surrender of this house near Beaumaris in Anglesea was signed by Friar John and three others on 19 August.[2]

The inventory is noted in *Letters and Papers*, XIII (2), 138.

On 22 November Sir Richard Bulkeley writes to Cromwell to renew his suit for a grant of this house which lay among his lands. He offers Cromwell one hundred marks for his pains in the matter. He wishes to make a dwelling-house of the convent.[3]

BRIDGENORTH (surrendered 5 August, 1538).

The warden and brethren in the deed of surrender say they could not live for the charity of the people was so small, that in three years they had not received in alms in ready money 10 shillings a year, but only

[1] *L. and P. Hen. VIII*, XIII (1), 1298.
[2] *L. and P. Hen. VIII*, XIII (2), 196.
[3] *L. and P. Hen. VIII*, XIII (1), 1298.

live by a service they had in the town in a chapel on the bridge. The surrender was made on August 5.

The inventory is as follows :—

A suit of red velvet. 6 copes ; yellow silk, green silk, silk with birds, and cloth of bankeng, 3 old vestments. 4 tenacles of banken. 4 surplices. 2 cross cloths, stained. 3 chasubles, 9 albs. A little altar cloth. 2 corporas cases with the cloth, one poor. A fair cross of copper and gilt with Mary and John. 3 great coffers. A silk cope with 2 old tunicles.

In the choir : 2 great candlesticks of lay metal. 4 candlesticks, a censer and a ship of laten. A cross of lay metal with a staff. A hanging lamp and holy water stoup of laten. 2 sacre bells. 2 small cruets. 2 bells in the steeple. A pair of organs. 3 old altar cloths. 13 books.

In the fratry : 5 tables.

Plate : a chalice and six spoons. 14½ oz. etc.[1]

On 7 August Ingworth tells Cromwell that the Grey Friars at Bridgenorth is the poorest house he has seen, not worth 10 shillings a year, all the houses at falling down. He recommends Nicholas Holt who wishes to have it.[2]

The site was granted 36 Hen. VIII to John Beaumont.

STAFFORD (suppressed 9 August, 1538).

Here is a good instance of what the process of suppression actually was. " Mem. This 9 day of August in the 30 year of our most dred Sovereign lord King

---

[1] *L. and P. Hen. VIII*, XIII (2), 41.
[2] *L. and P. Hen. VIII*, XIII (2), 47.

Henry VIII. Richard bp. of Dover Visitor under the lord Privy Seal for the King's Grace was in Stafford in the Grey Friars and also in the Austen Friars where that the said visitor said to the heads and brethren of both places these words :—

" Brethren, where that I understand ye have had information that I should come, by the King's commission, to suppress your house and put you out, fear not, for I have no such commission, nor I use no such fashion in my place. I am sent to reform every man to a good order and to give injunctions for the preservation of the same. If ye can be content and think yourself able here to live and to be reformed and to observe such reasonable injunctions as I shall leave with you, the which or that I require your answer, ye shall here and see in writing, then I am and shall be content that ye shall with the King's favour continue as before ye have do. If that ye be not able to live and observe the same then if ye of your own minds and wills give your houses unto the King's hands, I must receive them.

" The said injunctions were read to them, which were reasonable. The said heads with all the brethren with one assent, without my counsel or coaction gave their houses into the Visitor's hands to the King's use. The Visitor received the same, and of the houses and implements made inventories and delivered them to such as should keep them to the King's use, and so delivered to each friar a letter to visit his friends and so departed. This witnesseth John Savage, and Thos. Russell, bailiffs of the borough of Stafford, Wm. Stamforde and Ric. Warde gentleman and divers others."

The Franciscans in England

The inventory is as follows :—

The Sextry : 5 suits without albs, requiem dress silk, yellow say and branched green silk. 6 copes, 2 being of linen cloth stained with image work. 6 altar cloths, a pyx of laten etc.

The Church : 4 tables of alabaster, a pair of great candlesticks, a cross and censer of latten, 2 poor mass books, one printed, one written ; a pair of small organs etc.

The Visitor has a chalice and 6 spoons, 16 oz. . . . A Close with an orchard. . . . Half the choir leaded and a chapel.[1]

The sale took place on 27 September. The buildings were then sold to James Lusone Ideveson, the wall next the town to the township.[2]

PRESTON (surrendered ? February, 1539).

On February 23, 1539, Ingworth writes to Cromwell that he is about to go to the north to suppress some twenty friaries not yet disposed of. Among these, we may suppose, was Preston ; but we know no more of its fate.[3]

The site was granted 18 June, 32 Hen. VIII to Thomas Holcroft, esquire of the body for 126 pounds 10 shillings.[4]

Leland says : "The Grey Friars College in the north-west side of the town of Preston was set on the soil of a gentleman called Prestun . . . divers of the Prestons were buried in this house. But the original

---

[1] *L. and P. Hen. VIII*, XIII (2), 56.
[2] *L. and P. Hen. VIII*, XIII (2), 666.
[3] *L. and P. Hen. VIII*, XIV (1), 348, 413, 494.
[4] *L. and P. Hen. VIII*, XV, 831 (43).

and great builder of this house was Edmund Earl of Lancaster son of Henry III."

VII. Newcastle Custody

Newcastle (Observant house since 1499, suppressed as such 1534).

This house was in 1536 granted to the Austin friars. It was surrendered January 9, 1539, by John Crayforth, and ten friars, two of them novices. In 36 Hen. VIII it was granted to the Earl of Essex, James Rockby and others.

Leland says : " The Observant Friars house stood by Pandon. It was a very fair thing."

Hartlepool (suppressed February, 1539).

This house was dissolved about February, 1539, and is so mentioned in a document in the British Museum (Harl. MS., 604, f. 104).[1] It was doubtless one of the twenty convents in the north of which Ingworth wrote to Cromwell as we have seen.[2]

Carlisle (surrendered March, 1539).

This is another of the convents in the north, which Ingworth writes to Cromwell in February, 1539, he is going to suppress.[3] He mentions Carlisle by name. But on March 1 (?) when he writes Cromwell again, Beverley, Scarborough and Carlisle had still to be visited.[4]

Friars Court behind Devonshire Street marks the site of the convent.

[1] *L. and P. Hen. VIII*, XIV (1), 394.
[2] *Ibid.*, XIV (1), 348.
[3] *L. and P. Hen. VIII*, XIV (1), 348.
[4] *L. and P. Hen. VIII*, XIV (2), 413.

RICHMOND (Yorks) (surrendered 19 January, 1539).

The surrender of this house on 19 January, 1539, was signed by Robert Sanderson, doctor, the warden and fourteen friars, all but one of them priests.[1]

The lead on the church was three fother, the three bells weighed 2000 lbs, the plate was 31 ozs.

The site of sixteen acres within a wall was valued at 31 shillings a year, and was leased to Ralph Gower for twenty-one years in 1539.[2]

Leland says : " At the back of the Frenchgate is the Grey Friars a little without the walls. Their house, meadow, orchard and a little wood is walled in. Men go from the Market Place to it by a postern gate. There is a conduit of water at the Grey Friars, else there is none in Richmond. Not far from the Friars' wall is a chapel of St. Antony . . ."

> Quis desiderio sit pudor aut modus
> Tam cari capitis? . . .

---

[1] *L. and P. Hen. VIII*, XIV (1), 96.
[2] *L. and P. Hen. VIII*, XV, p. 556, and V.C.H., *Yorks*, III, 274.

INDEX

Abingdon, Abbey of, 37
— Abbot of, 40
Abraham, Father, 249
Agnellus, *see* Pisa, Agnellus of
Agnes, widow of Guydo, 44
Albert of Pisa, *see* Pisa
Albert the Great, 137, 138, 145
Alemaina, Bartholomew de, 166
Alessandria, Alexander of, 206
Alexander IV, Pope, 72, 73, 141, 146
Alexander, Master of Priests' Hospice, Canterbury, 21–24
Alexander of Hales, *see* Hales
Alfieri, Frate Enrico, 224
Amney, John, 250 *n.*
Andrews, Richard, 276, 308
Angelo, Friar, 11
Anglicus, Jocelinus, 35 *n.*
— Stephen, 35 *n.*
Anthony, Saint, of Padua, 127
Aquinas, Thomas, *see* Thomas
Aristotle, 137, 143–146, 153
Arnuleph, Brother, 119, 121
Ashburnham, Earl of, 283
Assisi, Church of St. Francis, 106, 111 *n.*, 118 ; General Chapter of, 208, 225 ; house of San Damiano, 224
Astley, Sir Francis, 302
Atelyf, —, 295
Austin Friars (Augustinians), 69, 137, 150, 153, 232, 239, 244, 253, 266, 268, 308, 311, 313
Austria, Frederick Duke of, 160
Auvergne, William of, 137, 138

Averroës, 145
Avignon, *Magna Disputatio* at, 206
Aylesbury, Convent, 285
Aylesham, Geoffrey of, 166

Babwell, *see* Bury St. Edmunds
Bacon, Roger, 128, 135–148, 153, 154, 158, 163
Baginton, " Inclusa " de, 22
Baldero, Francis, 289
Baldwin, Sir John, 286
Barkerfelde, Edward, 276
Barlow, Bp. of St. David's, 303
Bartholomew of Pisa, *see* Pisa
Barton, Brother, 90
— Elizabeth, Maid of Kent, 239, 240
— Martin de, 56, 58, 76
Basford, Thomas, 284
Basing, Salekin de, 29 *n.*
Bassett, Gregory, 300
Batenturt, Luke de, 81
Bath and Wells, Bishop of, 175
Beauchamp, William, Earl of Warwick, 88
Beaumont, John, 310
Beauvais, Laurence of, 17, 20
Bec, Abbot of, 43
Beckk, James, 248
Beckwith, Leonard, 294
Bedford, Isabella, 170
Bedford, Convent, 66, 68, 281
Bellow, John, 295
Belton, John, 285

282.42
H98

14968

3 4711 00184 0380